DEMOCRATIC PROSPECT

CHARLES FRANKEL

This is a book about the relation of the ideas and ideals of democracy to the new facts of life in the mid-twentieth century. It offers a chart of the American democratic prospect—the new agenda of things to be done to expand our democratic society.

What do we mean by "government by the consent of the governed"? By "an open society"? By "personal freedom" and "individual autonomy"? By "responsible government"? What, indeed, do we mean by the word "democracy" itself? These are the questions with which this book is concerned. Mr. Frankel explains why our faith in democratic ideals is troubled, and examines the theories which proclaim that democratic ideals are doomed. But he does not defend democratic ideals in abstract terms. He fills the abstractions with content, and indicates what must be done under contemporary conditions to give them meaning and substance.

According to Mr. Frankel, our present "politics of malaise" are the consequence

(*Continued on back flap*)

pening to him as a citizen of a democracy, and the place this generation can make for itself in democracy's historical career. To Americans and to many people elsewhere it will make clearer what our best aspirations are, and what they demand in the reconstruction of our ideas and the reform of our society.

THE DEMOCRATIC PROSPECT

BOOKS BY CHARLES FRANKEL

THE FAITH OF REASON
THE BEAR AND THE BEAVER
THE CASE FOR MODERN MAN

BOOKS EDITED BY CHARLES FRANKEL

ROUSSEAU'S SOCIAL CONTRACT
THE USES OF PHILOSOPHY: AN IRWIN EDMAN READER
ISSUES IN UNIVERSITY EDUCATION
THE GOLDEN AGE OF AMERICAN PHILOSOPHY

THE
DEMOCRATIC
PROSPECT

CHARLES FRANKEL

HARPER & ROW, PUBLISHERS
NEW YORK AND EVANSTON

To

HELEN

CONTENTS

	FOREWORD	ix
I.	THE POLITICS OF MALAISE	1
II.	THE NATURAL HISTORY OF DEMOCRACY	10
III.	IDEALS AND IDOLS OF DEMOCRACY	30
IV.	RECOVERING GOVERNMENT BY CONSENT	49
V.	THE DILEMMAS OF AN OPEN SOCIETY	72
VI.	THE REORGANIZATION OF WORK AND PLAY	93
VII.	THE WELFARE STATE: POSTSCRIPT AND PRELUDE	125
VIII.	THE RESPONSIBLE SOCIETY	145
IX.	EPILOGUE: WHY CHOOSE DEMOCRACY?	166
	ACKNOWLEDGMENTS	181
	NOTES	183
	INDEX	217

AUTHOR'S NOTE

In order to make the reader's life less difficult, I have put the footnotes in this book at the back and have also eliminated the worrying little numbers that suggest to the reader that he may be missing something. The footnotes are identified by page number and key phrase.

FOREWORD

On the ground that double meanings ought to be avoided, I have buried three meanings in the title of this book. I mean by "the democratic prospect," first of all, the social landscape that stretches out before us in the United States today when we stand back and try to get our bearings and to estimate where we are in the light of democratic ideals. Secondly, I mean by "the democratic prospect" the democratic perspective itself, the view of human possibilities which the democratic idea invites us to take. And finally, I mean by "the democratic prospect" the domestic business to which American democracy might give itself, the new agenda of things to be done on the American scene in the years immediately ahead. There is one kind of "prospect," however, which does not figure in this book. It offers no prophecies about the eventual triumph or defeat of the existing American system. I am not interested in speculations about the future. I am interested in the possibilities of the present.

According to Plato, the father of Western philosophy, democracy "is a charming form of government, full of variety and disorder, and dispensing a sort of equality to equals and unequals alike." In a democracy, he asserted, all fixed distinctions between better and worse are subverted. Subjects act like rulers and rulers like subjects, fathers defer to their sons, teachers fear and flatter their students, and old men ape the manners of the young. "Everything is just ready to burst with liberty." I have tried to take Plato's challenge seriously. Democracy is presented in these pages as an episode in the moral career of mankind, an assault on the forms of social authority that have been most customary in human history and an education in new and dangerous forms of social discipline. There is much that is descriptive in these pages: I hope that I am talking about facts. But my interest is not in the facts but in their connections and their ideal import. My point of departure is our present disappointments with the democratic revolution; my central concern is with unfulfilled possibilities of that revolution, and particularly of its American version.

Accordingly, the issues examined in this book are not the issues that are most often raised when the future of American democracy is discussed. Little is said about the threat of nuclear extermination, or the fateful and potentially fatal contrast between our wealth and the poverty of most people elsewhere, or the challenge that has been mounted against liberal democracy by that giant holding company in discontent, the Sino-Soviet bloc. Similarly, the racial question and problems of economic growth are more or less ignored. Obviously, this is not because I think these questions unimportant. But I have deliberately chosen to set them aside in order to concentrate on other issues which I think we neglect, to the discredit of our system and its resources.

These issues arise when we look at our society in the light of the expectations which the liberal and democratic revolution itself has taught us to have. They have to do with the savor of democracy, with what it means or might mean as a quality directly experienced in our daily lives. And if the savor that men find in a system has anything to do with its survival, then these problems, too, are crucial. The recognition that they exist may lead us to take a more jaundiced view of the status quo, but it would also allow us to face ourselves and the rest of the world as a society alive to its possibilities and charting its own course. Our preoccupation with external dangers has led us to take our lead increasingly from those we fear. But a social system worth preserving surely provides its own cues to passion and action.

The first chapters of this book, therefore, are an effort to see the democratic system in perspective—to set forth the social circumstances that produce and sustain it, the persisting issues which it has to face, the distinctive framework within which it has to settle its problems if it can. I have tried to indicate what democratic ideas and principles mean, not in the abstract, but when they are interpreted in the context of a democracy's actual institutions. Against this background, I turn, in the later chapters, to look at the relationship of our existing arrangements to the aspirations that democracy has turned loose. Implicit in the democratic revolution are the ideals of government by consent, an open society, the autonomous individual, and the responsible control by human beings of their own history. For reasons that I shall bare, I do not share the theory that these ideals are now anachronisms and that there is nothing we can do but fight a temporary holding action on their behalf. But the meaning and destiny of each of these ideals have become obscure. I have tried to say why, and to suggest a general approach to the reorganization of the democracy we possess.

A word should perhaps be said about the philosophy behind that approach. Like everyone who calls himself a liberal and a democrat, and like a good many who do not, I think that the central problem for democracy and for modern civilization is to preserve humanistic values and the possibility of freedom for the individual in a world now driven by the sovereign powers of science and technology. But I am not convinced that the way to approach this problem is to put humanistic values on one side of the fence and science and technology on the other. Our commitment to science and technology is irreversible. Moreover, it is difficult to think that the distinguishing characteristics of the scientific style of mind—a recognition of the need for evidence to support one's beliefs, a preference for qualified argument over sweeping generalization, a habit of acting on the basis of ideas examined in advance, a willingness to use our actions to test and revise these ideas—it is difficult to think that these have nothing to contribute to humane civilization. I do not in this book discuss the general question of the relation of the sciences to the humanities. That is a large question which deserves separate examination on its own. But I have tried to give one concrete example of an approach to the problems of our time which is both humanistic and sympathetic with the methods and spirit of the sciences.

I hasten to add, however, that I do not claim "scientific" standing for most of what I say. It is unapologetically evaluative and philosophical.

I am more than aware of what is involved in undertaking this effort to frame a coherent picture of the present setting and prospects of American democracy. I have left out a great deal, and I have also moved into many fields where I am an amateur. But where the purposes that a society should seek are concerned, there are no professionals. It is amateurs who will have to decide what American democracy can be and do, and I think there is something to be said for trying to pull problems together which are usually treated separately, and for trying to examine them from a single, consistent point of view. It is frequently affirmed these days that American liberalism has run out of issues. Nothing, I think, could be further from the truth. But what contemporary American liberalism lacks is a sure sense of its standards and language. They have been eroded by fundamental changes on the American democratic scene, some of which are the work of American liberalism itself. If there is a *fin de siècle* quality to present-day liberalism, if it is nostalgic in its mood and uninventive in the programs it has to offer, one reason, I think, is that it is still seeking the right terms for discussing—and indeed discovering—its problems. The old terms will not do. To find some of the appropriate new terms is what I have attempted.

CHARLES FRANKEL

THE DEMOCRATIC PROSPECT

I

THE POLITICS OF MALAISE

There is an intellectual mood in the air these days, and it is the mood of men and women who believe that the world is moving in a direction they do not like but cannot control. In an age that knows that it can do anything from eliminating poverty to exploring the moon, a large proportion of the intellectuals and the educated classes apparently feel overwhelmed by their problems and inundated by the tidal wave of events.

In Great Britain, angry young men, looking at the new social order that has emerged in their country, accept its parts—the Welfare State, the altered relations between social classes, the careers newly opened to talents—but pronounce a somber verdict on the whole: "Novocaine for the soul" is all they find. In France a generation of philosophers, novelists, and playwrights have informed us that the human spirit is a lonely and hunted thing in an impersonal world, and have suggested that individual rebellion, in and for itself and without any definite social end in view, is the only meaningful moral gesture that is left in human life. And in the United States the sense has obviously long since disappeared that, in Brandeis's words, we are all bound for Paradise in a perambulator called Evolution. A kind of moral weather that is new to these latitudes appears to have settled in.

The conversation of high-brows, middle-brows, and not a few low-brows shimmers with the same fashionable slogans of anxiety —"the lonely crowd," "the organization man," "the hidden persuaders," "the power elite," and, always and everywhere, "con-

1

formity." And the cures that are preached and that seem to be
most popular are not social cures, but individual ones. We are
urged to cheat on personality tests and to find some private way
of beating the system. The present state of mind of a considerable section of the educated American public is like a case study
in the disillusionments of success. In a society richer in physical
resources and technical skills than any that has ever existed, and
in one that has habitually scorned doctrines of fate and inevitability, the common complaint is that we lack a sense of purpose,
and the underlying fear is that we are in the grip of unalterable
imperatives which make all our purposes futile.

And at a moment in the history of that society when almost
all the most liberal programs of the preceding generation have
been realized, malaise and a sense of helplessness and drift have
become the badges of the liberal mind. Like Keats denouncing
himself for belonging to the tribe of dreaming poets, a large proportion of those who attach themselves to the tribe of liberal
intellectuals have been asking themselves for a decade or more,

> What benefit canst thou do, or all thy tribe,
> To the great world? Thou art a dreaming thing,
> A fever of thyself . . .

An organizing and inspiriting conception of democracy in America,
of what it might be, is missing. There are still, of course, significant issues. The acceleration of America's rate of economic
growth, the more rational allocation of American resources to
public purposes, the extension of our aid to the developing nations, are urgent and important questions. And yet the nagging
doubt plainly remains that these questions fail to get to the heart
of the matter, that they do not touch the sources of our present
anxieties.

Somehow the danger seems deeper, the contrast between ideal
and reality greater, than any existing liberal programs seem to
suggest. Not injustice but the absence of any cause to which we
can reasonably give ourselves, not insecurity but the prepackaged
career through life—these are the typical complaints, the standard, almost conventional, reasons we give for disaffection from
our times. In the decade since the Korean War, the United

States seems to have turned a corner in the history of politics. With the exception of civil rights for Negroes, the public imagination has left behind the politics of grievances, the politics impelled by the existence of large, definite wrongs crying out to be set right. It has entered the period of the politics of malaise, the politics of unfocused worries and moral ennui.

THE SPECTER OF A MASS SOCIETY

There are reasons for this mood, of course. Never has the pace of change been greater, or its scope, or the degree to which distant events play back and forth on one another. We are preoccupied and distracted by powerful rivals, disoriented by the shift in the balance of power among the continents, unmoored by our affluence and apologetic about it. The international scene troubles us not only with its perils but with its moral dilemmas. The threat of nuclear war, the sheer horror of the preparations in which modern governments are engaged, make ordinary prudence seem like madness, and exhibit a separation between mind and feeling that stuns the conscience. And there are other reasons besides. The twentieth-century intellectual has had a series of cruel lessons in self-distrust. He has seen how pallid and futile refined ideas can be when they are brought face to face with the ferocities of society and politics. And he has also seen that ideas can make men mad.

Yet no one of these reasons, nor all of them together, is quite enough to account for the sense of an oncoming doom, the feeling that all humane social ideals have been rendered irrelevant. The mood has a distinctive shape, it rests on attitudes and ideas, which suggests that there is still another reason for its existence. This is a view of the nature of contemporary industrial society and of the direction in which all societies that have been captured by modern techniques and slogans are relentlessly moving. The movement has many names—"collectivism," "Americanization," "mass society"—depending on who talks about it and where he lives. But the conviction is clearly widespread that this movement is taking place, that it is irreversible, and that it is turning words like "freedom" and "democracy" into sour ironies.

Behind this conviction there lie the authority, the ideas, and the metaphors of a long tradition of protest against modern industrial and democratic society. Such protest is one main theme of the literature and art of the nineteenth and twentieth centuries. Today it is put forward as something close to the *raison d'être* for the existence of literature, the arts, and the humanistic disciplines in general. The merest sampling of the names of those who have contributed to the image of industrial and democratic society that now dominates—and chills—our minds will suggest its power: Nietzsche, Ortega and Jean-Paul Sartre, William Blake, Wordsworth and T. S. Eliot, Jakob Burckhardt and Henry Adams, Balzac, D. H. Lawrence and Picasso. If they are to be believed— and they know how to make themselves credible—the modern world is embarked on a course, whatever the political name attached to it, that will leave men dehumanized and manipulated, and reduced in their power to feel, to imagine, and to act.

What sort of world is it whose birth throes, it is suggested, we are witnessing? Images of that world have furnished our imaginations for more than a generation. It is Charlie Chaplin's *Modern Times*, George Orwell's world of Doublespeak, Aldous Huxley's *Brave New World* with its mass-produced dreams. It is the world of Franz Kafka's K, looking for his hidden persecutor through a bureaucratic maze that is oppressively rational and wholly unintelligible; it is the organized country of policemen and jobs and Sunday excursions where Albert Camus' Stranger lives, moving among men but remote from them and knowing only that he is impenetrably alone. It is the social order drawn by E. M. Forster in "The Day the Machine Stopped"—a society governed by a machine, a rational, hygienic society, giving every man a job to do; but a society in which everyone lives in separate chambers underground, communicating by television with others, and never seeing the stars or touching another human being.

These, of course, are nightmare visions, warnings, and not predictions. But they are not isolated fantasies. Jeremy Bentham's model prison, Auguste Comte's Positive Society, the utopian Walden II which the distinguished experimental psychologist Professor B. F. Skinner has permitted himself to project—these indicate that some partisans of technology, bureaucracy and a "scientific outlook" have advocated the kind of "efficiency" and "organization" that most liberal men today most fear. And behind this fear there stands more than the intuitions of artists, poets, and novelists. The evidences of a "mass society" seem to be all around us—in the assembly line, the supermarket, the urban housing project, the suburban development; in the proliferation of rules and routines on every side, in the mechanically prearranged work we perform, in the prepackaged capsules of entertainment we consume; in the size of the organizations to which we belong, the bureaucratic machinery on which we all depend, the anonymity and remoteness of those who control this machinery; in the increasingly numerous high priesthood of experts who stand between us and everything we do, interpreting, guiding, arranging our lives because things are too complex for us to do so for ourselves. "Mass society" is seen in television with its anodynes against consciousness, in slick magazines with their decontaminated ideas, in Presidential candidates made by machine, in political debates, national and international, carried on before a vast, dispersed, and ill-prepared audience. It is reflected in the spread of a single style of life throughout a nation, and in the steady disappearance, so we are told, not only of all class distinctions, but of all distinctions of better or worse.

The vision is melancholy and melodramatic. Yet there is at least some evidence that it is not wholly invented; and there is even more evidence that it haunts our minds. The most widely read sociological analyses of our condition and the philosophical treatises that have attracted the widest attention from the educated public all give support to the thesis that something quite new is emerging in the democratic world which cancels all our old liberal bets. David Riesman has informed us that the present generation of Americans is "other-directed" rather than "inner-directed," and that consuming has replaced producing as the primary American value. William Holly Whyte, Jr., tells us that the Puritan individualism of our fathers is dying and is being replaced by the morality of the team and the group. And in one way or another, more irritably, more worriedly, more systemat-

ically, other respected and influential observers of the American
scene—Walter Lippmann, C. Wright Mills, Erich Fromm—have
reinforced this new self-image.

The notion that a "mass society" is emerging or that it has
already emerged has replaced the shattered complacencies of
Marxism as a main stimulus and matrix for systematic social
criticism in every advanced industrial country today. Like Marxism in the thirties, the doctrine can be accepted or rejected, but
it cannot be ignored. Indeed, the ideas of those who believe in
the coming mass society are spread by the mass media themselves, in America and abroad. When Eugene Ionesco's play
about the herd instinct triumphant, *Rhinoceros*, opened in London, it caught on, Mollie Panter-Downes reported, "to the point
of being serialized in story form for the man-in-the-herd reader
by Beaverbrook's *Evening Standard*."

The existence and influence of this image or nightmare, indeed,
is itself one of the important political facts on the current scene.
Behind the antipathy that most thinking men and women in the
Western world feel towards Communism there lurks the fear,
more often than is admitted, that Communism is only one form
of a deeper danger and that in this century only the simulacrum
but not the reality of freedom is likely to be retained anywhere
in the world. An emphasis on the limitations and delusions of
reason and science and a grim sense that there is an ominous
movement of events which is turning the traditional ideals of
liberal civilization into historical oddities define the present intellectual temper, or distemper.

Nor are these attitudes restricted to the professional intellectual. The specter of a mass society is plainly on the minds of
more and more people who have never thought of giving it a
name. It may be real or only a creature of our imaginations, but
like the ghost of Hamlet's father it plays an unmistakable part in
the thoughts and actions of the most diverse groups. Conserva-
tives, who have usually valued security and order more than they
have trusted liberty, now complain that we are sacrificing liberty
to security. Liberals who, a generation ago, were pleading for the
application of scientific methods to human affairs are now be-
moaning an era of engineered complacency. The mixed feelings

that greet every innovation in technology from tranquilizers to rockets, the extraordinary spasm of soul-searching touched off by revelations of fraud in radio and television, all the conventional, irritable jokes about Madison Avenue—these can be explained only if there is a suspicion that our technology is a trap and that manipulation and deception are not isolated occurrences but parts of a pattern.

Attitudes are arising among us, in fact, that are reminiscent of the Hellenistic Age in its weariness. Exotic cults have emerged which instruct us in how to remain serene though bewildered, and which promise an ecstasy that lies beyond both society and logic. There is a resurgent Stoic emphasis on personal integrity, on the kind of freedom that can be saved only if a man does not share the values of the world in which he must live. And over the clatter of a society busily and indiscriminately accumulating material goods, there are beginning to be heard the strains of a strange aristocratic, high-fidelity epicureanism counseling men of taste and discernment to turn away from the storm, to cultivate their gardens, and to pursue, as long as they can, their own decent private purposes.

A hundred and thirty years ago, at the conclusion of his *Democracy in America,* Alexis de Tocqueville asked, "What sort of despotism do democratic nations have to fear?" The picture he drew was of a society that gluts men with petty and paltry pleasures, separates them from one another, takes the means of social action out of their hands, and leaves them helplessly in the hands of a vast tutelary power. "I have always thought," he concluded, "that servitude of the regular, quiet and gentle kind which I have just described might be combined more easily than is commonly believed with some of the outward forms of freedom, and that it might even establish itself under the wing of the sovereignty of the people." This brooding vision is our own.

IMAGE AND REALITY

Is it a true one? The question cannot be answered in a word or a platitude. But it is the secret question that feeds our politics of malaise. And whether we think that the theory of a mass society is an accurate account of our condition or only the expression of a mood, it is a symptom of our pains and an index to where we feel them. We are feeling them where long-range and fundamental changes in the character of our social institutions are taking place. The specter of a mass society points to the emergence of a new sort of relationship between the individual and the groups on which he depends; to a new distribution of power within the community at large; to new kinds of relations between social classes. And it points as well to a major shift in our civilization's center of gravity—the emergence of science, technology, and bureaucracy as the great driving enterprises of modern society. A form of guerrilla warfare is going on at the heart of our civilization. The image of a mass society is the product and sign of a society at odds with itself, a society that has not managed to fit its new powers to its traditional standards and cannot accept the standards that seem to fit its new powers.

But to speak of standards is to speak of the second part of the problem. For it is only half the truth—and, on the whole, the less interesting half—to say that men live in society. They also live inside an image of their society. They hold beliefs about the facts which may be true or false, and they also judge these facts in terms of expectations of what is normal and natural and standards of what is right and proper. And these expectations and standards can be misleading. Men may cling to them, and probably will, just the same. But when men's expectations are baseless, when their standards do not show them where to get a grip on their problems or how to turn their vague hopes into definite purposes, there is one thing they do not have. They do not have the power to direct events or to shape their destinies.

This is the context, I think, in which our politics of malaise can be understood. Our image of democracy and the realities are out of accord. On one side, the facts are new and the standard descriptions of liberal democracy have lost their authority. On the other side, the old words are out of kilter and the classic ideals of liberal democracy have lost their unambiguous clarity and charm. There are ideas and hopes that have sustained the modern liberal mind since at least the time of the American and French revolutions. One by one, each seems to be denied or embarrass-

ingly parodied in the world on which we look out. We have lost
our assurance about what the facts are, and we have lost something even more fundamental—an assured language in which to
speak about the facts, to judge them, and to manage them.

Our democratic professions obviously diverge from our practices at many points, and at many points our practices are wrong.
But at many other points the trouble may lie not in our practices
but in our stars—in the obscure and mistaken conceptions of ideal
democracy that we hold, conceptions that tell us neither what is
possible nor what is desirable. Before we can begin to talk about
what has happened to leave us disappointed and disoriented, and
before we can think about ways of dealing with our problems,
we have to examine the ideas and standards we employ when we
declare ourselves disappointed and disoriented.

The first order of business, then, must be to stand back and
look at what we call democracy in perspective. What kind of
social phenomenon is it? What are the conditions in which it
emerges? What do cherished phrases in the democratic lexicon—
phrases like "majority rule" or "the consent of the governed"—
actually stand for? What are the expectations that democracy
provokes in those who live under it, and how do these expectations explain our present discontents? We must begin, in short,
by trying to come to terms with our terms.

II

THE NATURAL HISTORY
OF DEMOCRACY

Whatever ideals, human or divine, a liberal democracy may serve or misserve, it conducts its business in an unusual way. Those who hold power are expected to protect the rights of those who are trying to take their power away from them, and those who are trying to throw the rascals out are expected to accept the rascals' authority until they do. Magic, mystery, and authority have commonly been thought to be the indispensable instruments for the government of mankind. Yet democratic arrangements seem like a systematic device for tearing away these protective wrappings from government. A democratic government must compete in the hustings for votes; it must speak in the ordinary language of men and dwell in the market place and not on the heights; it must command while it is being heckled and lead while everyone recognizes that its days are numbered.

Perhaps all this is a puppet show. Even so, it is a strange ritual, and it has always seemed a mystery to some and foolishness to others. What is the natural history of this form of government, the drama it enacts and re-enacts? What is the context in which it arises, the problems that stay with it, the circumstances and the combination of accident and artifice that are present when it manages to sustain itself? Is there, indeed, any general pattern in the development of all the stable democracies?

THE PERMANENT PROBLEM OF GOVERNMENT

Anarchists, together with a large number of respectable people, habitually associate government with trouble. They are right, but for the wrong reasons. Governments make trouble, but they do not start it. Trouble starts them. Their existence testifies to the fact that the elementary and almost instinctive ways in which men ordinarily arrange their joint affairs have broken down.

Any functioning social order may be construed as a set of arrangements for helping men to know what is expected of them and how their fellows are likely to behave. In most societies most of the time, however, men fit their behavior to the behavior of their fellows spontaneously and effortlessly, like the crowds in old markets, avoiding collisions and following the flow of the traffic without the help of officials. Myth, ritual, emotional ties, common economic imperatives, the unmistakable concentration of superior power in definite hands, simple routine—these work automatically and silently, though not always painlessly, to cause men to live by common authorities and to fit their activities to a common mold. Men's lives are governed, and governed effectively. But government as such is as invisible and ubiquitous as the air.

Yet politics and formal government are distinct and specialized activities in all civilized societies. And the fact that they are is a sign that these societies are permanently disturbed. Politics is a substitute for custom; it becomes conspicuous whenever and wherever custom recedes or breaks down. It is an indicator of disequilibrium, of the existence of discordant interests and unsettled controversies, of the need to make deliberate decisions and to decide who is going to make them. The father who has to proclaim that he is master in his own house gives us reason to suspect that perhaps he is not. But governments are repeatedly proclaiming just this. They steadily assert their formal and legal authority, thereby testifying to the fact that authority as such is no longer a simple and unchallenged fact of life. It has to be declared—and it has to be contended for, located, and defined. That is why government and politics are invariably surrounded with apologetics and smothered in symbols and words. Government and politics are the signs that there is a struggle going on for men's allegiance.

What is the prize for which a government contends when it is engaged in this struggle? It may aspire to receive the consent of the governed, whatever that means, but most governments have been willing to settle for something much less than consent—just unpushed obedience, just a general disposition in the societies they govern to accept their authority, and to do so for reasons other than the fear of reprisal and punishment. This general agreement about who has the right to govern is always a precarious thing, and is based on a patchwork of motives and circumstances. Despite the dreams that Rousseau sometimes permitted himself, no society, and certainly no sophisticated or interesting society, is so radiant with a single conception of the common good that its government can get on with its business without ever resorting to violence or police measures. The club and the cop lie in the background of all political arrangements.

But the circumstances are rare when men obey their governments simply because they know their governments have supreme power. Their governments would not command that power if they commanded no voluntary cooperation anywhere. The so-called "realist" about politics, the man like Thomas Hobbes who cannot get the ubiquity of force and its threat out of his mind, prefers melodrama to observation. Normally, men accept the edicts of the authorities above them not simply or mainly out of fear, but out of habit, interest, conviction, and the simplest of all reasons—inability to get off the treadmill, to turn away for a moment from the desperate pressures of their daily lives. And over the long run the existence of an unquestioned center of power in a community generally tends in itself to generate some supporting sentiments.

Yet the "consensus" that supports any government is always limited. There is a reservoir of loyalty and confidence into which a government can dip only so far before powerful groups will withdraw their cooperation or undertake active resistance. The American government made this discovery when it tried to desegregate the schools; the French Fourth Republic almost constantly, and on almost every important front, for fifteen years. When a government meets problems of this sort, it can retreat, remain immobile, try to extend the area of agreement by persuasion, or resort to the surgery of force or the threat of force. But whatever it does, it has reached the boundaries of the consensus that currently supports it. It has been reminded of what it is likely to forget on the routine days—that some parts of the nation are sternly arrayed against other parts, that violence lies just beneath the surface, and that a government is constantly engaged in a struggle for men's allegiance but can never say that the prize is securely in hand. That is the permanent problem of all government, and it is where liberal democracy, like every other form of government, begins and ends.

MODERNITY AND DEMOCRACY

But if formal government is a product of disequilibrium, liberal democracy, the kind of liberal democracy we know today, is a sign of accentuated disequilibrium. It is the product of a culture in a peculiar and persisting state of tension. And such a culture is a prerequisite for the existence of democratic arrangements on a large scale. Nowhere in the world is democracy flourishing at present except in societies that have felt the shock of modernity and have had time enough to absorb its first effects. Democratic political arrangements are not the inevitable consequences of the modernization of a society. But they are precarious in any society that has not gone a long way down that path.

The modernizing of a society means changes both material and psychological. Materially, modernization means the commercialization and industrialization of an economy, or at least an open, mobile agricultural system; a rise in per capita income; a decrease in the proportion of the population engaged in providing the food supply; a shift in the center of gravity from the countryside to the city; the loosening of the ties of birthplace and birth rank, and a quickening of men's opportunities to move around on the landscape and up and down the social ladder; the rise in the importance of highly specialized skills for which long training is required; and, not least, the general spread of literacy and the growth of media of communication reaching all sections of the society.

But the deeper effects of modernity are felt underneath men's

skins. The modernization of a society means the emergence of
men and women who have new attitudes towards the past, who
make altered demands on the present and future, and who have
a radically different sense of themselves. The attitudes that define
a modern outlook are not complicated. But they spell an extraordinary change in the moral geography of the human scene. And
it is that change that makes democratic political arrangements
conceivable.

What is it to be "modern"? Few of us *are* modern, wholly and
unequivocally. But insofar as we are, we have broken free from
a simple and primeval assumption—the assumption that the world
follows its appointed rounds, repeating itself for ever and ever.
A man who is eagerly modern is aware that he has a place in a
sequence of changes. He has it always on his mind that he may
be out of date, and that it is dangerous—almost worse, it is laugh-
able—to be out of date. He has, in a word, more sense of history
and less respect for the past. And this attitude towards the past
means a new attitude towards the present and the future. The
status quo can no longer be regarded as something that is simply
given, a gift or punishment of the gods, a movement of things in
their predestinate grooves. To the man who looks at the world
with a self-consciously modern eye, the status quo is a set of
problems to be managed, something for which he and his fellows
have responsibility. And he is likely to think that if men do their
jobs the future will be better than the present. Moderns have dis-
agreed about whether or not progress is inevitable; but they usually agree that progress is the elementary duty of man.

To have a modern attitude, accordingly, is to have something
more than new ideals. It is to have a new attitude towards the
function of all ideals. It is to think that ideals have a human and
immediate purpose, and to be impatient and restless about putting them to work. In any developed civilization men possess conceptions of the world as it ought to be and judge the world as it
is in the light of these conceptions. But in a modern civilization,
Greek, Elizabethan, or twentieth century, men expect their ideals
to make a practical, worldly difference here and now, and they
have lost that willingness to wait which their fathers took or mis-
took for wisdom. To the extent that men aim to be modern, they

commit themselves to a war with the ancient gods and with the institutions that represent these gods on earth; or else they must secularize these gods and their institutions. In America, Tocqueville reported, you hear ministers speak mainly of the goods of this world, and you meet a politician where you expected to meet a priest.

But the impact of modernity is felt not only in the individual's attitude towards time and eternity, but in his attitude towards himself. The typically modern man develops the sense that he is disengaged from the past, separable from his home, distinguishable from any status he may occupy. The Christian belief is that each individual is judged for himself in the next world. A modern society translates this belief into the principle that each individual ought to be judged for himself in this world—a much harder thing to do, since the standards are fluid and men are doing the judging. Modernity is an education in self-consciousness, in the sense of uniqueness and separateness, in ambition and self-assertion, in uncertainty and embarrassment. The pain and mystery of selfhood, an experience best known to religious seers in most societies, becomes Everyman's experience when he enters a modern society.

For if a man thinks that the past is on trial, if he thinks the present is a test of his powers, and the future, his responsibility, he has put himself to the test as well. Life is a series of challenges to be met, a trial of one's powers, a career. The attitude shows itself equally in the Puritan ethic and the competition of Stakhanovites; it dominates the atmosphere of societies in which a modern spirit has been turned loose, explaining both their dynamism and their tension. "If human nature felt no temptation to take a chance," Keynes observed, "no satisfaction (profit apart) in constructing a factory, a railway, a mine or a farm, there might not be much investment merely as a result of cold calculation." But the "human nature" of which Keynes speaks is the human nature of modern-minded men somehow impelled to see what they can do. It is the spirit which made Odysseus, the man who was never at a loss, a hero to the modern-minded Greeks.

Moreover, there is another attitude which is likely to go hand in hand with this one. The individual who is on the move, not as a member of migratory hordes but on his own, has to throw down old associations and to find or build new ones. And in a society in which this experience is common, new attitudes towards social groups emerge. Like the individual himself, they are expected to show results. Their sanctity disappears, their authority becomes clearly provisional. Not only government, but even groups like the family and the church take on the character of practical arrangements, to be judged by their success in performing their specialized functions. Men in a modern society cannot act without the support of groups any more than men in any other kind of society. But the groups are inventions, devices, means to ends; and men tend to think of their membership in any particular group as a matter of quid pro quo. We may like this attitude or dislike it, celebrate it as elementary common sense or denounce it as the dissolvent of all social discipline. Undoubtedly, it deflates the meanings that men find in their social experience. But it is this attitude that makes democratic arrangements possible, and at least the show of democratic arrangements necessary, in all industrial societies. The censors of the city of Geneva condemned Rousseau's *Social Contract* and denounced its author because he considered "all forms of government to be only provisional, experiments that can always be changed. . . ." The censors misunderstood, as they so often do.

Accordingly, the habits of social discipline that prevail in a modern society are significantly different from the patterns of deference that hold traditional societies together. Men who are mobile, who have seen more than one place in their lives or who have fought through to a station in society different from that of their parents, are not so likely to regard the differences between social classes as sacrosanct. The lines between the classes can remain, of course, and the forms and even the feelings of deference as well. But even in modernized countries where the sense of class remains as strong as the sense of race in America, it would be strange to hear the old song that ordinary people were once expected to sing:

> God bless the squire and his relations
> And keep us in our proper stations.

The shoe is on the other foot:

High rank involves no shame—
We boast an equal claim
With him of humble name
To be respected!

Moreover, there is more in these new attitudes than resentment or hostility towards privilege. A modern man, a mobile and disengaged man, has a positive expectation. He resists fixed class lines because he thinks the public business his business, because he expects to share in the common wealth, because he has the attitudes of an active participant in society. The function of religion, according to Santayana, is to give men another world to live in. The ability to read serves the same function, as illiterate men everywhere recognize. A modern man can read, which gives him an expanded consciousness of the world; and he is exposed to the mass media, which gives him a sense of closeness to what is not directly his own affair. "How can you ask me such a question?" gasped the Turkish shepherd whom Daniel Lerner and his associates asked for an opinion on a public issue. But the modern expects to be asked, and expects a chance to answer. He has more active powers of empathy, and a more irritable demand for facts and reasons.

A modern society, in short, is an experiment in dissatisfaction, a wager on the benefits of discontent. It multiplies the pusher, the parvenu, and the snob; it also manufactures the man who makes it a point of honor not to be deceived. And liberal democracy can be understood as the product of men of this sort and as one response to the problem of governing them. It is an attempt to deal with such men in their own terms, to give them channels for complaint, the right to doubt out loud, and opportunities to advance themselves and their programs. It is an effort to take modernity in stride and to provide it with an appropriate discipline.

THE ECONOMIC AND SOCIAL MOLD

Modernity, of course, has its inherent dilemmas. It promises men equality, but it leans on methods of technological and economic organization that create new hierarchies. It promises them independence, and catches them up in social groups that are immense, impersonal, and powerful. And it generally raises men's expectations faster than they can be satisfied, and encourages new expectations as quickly as old ones are satisfied. With its emphasis on innovation and on results, modernity, indeed, can produce a disagreeable and dangerous tension between means and ends. On one side, it can foster an intense desire to move ahead, to have more and to be more; on the other side, it can obscure or erase the line between the legitimate and illegitimate avenues to self-advancement. And this situation is aggravated when the social system is unbalanced, and the legitimate avenues to success are available to some but not to others. There is a reason why the movie gangster generates sympathy. He breathes the modern ethic of aspiration and success. And while he uses illegitimate methods, it is because the legitimate avenues are closed to him or because he is not quite sure what the legitimate avenues are.

For a modern culture eliminates the major reason for the traditional passivity of the lower classes—which is simply the great difference and distance between the rich and the poor. The poorer a country, the richer its rich people are likely to be. Modernity removes the poor man's ignorance of any way of life but his own and upsets his inbred sense that nothing ever changes. It puts him in a world in which wealth is obviously growing, and gives him just enough of that wealth to make him want more. This is the situation that makes revolutions; and if it does not, that is because some way has been found to keep men from living in the limbo of desire without hope. Their desires have to be moderated or turned aside on new objects, or else their hopes have to seem not entirely unrealistic.

The struggle for the redistribution of wealth is therefore a perennial theme in the politics of all even fairly modernized societies. It has been one of the two or three persisting issues in the history of all democracies. But it can be met by other techniques than the straightforward redistribution of wealth. It can be met by making access to the upper classes freer—something that happens in all industrial societies, although the movement upwards is balanced by an equal movement downwards. And it can also be met simply by providing a steadily rising standard of living from which most sections of the population benefit. Perhaps most important of all, the key social goods, the prerequisites and symbols of social advancement—whether they are education or automobiles—have to be generally available to all classes. A democracy succeeds in its struggle for the allegiance of its citizens when it can convince them, by words and by works, that they are getting a fair share of what is coming to them. And as the worriers have noted, there is a tendency for the conception of a "fair share" to expand. Economic abundance is therefore a general condition for democratic stability.

More than abundance is necessary, however, if the strange, odd democratic etiquette of mutual criticism and forbearance between different kinds and conditions of men is to grow and be maintained. A certain balance in the distribution of social power and opportunity is also necessary. When a man has an invention to sell, a career to make, a cause to promote, or just a complaint to utter, he needs another man's ear. His opportunities and powers to achieve his purposes depend not only on himself but, as the folk wisdom of moderns recognizes, on his connections or chances to make connections. And when he finds others who can help, the quality of the help they can give depends on their money, influence, education, and talents. A democracy must have a social structure, therefore, which puts powerful groups and organizations at the disposal of most individuals, and thereby makes it possible for them to get into the democratic act.

A recurrent issue has therefore dominated the history of democracy in all countries, extending from the struggles of religious minorities through the struggles of labor unions for recognition to the contemporary struggles of American Negroes. It is the quarrel between those who already enjoy full citizenship in democratic society and those to whom the tokens and powers of full citizenship have not been extended. Modernity galvanizes that struggle; democratic ideas give it legitimacy; and the practical conditions for stable democratic government usually require that those who want admission to the democratic community badly enough be granted such admission. Where this issue has been solved fairly speedily, and without leaving stubborn distrust and resentments behind, the democratic form of government has been

durable. Where the issue has not been solved, or solved slowly
and bitterly, democratic institutions have been precarious. The
poison that destroys a democracy—the poison that Marx was sure
was going to destroy Western democracy—is the growth of the
feeling that some people are in and others are out. It creates a
division around which most other issues come to turn, and inflates
otherwise manageable problems into quarrels between two irreconcilable camps. For democratic government, in the course of its
natural history, throws down a gage to fate. It invites men to be
troublesome. It can command their disciplined allegiance only if
it can also convince them that they are being consulted, and that
there is an effective way of making trouble within established
arrangements and not despite them.

THE THEATRICAL ASPECT OF DEMOCRACY

The conditions that sustain democracy involve more, however,
than the distribution of wealth, power, and rights. When men
struggle for admission to a community, or when they struggle to
throw out what they regard as an alien government, they do not
do so simply to advance their practical interests. They are struggling for and against symbols—symbols of honor or humiliation,
symbols that excite or that outrage their imaginations. As Walter
Bagehot pointed out a century ago, a government has its "efficient" side. It has to marshal power, solve problems, enforce decisions. But it also has its "theatrical" side. It dramatizes men's
memories and commitments and embodies values and attitudes
held or rejected by the community or by sections of it. It is itself
a symbol, and it leans on symbols. And its power to secure allegiance depends not only on its efficiency, but on its command of
the symbols that are most contagious.

For a form of government can be relatively efficient and still
not have the staying power it needs. On its "efficient" side the
Weimar Republic stood comparatively high. But it symbolized
defeat, and it spoke a language and seemed to represent an outlook—modern, utilitarian, democratic—for which important groups
in the German nation felt a profound antipathy. The history of
the most stable democracies, in contrast, shows a continuity in

symbols. The United States, of course, was born and baptized in liberal original sin: its symbols of democracy are identical with its symbols of nationhood. But other democracies with an undemocratic past—for example, in Britain or Scandinavia—have managed a social alchemy that absorbs the new to the old, and that changes the interior of things while leaving their surfaces agreeably unmarked. They have superintended the movement of their nations towards modernity and the uprooting of the powers and privileges of traditional classes while maintaining the old symbols and allowing the retired soldiers to wear their old uniforms. They have therefore succeeded in keeping within the democratic system groups that might otherwise associate this system with their own defeat and disgrace.

Even the United States has had to manage that sort of miracle: it has somehow converted symbols of rebellion into symbols of patriotism and put Lee alongside Grant in its pantheon of heroes. It is when the symbols of a democratic regime become identified too clearly and exclusively with one side in an old argument, as in France, that agreement about the validity of democratic institutions is difficult to achieve. In most countries, indeed, these symbols have to be mixed with the symbols and ideology of nationalism. For modernization is a traumatic experience. Without symbols and ideology it is difficult to cushion the shock.

But successful democratic regimes do not simply preserve old symbols. They develop symbols of their own. Liberal democratic regimes, to be sure, commonly adopt the posture of businesslike efficiency and parade the symbols of ordinary middle-class morality. Because this is so, and because magic and mystery are important in the government of men, it is often thought that liberal democracy is a quixotic adventure based on the idea that all that men want from their government is modesty, respectability, and results. "Mystic glamour," Joseph Schumpeter remarked, "is what counts in the ruling of men. The stock exchange is a poor substitute for the Holy Grail." But the stock exchange generates an excitement that transcends the purely practical, and so do production graphs on a chart. Men have been known to see the hand of God in them. And there is mystic glamour about Lincoln, about democratic games and ceremonies, about the celebrities a democracy creates, and, for that matter, about Roberts's *Rules of Order*. Liberal democracy undoubtedly gives further encouragement to the debunking and demasking tendencies of modern cultures. But it does not necessarily remove magic and mystery. It simply finds them in unusual places.

DEMOCRACY'S PECULIAR ARRANGEMENTS

Beyond wealth and the distribution of power, and beyond symbols, moreover, the democratic system also leans on some artifices of its own. Two in particular are decisive. The first is civil liberty; the second is a special form of social organization—a pluralistic society.

There are two ways to drive a man to subversion. The first is to require him to sacrifice or compromise what he cannot sacrifice or compromise while keeping his self-respect. The second is to deny him legitimate avenues for registering his complaints and trying to improve his condition. The basic civil liberties are therefore curiously effective instruments for maintaining men's fundamental loyalty to a political system even when they disapprove much that it does. Conventional opinion imagines that civil liberties exist only to make dissent possible. But in maintaining a loyal opposition, and in taking elaborate steps to protect organized disagreement with its programs, a democratic government also contributes to social cohesion. It offers its citizens instruments for changing the system that are themselves part of that system, and does not push dissent into disloyalty by refusing to draw a line between the two. To the cynic all this may seem simply a clever device for converting dissatisfaction with some part of the system into a reason for allegiance to the democratic system as a whole. The cynicism is gratuitous, but the cleverness is there.

Civil liberty, however, is the legal framework for a social order of a special type. Even if a man stands alone, his liberty to think and speak as he chooses is still a comfort. But it is only to the extent that a man does not have to stand alone that he can exert social influence and power. And it is only to the extent that he can choose among different groups, and can leave one and join another, that he can be at once drawn into the community and still retain his autonomy. The liberty to think and speak as one chooses has a bite to it, in short, only when it is matched and supported by the liberty to choose one's associations and by the existence of a social order which offers the individual a broad spectrum of diverse, independent, and powerful groups among which he can choose. Such a society is a pluralistic society. It is marked by a considerable decentralization in its decision-making processes, and the groups available to the individual have a distinctive character.

In the first place, they are usually specialized groups—a veterans' association, farmers' cooperative, or consumers' union—representing only a section of the individual's total interests. In the second place, these groups have hard shells. They are relatively autonomous, and have their own base of support. Accordingly, they have power to make decisions on their own and to take independent action for their members without leaning on other groups or the government. Moreover, since they have independent resources, they also have the power to influence the calculations of others who make decisions. It is the existence of such groups that makes the political struggle in a democracy a struggle in public and a struggle for the approval of organized publics. And it is also the existence of such groups that provides individuals with avenues into the community and into the general stream of social life. Not least, the individual who can enjoy such pluralistic arrangements has the chance to spread his interests around so that few setbacks need be ultimate disasters. He is not totally dependent on any group and not wholly insulated by any group. And he has protection against being manipulated by any single center of opinion or authority.

Such a form of social organization is what protects individual autonomy. But it has another and equally important function as well. It encourages the special aptitudes and skills, and also the special frame of mind, on which political democracy depends. The voluntary organizations that mark a democratic society are— or can be—training grounds for democratic habits. And they also provide the framework that makes compromise possible. For a pluralistic society is an arrangement for preventing any single center of power from embracing all the others. Although it produces conflicts, and often rancorous conflicts, between limited and specialized interests, the conflicts are localized.

Aristotle thought a large middle class the leaven of democracy, modifying and tempering the conflicts between rich and poor, and making negotiation and compromise possible. A pluralistic society carries this principle one step further. The individual who has many interests and who belongs to many associations has room to compromise, a reason to do so, and a perspective that invites him to think in compromising terms. Though committed to a particular group, some of his other interests are likely to overlap those of innocent bystanders or of members of the group directly opposed to his own. This encourages second thoughts. The rhetoric which makes the phrase "divided loyalty" a term of reproach is inimical to a democratic ethic. Democracy thrives on divided loyalties.

THE NATURE OF A DEMOCRATIC CONSENSUS

A modernized economy and culture, a reasonable distribution of wealth and power in the community, symbols and forms that have continuity and that speak men's language, civil liberties and a framework of vigorous private groups and associations—these, then, are conditions that sustain democratic government. And when they are present, a democratic consensus is the prize. It shows itself in the feeling—an odd feeling when we think of the animosities that politics engenders—that one's principal rivals in any dispute, though they are wrong, are at least sane and sincere. Their sanity is proved by the premises they accept for the discussion, and their sincerity by their obedience to established rules. It is exactly to the extent that men hold this attitude towards their opponents that a political community may be said to exist in a democracy.

A democratic consensus, in short, has two parts. The first part is an agreement or a convergence in belief. At no time are men forced or legislated into such a consensus, and no one can be required to accept it. But habit, sentiment, common experience, and commonplace political expediencies contrive to produce it. Such a consensus is simply an informal and uncodified agreement among all the major parties to the political competition about the principal issues that must be met, the place where discussion must begin, and the limits within which any proposed solution must fall. The agreement is a merely practical agreement. The beliefs that compose it have to do with mundane matters, and are subject to change and do change. But at any moment it is this working consensus that gives cohesion and coherence to the democratic debate.

Thus, political controversies may exist about taxation; but only groups not generally credited with political sanity will call the income tax into question. Men may quarrel about "the Welfare State"; but few will propose that old-age and survivors' benefits be abolished. In unstable democracies politics has the shape of a play by Chekhov: everyone carries on a loud monologue with himself and nobody ever answers anybody else. In stable democracies, in contrast, the political process has something closer to the shape of a dialogue. Few groups live in a world by themselves, extremist groups are weak, and all serious contenders for power and position have the inestimable advantage of knowing fairly clearly where they must begin and where they had better stop. There is, of course, nothing sacrosanct about this consensus: it may rest on nothing more than a tired agreement to define "reality" in terms of the illusion that everybody shares. The criticism of any working consensus is therefore indispensable. Nevertheless, when such a consensus exists it allows men to talk to each other rather than past each other, and gives democratic politics a spine and a cumulative direction. It is democracy's substitute for an official ideology.

But this working consensus is intertwined with a more basic consensus, and the strength or weakness of one affects the durability of the other. In constitutional democracies obedience is given to commands because those who issue the commands occupy their positions in accordance with certain procedures and issue the commands according to form. The existence of generally recognized rules, some written but the greater part unwritten, is the key to the basic consensus that marks a successful democracy. That consensus consists in a shared allegiance to the rules of the democratic game.

The influence of this "democratic mold" goes far beyond the official political process. In societies where democratic arrangements are well established, corporations and country clubs as well as governments conduct elections, consult with their constituencies, and accept, at least nominally, the supremacy of elected officials over professional managers. The rules may in many cases be only rituals; and many of them, of course, are hazy. But obedience to these rules is what conveys legitimacy to the social decisions that are made. When President Truman removed General MacArthur from his command in Korea, there was no effective challenge to the President's authority to do so. In contrast, when the elected leaders of the French Fourth Republic tried to control the army in Algiers, their right to do so was questioned, and questioned effectively. And when a government enjoying something like a consensus was finally restored, it was based as much as anything on a consensus around a man. The difference between these two cases is the difference between the presence and the absence of a basic democratic consensus.

And yet, though the difference is clear, it is a matter of degree. A basic democratic consensus, though it shows itself in a common respect for the rules of the democratic game, is supported—or distorted—by allegiance to personalities, by loyalties to subordinate institutions, by the efficiency of democratic governments in dealing with the public business, and by the success that individuals have in using the rules to advance their own private interests. It is not necessarily fragile, but neither does it sustain itself by its own sheer momentum. And a basic democratic consensus can very easily be destroyed by the simple device of trying to stretch it too far.

THE LIMITS OF CONSENSUS

For there is a final question to which we must turn. It is a question suggested by prevalent images of democracy, by everyday political discourse, by democratic ceremonials in the United States, and by habits of thought so inbred in us that they approach instincts.

Is this all that supports a democracy—a certain convergence of mundane opinion that may change, plus an etiquette and a moral attitude? Is not something more necessary? Is it possible to believe that there can be allegiance to the rules—does such allegiance even make sense—without a common philosophy, without shared beliefs about the nature of God and the final destiny of man? Is not a "consensus on first and last things" also required? According to Walter Lippmann—and he is only one of the notable figures who holds the view—the absence of such a consensus is the principal source of contemporary liberal democracy's maladies.

Those who are disturbed about the untidy philosophical character of democratic arrangements are seeking a kind of meeting of minds that would please the heavenly hosts. Heaven does not have democracy, and has no need for it. On this half-illuminated planet, a consensus on first and last things will not by itself produce the agreements necessary for an effective polity. And conversely, agreement on the kind of questions with which democratic politics are concerned is perfectly possible even when men start from different cosmic premises. Protestants, Catholics, Jews, and freethinkers have all found it possible to make common cause under liberal democracies; so have Platonists, materialists, skeptics, and hylozoists. And men who have started from the same abstract principles—for example, the belief in Natural Law to which Mr. Lippmann urges that we return—have opposed each other about such specific questions as slavery, free elections, or the limits of religious and intellectual toleration. Before a consensus on "the higher generalities" (as Mr. Lippmann calls them) can produce a practical operating consensus, it has to be supplemented by the establishment of some special group of men—a Party, a Church, or a Committee on Ultimate Truths—as the only group with the authority to say what the consensus means when it is applied to day-to-day affairs.

For the air is thin in the land of higher generalities. Everything depends on the interpretation we give to our beliefs about first and last things. Believers in Natural Law place great stress on the significance of such utterances as that justice ought to be done, or that a man's property ought to be respected subject to considerations of the public interest. But Mr. Khrushchev could assent unreservedly to both these propositions. It is when we try to give them some content, when we apply them to concrete cases in the here and now, that the trouble begins. The abstract formula has to be filled in, and at this point individual judgment and personal preference reappear. The insistence on the necessity of an ultimate philosophical consensus converts arguments about practical matters into arguments about the nature of the universe and the ultimate purpose of human life. No doubt it introduces passion into politics. But it can do so by turning minor disagreement into a question of ultimate conscience and ultimate loyalty. This does not cement a democracy together, it breaks it apart.

In fact cohesion is achieved in democratic societies precisely because certain questions, the most important questions, are kept out of the arena in which agreement is expected or required. This is the condition for democratic stability as well as for democratic freedom. "Ask a man of orthodoxy anywhere, what is fundamental?" Bentham once remarked. "His answer comes to this—it is what I am most earnest about." The tension which a democracy maintains between men of different orthodoxies is what keeps any one of them from running respectably riot.

And that tension also makes it possible to treat the most important human enterprises—art, science, religious belief and disbelief, the family, and the voluntary association of human beings with one another—as independent of politics and of the claims for a higher solidarity. This is why conscientious men can play by the rules of the democratic game. The rules do not ask them to sacrifice what they cannot sacrifice and keep their self-respect. In the end, the plurality of ultimate beliefs in a democracy produces a climate in which ultimate beliefs are seen to be what they are—choices and commitments. And it encourages an attitude that makes democratic government a little more possible. This is the attitude that politics is not a sacred process but a profane one.

The language of ultimates, of course, is inevitable. But when we hear the language of ultimates we hear the natural ritual and poetry of politics. We are listening to the overture to the democratic political performance and not to the performance itself. The agreements that hold a democracy together are agreements on a much lower level. If a man agrees with you on a concrete issue, then he does. His willingness to cooperate will not be improved if he is told that he does not have a logical right to agree because he holds the wrong metaphysics. There is no official or quasi-official doctrine about God, the universe, or man's ultimate destiny on which democratic arrangements necessarily depend. And that is only a way of saying that democracy is an arrangement aimed at preventing a society from being locked in by any single doctrine. It is a method of government based on the recognition that men are diverse, that ultimate questions are hard to answer, and that all human arrangements are fallible, including its own.

III

IDEALS AND IDOLS
OF DEMOCRACY

First and foremost, "democracy is a political term." It is a name for a particular set of conditions under which the right to coerce others is acquired and held. To be sure, there are many definitions of democracy, as many as there are men with causes they want to coat with legitimacy. Democracy is defined as rule by law, as a society that makes the individual central, as government by the people, as government for the people. Many conceive it as a great process of turning history around, a lifting of the masses from their ancient condition. And there is a point to most of these definitions. By and large, democracy works towards such ends, though not unfailingly. But to try to pin down the meaning of democracy by talking about these products of democracy is like defining the game of bridge in terms of brainwork and pleasant evenings. The one incontrovertible sign of a democracy is the way in which it makes the sticky decisions that are the business of politics. In its primary meaning, democracy is a system in which men acquire the right to govern through a system of free and open competition for votes, and in which they make their decisions while under the pressure of outside groups whose right to put them under pressure they must protect.

Yet politics is only machinery. Elections, parties, political bosses, and pressure groups are the unmistakable signs of the existence of democracy, but they have obviously not been the reasons why democracy has excited men. Something else, a change in the character of their experience at a deeper and more intimate level, has been what democracy has seemed to promise them. It is traditional to speak of the ideals that are presupposed by a political system—a habit of thought at once flattering and misleading, since it suggests that men know what they are about when they commit themselves to a political system. It is more appropriate to judge a system by the character of the ideals and expectations it encourages men to hold, and by the degree to which it fulfills these expectations. It is time for us to turn, therefore, from the framework of democracy to the aspirations that give it its reason for being. What is all the shooting about? What is the democratic system an attempt to accomplish?

To ask these questions is to begin to find out why so many devoted partisans of the successful democracy we enjoy in the United States today are nevertheless disoriented and disturbed. For the democratic system depends on a population that has certain expectations, and encourages them to have these expectations. And changes of geological proportions in the social terrain on which we move have challenged these expectations.

THE DEMOCRATIC BIAS

The way to begin, I think, is not with abstract ideals but with something simpler and more fundamental—a state of feeling and sentiment, an emotional posture. Beneath democratic ideals there is an elementary bias, an attitude that belongs to men who, without taking thought or giving reasons, look at the world in a certain way.

Our everyday use of the word "democratic" suggests what this attitude is. A man with democratic feelings habitually judges his fellows without regard to their rank or status. He looks on them as members of a single moral community in which all possess the same fundamental rights and obligations. He is suspicious of the sweeping social distinctions that place men in separate boxes. But he is also suspicious of universal formulas that place all men in the same box. He looks skeptically on any effort to define the good life for everyone. The ideal democrat is egalitarian not because he thinks all men are the same, but because he doubts, when the chips are down, that there is any single comprehensive standard of human excellence by which all men can be measured and compared. He is ready to assign all men the same rights without insisting that they all live by the same lights.

Democratic cultures, therefore, are normally the scene for a kind of moral drama, a recurrent contest between Babbitts and Bohemians, conformists and freebooters. There is a tension within them between gregariousness and a respect for privacy, between hostility towards the man who sets himself apart and admiration for achievement. Thirty years ago moral criticism in the United States was principally directed against unchecked individualism, particularly in the economic sphere. Today criticism is directed against a sentimental egalitarianism that denies the differences between individuals. By and large, indeed, there are two democratic traditions, not one. The Continental democratic tradition has in the main stressed the equality and fraternity of men—the falseness and injustice of class distinctions and racial barriers, the essential identity of all individuals as possessors of the same fundamental rights. The Anglo-Saxon tradition, in contrast, has stressed liberty—the intrinsic value of freedom of choice, the irreducible diversity of persons, temperaments, and talents for which a just society must find room. But the quarrel between these two traditions is a family quarrel. The belief that men are members of the same moral community and the belief that each man has his own singular good to pursue both represent the effort to escape the gravitational pull of a simple and stubborn human inclination—suspicion of the outsider, hostility towards the man who is different.

Far from being the expression of an aboriginal human preference, a democratic moral outlook is an instrument and symptom of the breakdown of the traditional moral codes which have divided men into members of the tribe and strangers, believers and unbelievers, U's and non-U's. Although democracy has been said to rest on the doctrine of natural rights, it is an acquired taste. The democratic outlook occurs only to those who have learned to look upon the existing lines between men as conventions, who want to redraw these lines, who think they may have some business on the other side of any line. And it is the attitude of men who have learned to take human diversity in stride, and who think that the man who sets himself up as a watchman over his neighbors is precisely the man who bears watching.

These are the twin attitudes—the belief in a moral community, the regard for individual difference and privacy—that generate the characteristic ideals of democracy. And there are many ways of describing these ideals. But if we examine the sources of our present anxieties, if we try to bring together the experiences that have led us to suspect that the democratic image and democratic realities do not fit together, certain central themes emerge. Political democracy may be conceived as an instrument for the construction of a civilization in which four ideals are pursued.

THE CONSENT OF THE GOVERNED

The first is the ideal of the consent of the governed. If the lines between men are to be softened, then the most irritating and dangerous line of all—that between those who command and those who obey—has to be redrawn. It cannot be erased, but it has to be made emotionally and morally digestible. And this can be done, so democratic theory has held, only if government rests on the consent of the governed.

Yet the phrase "the consent of the governed" is not an easy one to unravel. If those who are governed always consented to the decisions of their rulers, there would be no need for government, for police and taxes and penal sanctions. And no actual government, after all, can be absolutely even-handed in the way it conducts its business. The beginning of political education might be said to lie in the recognition that there is no such thing as an entirely equitable law. Ordinances against walking on the grass fall more heavily on dog-owners than on those who keep goldfish for pets, and rules against smoking in elevators ask smokers to sacrifice themselves while allowing nonsmokers to enjoy the benefits without cost. Even the recognition of everybody's right to free speech creates difficulties, after all, for the man who treasures silence. With the best will in the world, government is inevitably a process that takes more from some and gives more to others. And democratic government is simply one technique for determining who the winners and who the losers in the political fray will be. "Government by consent" cannot be interpreted to mean that those who are governed necessarily agree with what their rulers decide to do. Nor can it mean that "the majority" agrees. For in a democracy the minority, too, is presumably governed by its consent.

But to speak of majorities and minorities and the inevitability of disagreements is to suggest what "government by consent" expresses. It expresses the hope for a society in which ordinary people can influence the actions their leaders take. This means that they can exercise some control over who their leaders will be. And it also means that they are required to obey only after having been actively consulted by those who issue the orders. Coercion is implicit in all forms of government, but democracy nevertheless promises a peculiar prize to the individual citizen. It promises him that he will be present, personally or through a representative, when decisions that concern him are made, and that he will have instruments at his disposal that will give his presence some force.

The inside story, the experienced substance, of government by consent is told, therefore, when we describe the distribution of power and opportunity in a society, when we look at the internal structure of the groups that take part in the political competition and at the people they represent and the powers they command. The ideal of government by consent, to be fully effective, demands a society in which individuals who want to do something about their condition can find the allies, money, and talent to help them. It requires a social system which places weapons at the disposal of the ordinary citizen that force his rulers to deal with him as a party to a bargain and not as a passive instrument of their own purposes. The promise of government by consent does not imply that the individual will ever inhabit a social order in which all gradations of power and prestige have been abolished and everyone enjoys precisely the same amount of influence and authority. But it is a promise whose fulfillment requires much more than just one vote to every man or legal guarantees of personal freedom.

Accordingly, if significant sections of the community are unorganized, or if their opinions and interests are not brought insistently to the attention of the decision-makers, government by consent is absent to that extent. Similarly, if those who are attempting to press their opinions and interests have no powers to reward or punish those who make the decisions, their consent becomes gratuitous. Again, if there is a sizable imbalance of power between contending groups, then the settlement that is reached is an imposed settlement and not a free bargain. And if individuals cannot make their voices heard in the groups that claim to represent them, then they are not active participants in the processes by which the decisions that affect them are reached. "Government by consent," in short, is a function of underlying social arrangements.

But if this is true, then one reason for our present uneasiness becomes plain. The fundamental social arrangements in which government by consent has traditionally been embodied have undergone a radical alteration. The ideal of government by consent defines one major area in which we are in trouble.

THE IDEAL OF AN OPEN SOCIETY

Closely connected to the ideal of government by consent is the ideal of an open society. "Democracy" designates at least this much—a social order that deliberately protects men and agencies whose function it is to criticize what exists and to indicate other possibilities. The ideal of the open society proposes that men live under arrangements all of which are open to question. It holds that loyalty should be given to a social order precisely because it permits this process of criticism to take place. It insists that the process should be public and that everyone is in principle qualified to take part in it. And finally, it assumes that criticism and judgment are the preludes to corrective action.

To want an open society is thus to reject the classic view that men ought to expect a radical disparity between their hopes and the facts. There is a quality of impatience in a democratic culture. It eats away at any interest its members may have in consolation prizes. And in a community in which the ideal of an open society is widely accepted, those who have power or special knowledge must respond to a new imperative in human affairs. They have to provide those who do not have as much power or knowledge with information about what they are doing; worse, they have to appear to listen when their audience reports its reactions. In an open society, messages flow in two directions—from followers to leaders as well as from leaders to followers.

Even more than the ideal of government by consent, such an ideal presupposes social arrangements which cannot be secured simply by guarantees of freedom of speech and thought. These are essential but not sufficient. For communication is a complicated process. It depends not only on having something to say and knowing how to say it, but on being able to find an audience, and one that can do something about the message it receives. Freedom of speech serves a useful purpose even if it does nothing more than give men the chance to release their feelings by sending sounds out into the air. But the ideal of an open society encourages men to expect that freedom of speech will have other uses as well. In order for it to have these other uses, however, access to the instruments of communication has to be open, audiences have to be available that are organized and have powers of action, and the various participants in the discussion have to know the things they ought to know in order to speak intelligently and usefully. A bill of rights, therefore, provides only the supporting skeleton for an open society. The practical conditions for making such a society work lie outside the area of legal formalities.

And this is why the ideal of an open society is now not simply a promise but a provocation to cynicism. For the structure of the communications industry, the character of the groups that take part in the public debate, and the very nature of the issues that must now be debated do not fit our traditional assumptions. To say that what we now possess is an open society is not false. But it is a statement that requires a certain exercise of the imagination.

INDIVIDUAL AUTONOMY

The ideals of government by consent and of an open society bring us to another ideal—the one that is at the center of the democratic vision of human possibility. This is the ideal of individual autonomy.

One way to understand the emotional and moral impact of democracy is to see that it encourages great numbers of men to hold an expectation which only a life of privilege has bred in the past. Like the members of hereditary aristocracies in other days, a contemporary citizen of the United States is likely to grow up with the feeling that he counts just because he is who he is. And if his family is respectable and his skin not too heavily pigmented, he will probably feel that he is entitled to lead a life that he has chosen and made for himself. This, to coin a fresh and youthful phrase, is "the American dream." And pushed far enough, it is also the American fantasy. Scott Fitzgerald drew the picture of the pluperfect American in the great Gatsby—the man who interpreted the American ideal of the self-made man so simply and literally that he made himself up, inventing his past, writing his own ticket of admission to the great world, and creating a personality for himself as he would create a character in a romance.

But this pipe dream, this fantasy of self-creation, of perfect control over one's own nature and the conditions of one's life, does not prove that democratic ideals are immoderate and adolescent in their essence. Every social order produces its own special form of mad dream. Medieval society existed to make the journey of the soul to God more possible, but it was forced to organize monasteries in order to tame and socialize the extremists who took this promise too simply and literally. There is a kind of extremism proper to every society. The source of the Gatsby fantasy lies in the special sort of promise that a democratic culture makes to its members. It promises them that they will have personal autonomy—that they will be able to make uncoerced choices in terms of standards they choose for themselves. That no man can be free to adopt any standards he chooses is evident. But the presumed point of democracy, the consequence which those who have believed in it have claimed that it has, is that it gives its citizens the chance, more generously than any other system, to find themselves and their own talents and tastes, and, within reason, to seek their own ideals.

Yet not only the extremists, the moral purists and the morally insatiable, are doubtful today that democracy has this consequence. The realistic and the modest are also disturbed. Personal autonomy, so far as most men are concerned, seems to have been moved to the fringes of contemporary life. The packaged arrangements that are offered for our work and play; the massive industries that exist to manufacture opinion and engineer consent; the interventions of the State; the growth of technology and bureaucracy; the complexities of organization and regulation; the sheer pressure of our existence together in a crowded society—if the dim view of our future that now prevails has any substance, all these have weakened the ideal of personal autonomy and left the conditions in which it thrives in disarray. If the moral vision of liberal democracy is to be renewed, the prospects of individual autonomy on the contemporary scene have to be re-examined.

THE IDEAL OF RESPONSIBLE GOVERNMENT

Finally, there is a fundamental ideal in democracy which does not belong to democracy alone, but to all efforts to connect politics with the life of reason. What is it that the Greek meant, Mr. Kitto has asked, when he called himself "free" and the barbarian a "slave"? "Politically it meant not necessarily that he governed himself—because oftener than not he didn't—but that however his polity was governed it respected his rights. State affairs were public affairs, not the private concern of a despot. He was ruled by Law, a known Law which respected justice. . . . Arbitrary government offended the Greek in his very soul." To avoid arbitrary government, to live under laws that have reasons behind them that reasonable men can accept—this is not all there is to the idea of democracy. But it is the hope that allies democratic politics to other enterprises of liberal civilization. One large element in what men have meant by "freedom" is not the absence of external restraints on their behavior, but simply the chance to live under restraints they find intelligible rather than senseless and demeaning.

Liberal democracy has given a specific interpretation to this ideal of rational government. Rational government has meant, above all, responsible government. A responsible government, like a responsible man, is one that knows its limits. It conducts its affairs in accordance with the rule of law and with respect for the fundamental rights of individuals. Secondly, it is responsive government—government that is alert to the legitimate wants and potentialities of those it governs. And finally, it is a government that must respond satisfactorily when it is asked to account for its decisions. By responsible government liberal democracy has not meant simply government by responsible men. It has meant a government embedded in a certain sort of social structure, a government that is accountable to a larger society.

This is the basic ideal that justifies the curious organization of liberal societies. They are "dual societies," societies deliberately arranged to be at conflict with themselves. In all societies there are groups outside the official government—clans, businesses, clubs, cliques, and gangs—that lay down rules which control the behavior of men; and these groups, in all societies, possess sanctions like excommunication, expulsion, economic penalties, or the withdrawal of privileges, by which they enforce obedience to their rules. But in a liberal society these private governments do not exist through the weakness or indifference of the State. They exist as a matter of policy. They are conceived as checks against arbitrary government by the State, instruments that compel those who alone have the legal authority to use force to think twice before they resort to force. The existence of such private governments, indeed, is not only a condition for responsible government by the State. It is the source of one of liberal democracy's outstanding problems. For these private governments are also governments, possessing coercive powers, and powers sanctioned and supported by the State. If they exist to control the State and to keep it accountable, they, too, need to be controlled and held accountable.

And this seems to be the difficulty. Despite the persistence of elections, an independent judiciary, and all the institutions of free social inquiry and criticism that characterize liberal democracy, the process of holding the public and private governments that rule us to some effective system of accountability seems to have become increasingly complicated and uncertain.

SETTING WORDS ARIGHT

Before we can turn to examine the problems that now beset these ideals, we have to look carefully at some of the words we use to describe the democratic political method. For we shall have to deal with these problems democratically; and our discontents, indeed, are the consequences of what we think to be democratic standards. Yet there are easy but confusing misconceptions which lead us to diagnose our ailments improperly and sometimes to confuse symptoms of democratic health with symptoms of disease. There is good reason for many of our present discontents; but some of them are the products of our own unexamined and faulty ideas about democracy. Let us pass a number of them in review as a first step in putting our political ideas in order.

Begin with the most obvious mistake of all. It is the notion that government by consent, participation by the governed in the making of public decisions, means referenda, plebiscites, direct appeal to the people at every turn—in brief, a kind of giant and continuing town meeting. The idea has deep roots in the Western tradition. It is an inheritance from the theory and practice of democracy in the Greek city-state and the Puritan congregations of the seventeenth century. And it is a conception that is implicit in much that Rousseau, the prophet of popular sovereignty, had to say about the nature of political freedom. But it is plain, once the idea is made explicit, that the model of a town meeting is inapplicable to the processes by which the government of a modern nation-state can or should carry on its business. It expresses the hope, and the still realistic hope, that between the State and the individual, and between the large organization and the individual, there will be smaller, more manageable associations which the individual can join, and which will offer him the experience of face-to-face cooperation in dealing with immediate problems. But when this hope is inflated many times over, when it is applied to a modern nation-state as a whole, it overlooks the sheer size of modern societies, the fact of factions, the need for professional leadership, and the advantages that are bound to accrue to the specialist who can give the political business his full-time attention.

Yet despite the quixotic character of this ideal, it is invoked more often than we think. It is not invoked to say what should be done, but it is tacitly invoked to condemn what is done. Thus, some serious critics of the American scene have offered the fact that there was no general public debate before the atom bomb was dropped on Hiroshima as evidence that democracy in the United States is more advertised than real. But such criticism does more than skirt the question whether a popular referendum—and, necessarily, a secret referendum—in the middle of a war was possible. It overlooks the implications of the fact that there was widespread discussion after the decision. It treats as a lapse from democracy the legal fact that those who made the decision had the Constitutional responsibility to do so, and were prohibited from passing this responsibility on to others. And not least, it appears to rest on the cheerful assumption that the decision of the electorate would have been more gentle and humane than the decision that was actually made. It is an undeniable fact that our existing system assigns extraordinary power to a relatively small number of men. But the fact is not surprising. It is true of all large societies and of most small ones. To condemn this state of affairs as a distortion of democracy is to wash out all important distinctions in a bath of indignation. It is to employ a concept of democracy that could have no possible applicability. A man may complain if he thinks the wrong people have great power. But some people are going to have such power.

More plausible notions than that of the town meeting, however, are also capable of causing misformulations of the issues. The apparently simple idea of "majority rule," for example, is full of pitfalls which become noticeable only after the idea has been held in the air for a moment and examined. The majority of those who vote surely do determine who wins. But that majority is not a cohesive social group that persists once the election is over. It is an abstraction, a creation of the electoral procedure itself. Once the vote is counted, it is replaced by more palpable entities like political parties, businesses, unions, and the inevitable individuals who take it upon themselves to speak for "the majority." And if the idea of a majority is elusive, the idea of majority rule is doubly so. For an electoral majority registers no single definite

opinion on any question but that of the candidate who is pre-
ferred. And even this preference is governed by the alternatives
presented. "The people's choice" need not be the man most pre-
ferred. He may only be less dispreferred than his opponent. In
between elections, furthermore, the decisions made in a democracy are also influenced by the advice of administrative officers,
the pressures of different groups, the necessities for compromise,
the interpreted information about "public opinion" that comes
to the decision-makers, and the simple and not-so-simple play of
events. No political leader can say what his policy will be with
regard to questions that no one has foreseen at the time of the
election; and he cannot stop and turn to the electorate for its
judgment when such questions arise.

This is not to say that elections have no influence over events.
The announced programs of contending parties have more to do
with the decisions a government makes than the cynics say. At
the very least they tell the electorate where the candidate would
like them to think his heart lies, and sometimes they tell the candidate, too. In the end "majority rule" has a meaning, but it is
metaphorical rather than strictly literal. It describes a society in
which the fact that there are elections exerts a general climatic
influence on the decision-making process, requiring those who
make the decisions to keep themselves aware of the reactions of
ordinary citizens. It points to the fact that while decisions in a
democracy may be made behind closed doors, there is always
someone pounding at the doors. "Majority rule" is in this sense
an arithmetical figure of speech describing a government that can
be discussed, investigated, and scolded. And most important of
all, "majority rule" points to a fundamental characteristic of democracy. Democracy is not exclusive rule by any minority.

In the American democratic system most of the organized
groups in the community are able to make themselves heard in
the elaborate process by which the decisions of government are
finally made. The statement has to be read as it is written. It is
the organized groups, not the unorganized ones, that make themselves heard; they make themselves heard mainly through their
leaders; and we can only be reasonably sure that they make themselves heard, and not that what they say necessarily makes a dif-

ference. Still, such a process is one of extended competition among different interests, no one of which has a clearly secure position in the forefront, and every one of which has to fight for the approval of the bystander.

"Majority rule," in short, expresses the democratic attempt to give ordinary people a large measure of control over their leaders. It speaks for the effort to organize a society in such a way that it will not be dominated by any single center of power. And it describes the historical direction in which democratic governments, with slips and falls, but steadily over the long run, have come to serve the interests of ever larger sections of the nations they rule. But, strictly speaking, the phrase "majority rule" is a misnomer when applied to the democratic process. The proper phrase, as Robert Dahl has suggested, is rule by minorities. For every interest is in the minority when set against all the other interests with which it competes. It is cant, therefore, to condemn the victory of any interest in a democracy simply because it is a minority interest. There is no other kind.

This examination of what we can mean when we speak of "majority rule" leads us to an even more crucial idea in the lexicon of democracy—"representative government." The classic idea of representative government, and the idea that still forms our image of what democracy is or should be, is that of an electorate which chooses representatives who carry the popular will into effect. It is not an idea that stands up to scrutiny, and it causes unnecessary and debilitating anxieties and complaints when it is not scrutinized.

The first of the difficulties with the conventional belief that a democratic government exists simply to carry the views of the electorate into practice is that it rests on the concept of a "popular will." In large modern societies, political parties, the media of communication, voluntary organizations, and government itself act to define the questions to which the electorate addresses itself; they propose the alternatives between which the electorate makes its choice; they give the "popular will" its preoccupations, organization, and principal modes of expression. To assert under such conditions that "the people," or a majority of the people, have wholly self-engendered and precise demands to make on their leaders is to venture into the occult. And a second and even more serious difficulty with the theory that government should simply do what the citizens say is that it rests on an ideal that is clearly unrealistic—the ideal of the omnicompetent citizen, the man with a formed and informed opinion on all major issues.

The ideal is unrealistic not only because it demands a degree of omniscience which no citizen can have. It is also unrealistic because it overlooks a fact about human psychology. Few arguments are more difficult or dubious than those about the rationality or irrationality of the so-called "common man." But it is unnecessary to enter into such arguments. Imagine that all voters are reasonable and disciplined and have the necessary facts at their easy disposal. The views they hold about matters that are remote are formed under conditions that are significantly different just the same. For while the principle is not ironclad, a certain state of mind is generally a prerequisite to responsible judgment.

Normally, the individual making the judgment has to feel that the question under consideration is his personal business and that he will pay a personal price for giving the wrong answer. And this is the attitude that is bound to be attenuated in a contemporary polity. The housewife who has to decide whether the corner grocer is honest is under some compulsion to make a judgment that rests on more than a platitude about the honesty or dishonesty of all grocers. And besides, she has the inestimable advantage of being able to observe the grocer's behavior directly. These fundamental conditions do not hold in the relation of a contemporary citizen to his government. He may be concerned and informed, he may recognize the bearing that public issues have on his everyday life, but his identification with the issues is still mainly vicarious rather than direct.

This does not mean that education and public spirit have no bearing on the success of a democracy. It makes them more important, not less. If men are to make intelligent judgments about their leaders, they need a general understanding of the main drift of the issues, they need to have some shrewdness about the people they listen to, and they need to be able to tell the difference between sense and nonsense. And if democracy is unworkable, it is because the electorate cannot be counted on to have even these qualities. But the recognition of the difference between the two kinds of space in which men's minds move allows us to fix our sights more modestly and intelligently, and less discouragingly, on the proper objectives of democratic education and public spirit. Democratic government does not require an all-knowing electorate any more than any other system of government does. The theory of democracy that demands such an assumption is in error. Democratic government is simply a system in which the authority to govern is acquired through competition for the people's votes. The function of the electorate is to choose and remove a government. It is the function of the government to govern.

Nor is this a state of affairs that ought to be mourned. In the best of all possible worlds the ordinary citizen, we may hope, would still have his own work to do, and his own intimate and absorbing sphere of private experience and responsibility. The image of a society in which all men are wholly devoted to the great public business is worse than utopian. It is disagreeable.

But to point out that representative government means nothing more nor less than government chosen by free elections is not to finish the story. For the concept of a "free election" carries a whole baggage of notions with it. The liberal democratic tradition can be justly criticized for having frequently entertained an abstract and legalistic conception of representative government. Elections do not become free elections simply because legal safeguards may surround the exercise of the franchise. To speak of "representative government" is to presuppose the existence of appropriate social conditions as well. The distinction between a state of affairs in which an electorate is presented with actual alternatives and one in which it is only given the chance to acclaim the powers that be is fundamental. No reflections on the sociological conditions for free elections can erase that distinction. "Representative government," nevertheless, always refers to a relative state of affairs. Even mature liberal democracies never perfectly fulfill all the conditions that make government a representative process.

In estimating the degree to which elections are free and government is representative, the education, composition, and social circumstances of the electorate have to be taken into account.

Will voters suffer ostracism if they support a particular slate? Is there an alternative in which a large number of them are vitally interested, but which has been excluded from the alternatives on which they vote? Has relevant information been systematically withheld from the electorate, or does any single agency monopolize all the important channels of information? Have representatives of all significant groups had a chance to formulate the issues under debate? The failure to raise such questions has been responsible for the fetishistic application of the principle of free elections to societies where the conditions for such elections are not present. It partly explains why the gospel of free elections has had less resonance in many parts of the world than liberal democrats habitually assume that it will.

For the conditions that make elections free and government representative include a cultural climate that is relatively open and tolerant; an electorate that understands the purpose of voting; broad participation in the organization of the election and in the formulation of party programs; a press that gives expression to enough crosscurrents of opinion to put any single interpretation of the facts under pressure to defend itself; and not least, a reasonably broad and balanced distribution of powers in the community, so that all important groups have a chance to get into the act. Indeed, the most important condition of representative government lies outside elections and the official representative institutions of democratic society. The decisive representative institutions of democracy are unofficial.

They are the political blocs and the pressure groups; it is these that carry most of the democratic mail. Representative government is of course a matter of elections, competitive party politics, public discussion, and civil liberties. But these are thin and precarious without the existence of social groups that make it probable that those who are going to be affected by a social decision will be seriously and honestly consulted by those who make the decision. That aspect of democracy which most regularly troubles its partisans—the open struggle among special interests —is precisely what marks democracy as a system resting on the consent of the governed. The politics of pressure groups is the essential feature of the politics of democracy. The only alternative to the politics of pressure groups is government that rules over isolated and rootless individuals who have no groups other than the government to protect them, and no autonomous social power of their own.

That is why a democratic system of government cannot promise what most other systems promise. It cannot promise to do away with the dirty business of politics and to melt all men together in love of God, country, or historical necessity. Politics is a democracy's official business, and not, as in other systems, an unofficial and hidden business. The basic instrument of the democratic citizen is the organized group with enough power and influence to command the attention of those who make the decisions. The basic instruments of democratic government are the bargain and the compromise. And the one unmistakable goal of all democratic governments, when they arrange their bargains and compromises, is to win the next election.

This is the context in which every discussion of planning and of the development of consistent policy in a democracy must be placed. It does not make planning or consistent policy impossible. But it gives the formation of plans and policies a quality of responsiveness—or, if one prefers, of opportunism—which is not so likely to be present in systems that do not have to worry about elections. To ask the living to sacrifice themselves for their grandchildren is easier in a dictatorship than in a democracy. And since it is not easy, in a world of accelerating changes, to predict the condition or desires of our grandchildren, this democratic state of affairs has some manifest virtues.

But it is for this reason too that democratic politics requires ideas. Unless men have some coherent conceptions of their existing condition, unless they can imagine the long direction in which they would like to move, the politics of the bargain, the politics of equilibrium, can be a deadly affair—unfocused, uninspired, and, for all its realism, unrealistic. It can settle down, not simply very close to the center, but to a dead center, quarreling over issues that are ghosts of the past and tinkering with problems that lie at the fringes of the questions that have to be faced. With reservations, that is the picture of American politics at present, at any rate so far as domestic politics are concerned. Were it not for the

Russians, we could not be sure that we would have a purpose in life.

No doubt we can get rid of some misconceptions about democracy and, when we do, some of our discontents may be removed. But these are not the major reasons for our unmistakable dissatisfaction with things as they are. At bottom, our present uneasiness, our curiously embarrassed prosperity, is the consequence of the unfulfilled demands which democratic civilization itself has set in motion. The ideals of government by consent, of an open society, of individual autonomy, of responsible government, have become problems rather than promises, sources of disillusion rather than aspirations. For the social conditions on which they lean seem to have been subverted. Each of these ideals defines a major area in which image does not fit reality.

IV

RECOVERING GOVERNMENT
BY CONSENT

Is the democratic performance a masquerade? Are the televised political conventions, the "great debates," the exposés, the solemn appeals to "public opinion"—are these all parts of a pageant disguising the fact that most citizens do not have instruments by which they can exercise any significant leverage on their everyday environments? The question, clearly, is on the minds of an increasing number of us. On the right, there are fantasies that we have been taken over by a conspiracy. On the left is the murmur that ordinary men have been expropriated, that a power elite has taken all real power into its own hands. And everywhere there are anxious beatings-about for a cause, and recurrent complaints that there are no causes, for no one can do anything anyway.

In Sartre's *The Age of Reason* Mathieu walks along a Paris street in 1938, reading the news about the bombing of Valencia.

> There were thousands of men in France who had not been able to read their paper that morning without feeling a clot of anger rise in their throat, thousands of men who had clenched their fists and muttered: "Swine!" Mathieu clenched his fists and muttered: "Swine!" and felt himself still more guilty. . . . He was empty, he was confronted by a vast anger, a desperate anger, he saw it and could almost have touched it. But it was inert. . . . He was left in solitude, walking with the measured and decorous gait of a man in a funeral procession in Paris, not Valencia. Paris, haunted by a phantom wrath.

These emotions—a phantom wrath, a feeling of responsibility without power, the emotion of sitting on one's emotions—have become the apparent hazards of life in modern democratic society. The fact that so many things are well arranged for its citizens has not allayed these feelings. On the contrary, the comforting securities provided by corporations, unions, and the Welfare State seem only to have reinforced the suspicion that the democratic citizen has become a well-tended and well-shepherded animal, that he is on the end that receives but not the end that controls. What has happened to the democratic promise of government by consent? What are the reasons for the growing conviction that this ideal is a thing of the past?

SOME REASONS, GOOD AND BAD, FOR OUR DISILLUSIONMENT

In part, the facts have changed; in part, quixotic dreams have been exploded. There has never been a time when any but a tiny minority of men have had any significant influence on public events. But now the awareness of the world that most of us carry around with us has been intensified and magnified by modern communication, and an additional irritant has been added because we are told that it is we, the people, who have the power and we who ought to feel responsible for the state of things. Moreover, in the course of hardly a generation, the political arena on which our imaginations are focused has lost its local character and has become national and international in scope. The individual is bound to feel at once more closely tied to what is far away and less able to exercise any influence on it.

Nor is this all. The feeling of many men that they have lost power, that their giving or withholding their consent makes no difference, has been aggravated by still another change in the political scene. It reflects the fact that a great many more people, and new people, have actually come to enjoy a larger measure of government by consent. The American democratic process has been making good on its promise of government by consent in some obvious and important ways. A steadily larger number of diversified groups have entered the active political competition and are throwing their weight around. Whatever beliefs we may hold about the degree to which power is centralized in the United States, few serious decisions are made either by public officials or by those who wield power in the private sector—and this includes major diplomatic and military decisions—that do not take account of the opinions and probable reactions of a great many people on the outside. If this were not the case, the normal political temperature would be somewhat lower and the public-relations industry would be less prosperous than it is. Yet all this has its discouraging side. For a man will attach less significance to his vote when millions vote instead of thousands. In brief, if many men now complain that the individual's influence over events is infinitesimal, this is in part because the number of those who are represented in the democratic political community has been expanded.

But beyond these changed circumstances, there are also deep illusions that have been shattered. Some of our doubts about the reality of government by consent reflect the still undigested disappointments of a people that has been used to getting its way. In view of our history, it is not surprising that Americans should feel suddenly dispossessed, powerless, deprived of their birthright, when events in Cuba or the Congo do not go as they like. The assumption that the United States has the power to shape events as it wills has diverted and dissipated our energies since World War II. It explains the recurrent charge that a conspiracy has taken over in Washington, a charge that is based on the assumption that if our government were really *our* government the world would be marching to our music. And our sense of frustration has been further aggravated by the continuing influence of populist and town-meeting conceptions of democracy. They encourage the notion that democratic citizens need only ask and they will be able to change the world quickly, directly, and just as they please.

Yet neither this reason, nor all of those we have mentioned, is enough to explain our current uneasiness about the condition and prospects of government by consent. There are objective reasons why sober and serious men, men with a sense of history and a disciplined view of what is possible, might also think the democracy we possess is in the process of losing its solid substance. In at least two significant respects, the social instruments for realiz-

ing government by consent have been drastically altered in the
course of the last generation. First, scientific research and technological innovation have enormously accelerated the processes
of social change, and have rendered the instruments we have inherited for guiding this change even less adequate than they have
been in the past. This is a subject to which we shall return. Second, the major practical agency by which the citizen has traditionally exercised influence on the centers of power in democratic
society has lost the character which classic democratic theory
supposed it would have. This is the voluntary association.

THE VOLUNTARY ASSOCIATION AND GOVERNMENT
BY CONSENT

The independent voluntary organization—the trade association,
the veterans' society, the consumers' cooperative, the political
party—is the most distinctive feature of a democratic social system
and an indispensable practical instrument of government by consent. It represents the response of democratic society to radical
changes in the historical conditions that have normally protected
the individual in society and that have given him what power he
has had to influence his environment.

Over the long course of human history men have not had to
ask themselves those questions which are the marks of modern
man's freedom as well as of his malaise. Is there a place for me
in society? Do I belong to the group? Do I wish to belong? Will
I be submerged in the group? These questions were settled because they had never been raised. The individual's chances in
life were determined by the kin group into which he was born
and the position in society he inherited. The family, the local
community, the guild and the parish provided the individual with
his schooling, his work, and his security—more or less—against
illness, bad times, old age, and external aggression. They incorporated the individual into society, assigning him his station and
duties, without any act of choice on his part.

On one side, the individual was not left out, as so many members of modern societies are left out. He had his place in the
great social procession. On the other side, he had that place

whether he wished it or not and whether he wished to leave it or not. In a fully traditional society, a man's associations can be called neither voluntary nor involuntary. He neither chooses them nor is forced into them. He falls into them, and by an accident so vast, arbitrary, and inevitable that it has the shape of a natural necessity. And what influence he can exert on his environment depends on this accident—on the groups to which willy-nilly he belongs and on the status he possesses in these groups.

But industrialism and the growth of cities has shattered these groups or drained the strength from them. Economic mobility, democratic political rights, changes in moral standards and in the power of religious groups, revisions in the laws governing marriage, divorce, and inheritance, have changed the individual's relation to even the most intimate groups to which he belongs. The tie between household and occupation has been broken, and the link between one's family name and one's social status weakened. And partly as a result, the traditional forms of association like the family and the neighborhood have themselves lost their traditional character. They are not quite the involuntary forms of association they once were. The family into which a man is born and the environment in which he grows up are still enormous influences over his life, and not even the most imaginative social planning is likely to find a way to give men a choice about such matters. But these associations are no longer wholly inescapable.

Nor can they provide the individual with adequate social protection. If he wishes some control over the conditions affecting his fate, he must look for instruments of social power elsewhere. The great instrument has been the voluntary association, formed by deliberate choice for specific, definite, and limited purposes. Ruled by considerations of efficiency not tradition, of utility rather than inherited authority, the voluntary association introduces a new and necessary kind of social discipline into areas of life and work that have been cut loose from the governance of custom and wont. And it represents a new way of connecting the individual to his fellows, a way that gives him some choice about the persons to whom he will be connected and the conditions under which his obligations to them hold. A society full of voluntary associations thus creates the kind of experience and the kind of psychological perspective that give the idea of being governed by one's own consent a chance to take hold.

Beyond the decline in the power of traditional forms of association, furthermore, there are special reasons for the decisive importance of the voluntary association in a modern democratic social order. In an industrial society the exercise of significant economic or social power requires access to large amounts of wealth. The pooling of individual resources is usually necessary, and if any reasonably ambitious social purpose is to be accomplished, the efforts of large numbers of people must also be coordinated. In such circumstances, the individual with an ideal to promote or an interest to protect is likely to be powerless unless he can form or find an organization to support him. And he generally needs more than just the help of others with common interests. He needs the guidance of men with specialized knowledge, and a system of alliances between his own group and other groups which only those who make a profession of such things can arrange. Moreover, in democratic societies educational opportunity, wealth, and social power are likely to be more evenly distributed than in other societies. Though more men have some power, fewer people have sufficient power all by themselves to achieve what they want. More than in most other kinds of society, therefore, power in a democracy must be the power of associations before it is likely to count. "In democratic countries," as Tocqueville remarked, "the science of association is the mother of science; the progress of all the rest depends on the progress it has made."

The word "individualism" was first used by Tocqueville. It was the word he found it necessary to invent in order to explain democracy. But the other side of democracy's individualism, of its assault on the traditional ties that bind men to one another, is the voluntary association. It has been the agency that has protected individual rights, extended the range of the individual's social powers, and given concrete embodiment to the view that a democratic society is a self-governing society. Elections, parliaments, and civil liberties are the supporting skeleton of democratic society; the flesh is provided by the multiple voluntary societies that exist within this larger framework.

And this is one principal reason why government by consent, as we actually experience it, has come to seem increasingly thin and abstract. Although we employ the same old words when we talk about voluntary associations, they have changed in fundamental ways. A large number of the most powerful are voluntary in only a Pickwickian sense of the term. Considered as case studies in democratic self-government, many of them, to say the least, are disconcerting. And some of the most influential voluntary associations we possess elude all the categories: they are voluntary associations in fact, and most of us belong to them, but they are not associations in theory, and few of us know that we belong to them or have done anything deliberate to associate ourselves with them. In sum, the classic conception of the voluntary association no longer fits the facts. Both our ideas and the facts need to be refashioned. Our politics of malaise may be said to begin here.

THE TRANSFORMATION OF THE VOLUNTARY ASSOCIATION

The classic conception of a voluntary association envisages a group of people who have deliberately come together to promote some idea or project which they share in common. According to this conception membership in a voluntary association differs from membership in a family, which is simply inherited, and also from membership in the State, since the individual is under a legal obligation to accept the State's jurisdiction. In short, a voluntary association, in traditional terms, is an association a man is legally free to join or to leave. He may suffer penalties when he does leave—for example, excommunication if he defies the authority of his church. But the State does not take a hand in enforcing these penalties, nor does it insist that the individual enter into relations with any purely voluntary group. From this point of view, political parties, trade associations, or veterans' leagues all appear to be voluntary associations.

To this traditional conception of a voluntary association two other ideas were also usually added. First, the typical voluntary organization, it was tacitly assumed, would be small in size, and would be composed of people who took an active interest in its affairs and participated in the formation of its policies. Second, it was naturally assumed that a voluntary association was always a definite and formally identifiable organization, with a specifiable membership, an official set of rules, and a clearly understood and sharply defined mission. None of these assumptions, however, is any longer a dependable guide to the nature of the most important voluntary associations on the contemporary democratic scene.

Let us look first at the principle that a voluntary association is one which the individual is legally free to join or to leave. In abstract terms, the principle is still valid: the individual is legally free to join, leave, or ignore clubs, churches, unions, professional societies, or trade associations. But if our livelihood depends on joining an association, it is cold comfort to be told that no one has ordered us to be a miner, teacher, or construction worker. In the nineteenth century the legal abstraction "freedom of contract" was invoked to protect the arrangements imposed on individual workers by their employers. Collective bargaining has corrected that state of affairs, and if there is any substitute for it as an instrument of countervailing power in the government of the economy, it has not yet been found. But the use of the protective label "voluntary association" to describe organizations like labor unions is our own era's contribution to the history of stretched words and deceptive abstractions.

The legal freedom to join or leave an organization like a labor union does not touch the concrete pressures that bear on the individual and that prevent him from treating his membership as a matter of choice. And the laws themselves have made the distinctions between voluntary and involuntary associations doubly difficult to draw. They have made labor unions organs of public power, investing them with a special status as the recognized instruments for making and maintaining the rules and agreements on which the work of our society turns. Under these circumstances, the individual union member pays his dues as he pays his taxes, and the justification in both cases is much the same— the common defense, the maintenance of secure and dependable arrangements, and the preservation of a system that determines the distribution of social burdens and rewards through a process of bargaining rather than coercion.

Nor is the labor union the only form of voluntary association that can no longer be said to be sharply and clearly voluntary. The pressures that professional and trade associations can mount to compel membership are formidable, and the ties that bind individuals to the corporations for which they work are also increasingly tight. Although there is much to be said in favor of fringe benefits and similar practices, these deprive the individual of a measure of control over what he does with his income and over his plans for saving and investment. He is a beneficiary, but a passive and involuntary beneficiary, of the organization. Moreover, when an individual has accumulated a large equity in a pension fund and cannot take the equity with him if he leaves for another job, his employer has a collar, albeit a velvet collar, around his neck. The belief that our relationship to the major groups that frame and shape our lives is "voluntary" can perhaps be justified. But the justification will depend on casuistry as much as on simple observation.

This brings us to the second respect in which voluntary organizations now escape our native democratic categories. The most important voluntary associations are large-scale organizations, and such organizations are unmanageable without the development of bureaucratic methods of administration and the concentration of considerable power in the hands of a small group of full-time professional leaders. Moreover, the problem of building democratic procedures into large voluntary associations is aggravated by the fact that the more successful the association is in achieving the purposes for which it exists, the less the rank-and-file members feel impelled, so most of the evidence indicates, to take an active part in its affairs.

Robert Michels argued long ago that an "iron law of oligarchy," an irreversible tendency towards the centralization of power in the hands of the few, governed all large human organizations and made the democratic ideal a utopian dream. The law may or may not be iron and inevitable. But the contemporary labor union, political party, veterans' association, or corporation is typically composed of a large inert membership controlled by a small active minority governing through a one-party or a no-party system. Such organizations may serve their members or stockholders well.

But they are service organizations, not participant organizations. Their members are not citizens of the organization but clients, not makers of policy but its customers.

When we recall that the democratically organized voluntary association has traditionally been conceived to be the indispensable practical instrument for achieving genuine government by consent, the reasons for our uneasiness about the status of this ideal become evident. Our inherited conception of the voluntary association has been challenged not only by the rise of associations that are voluntary in only a narrow sense of the term, but also by associations that have a democratic and constitutional structure on paper but not in fact.

But the most serious assault on the orthodox democratic image of the voluntary association comes from still a third source. A kind of "association" exists that eludes our inherited categories entirely. It is not an explicit form of organization at all. It is an implicit association, a shadow organization; yet its significance and influence on the processes by which social decisions are made is as great and perhaps greater than the influence exerted by actual organizations whose formal existence is recognized. There are voluntary associations in which membership is quasi-obligatory. But as we move along the spectrum, examining the social groups that significantly influence the course of contemporary democracy, we come finally to a kind of massive association which we do not have to join consciously in order to be its member or client. A chain store and its customers, a television network and its viewers, a politician and those who regularly quote him, or a newspaper, which, as Tocqueville observed, "always represents an association that is composed of its habitual readers"— these are all instances of *implicit* voluntary associations. They are groups or individuals with a following, real or imputed. And they speak for us whether we tell them to do so or not.

One of the more interesting stories in the recent history of American government, for example, is the role played by scientists and scientific interest groups in the formation of public policy. In part, this job has been performed by the representatives of organized groups; but in part it has also been performed by eminent scientist-statesmen such as Mr. Conant or Vannevar Bush.

Though they may make no such claims for themselves, such men are taken to be spokesmen of "the scientific community." Their power is the power of leaders and representatives, although no formal procedures have been adopted for choosing them. Indeed, "the scientific community" as such is an undefined entity. And yet the power of these men is comparable to the power of leaders of explicitly organized associations of scientists. Explicit and formally organized associations, indeed, can also function in the same shadowy way. Part of their power comes from the fact that they are also implicit associations. The American Medical Association speaks for American doctors although many American doctors do not recognize their voice when the Association speaks; the American Legion speaks for veterans; the American Association of University Professors speaks for professors. The individual who does not belong still has his case made for him, and his support is tacitly invoked.

In short, the processes by which decisions are made on the contemporary democratic scene can be explained in terms of the competition of "interest groups" or "voluntary associations" only if the concept of the "interest group" and the "voluntary association" is greatly expanded. If we look at our society and ask what groups have an obvious power to make their weight felt in the democratic process, we find a large number of groups that are formally organized, that exist to serve selected and specifically declared purposes, and that state precise conditions defining the responsibilities of their officers and the qualifications for membership. Trade associations, veterans' groups, political parties, and labor unions are examples. But if the decision-making process of a democracy is explained in terms of the pressures exerted by different groups, then more than these formally organized associations must be taken into account. We also have to mention the power of corporations and great industrial complexes, of television and radio networks, of national magazines and newspaper syndicates, of banks and pension funds and chain stores. These social agencies have at least as much to say about how the citizens of a contemporary democracy will be governed, what sort of work they will do, what their cities and countryside will look like, what they will buy, and what they will read and see and

talk about. It is on the basis of their say-so, too, that we form
rather a large number of our judgments about what the desires
and opinions of the citizenry are. And the social power of these
organizations is in part a derived power. It depends on the fact
that they have a following. In social fact, though not in name or
in law, they are voluntary associations.

The implicit voluntary association thus carries even further
the tendency which the large, explicitly organized voluntary association also exemplifies. On one side, decisions affecting great
numbers are made by a relatively small group of individuals
occupying key positions, official or otherwise; on the other side,
the influence of these individuals derives from the fact that they
"represent" a large and inactive following that can only infrequently do anything but take what it gets. It is wise not to exag-
gerate this state of affairs. Undoubtedly, there is some play back
and forth between the opinions and interests of leaders and those
of their following. We face here, nevertheless, the emergence of
conditions in which a modern population may be well served and
the external forms of democracy preserved, but in which relatively few citizens are in fact active agents in determining the
alternatives that will be put before them and the conditions they
will find in their work, their neighborhoods, their leisure-time
activities, or their civic projects.

Adolf Berle has talked of the development of modern capitalism into a system of "power without property"—a system in which
a relatively small group of men, the officers of the large pension
funds, insurance companies, and mutual investment corporations,
have the power, along with government, to determine the shape
of the American economy and the way in which its resources will
be allocated. But this system of "power without property" is part
of a much larger trend in which some men hold power as trustees
and representatives of other men though other men hold little
control over them. The involuntary character of many associations officially called voluntary, the weakening or disappearance
of democratic processes within them, and the rise of shadow associations whose power is very great have all challenged the
assumptions on which the image of the voluntary association—
and, behind it, the ideal of government by consent—has rested.

The present position of the voluntary association raises questions as fundamental as any that can be asked about the prospects of the democratic idea.

SOME MISLEADING STEREOTYPES

It is important to see these questions for what they are. What has been said does not imply that we are in the grip of a new ruling class or power elite. It is true that men are organized today into massive social formations, formal and informal, which are governed by relatively few men occupying key positions. But this does not mean that those who have such power comprise a single group with common interests and intentions. The conditions of their power are different and often throw them into conflict with one another. Walter Reuther and Richard Nixon, Edward Teller and Robert Oppenheimer, David Sarnoff and Henry Luce, Admiral Radford and General Taylor, James Hoffa and Robert Kennedy, have all exercised considerable power in the United States. It is difficult to think of them as a "ruling circle" harmoniously seeking the same general objectives, or arrayed as a unit against those on the outside. "Every body politic," the British philosopher Collingwood observed, "consists of two parts, a politically active or ruling class, and a politically passive or ruled class." It might also be said that all humanity consists of two classes—those who like to divide humanity into two classes and those who do not. In a society that consists of many bodies politic there are many politically active, or ruling, classes and many passive, or ruled, classes. And a man who is a member of an active class in one context can be a member of a passive class in another context.

It is equally misleading to assume that the bureaucratic organization of most voluntary associations automatically turns them into undemocratic or antidemocratic organizations. Bureaucratic management is compatible with the democratic control of an organization, and in some places the two coexist. But even when bureaucratic management and centralized professional leadership eliminate democracy from the internal structure of an organization, the organization may still be an instrument of democratic control in the larger community. For there are two different senses in which a voluntary organization may be said to be "representative." On the one hand, its leaders may be chosen as the result of a genuine democratic competition, and the policies of the organization may be worked out by procedures that permit the widespread and active participation of the membership. On the other hand, an organization may not enjoy this kind of government, and yet its leaders may still truly express and work for the interests of the membership. Despite the absence of effective democratic arrangements in most unions, for example, labor unions have introduced the constitutional principle of checks and balances into the government of the economy, and there is little doubt but that they have improved the living conditions of their members and that most of their members think so.

Professional leadership and bureaucratic management, furthermore, have another virtue. They help to maintain the texture of a pluralistic society. In such a society the organizations that represent the citizen's interests must be capable of resisting external infiltration and manipulation. That protection is provided by a permanent administrative machine manned by people who have a vested interest in preserving the organization's autonomy and visibility. In sum, although it is true that the great majority of citizens have little direct access to the processes by which major social decisions are made, it is not true that they do not have indirect access. Their interests are expressed, and quite often accurately expressed, through their organizations. Through these organizations they can help or hurt, reward or punish, if not their own leaders, then at least the leaders of outside organizations. And this affects the calculus of power in the society as a whole. For it is not enough to note that men hold positions at the top of some hierarchy in order to understand the kind of power they have. One must also take account of the people and groups, on the inside or outside of their organizations, who possess sanctions that can make them sit up and take notice.

Nor should a fetish be made of the genuine democratic value of participation. If the available evidence is accurate, for example, relatively few union members are interested in participating in the affairs of their union. And with some variations, the same generalization applies to members of professional associations and most other large national voluntary organizations. But what is surprising about this state of affairs is not the fact that it exists. What is surprising is the unmodified concern it arouses.

There are limitations, after all, on the time and energy of most citizens. They have homes, families, and jobs. So long as they are satisfied with the performance of their voluntary organizations, they may wish quite legitimately to put their energies into other activities. The best and simplest reason for welcoming the professional government of one's union, political party, or civic association is that life is short and one may have better and more useful things to do than to serve on another committee. There is no magic in universal participation. From the point of view of the organization, there are always some people who are simply nuisances. From the point of view of the individual, there are surely gentler forms of torture than an unremitting round of meetings.

Indeed, if an unhurried pace, a chance for contemplation, and an opportunity to pursue purely private interests are among the elements of a good life, and if they contribute anything to the quality of a culture, a good case can be made for the view that many middle-class citizens of the United States are suffering from an excess rather than a scarcity of "participant activity." It is undeniably true that in any large organization power is likely to drift into the hands of those who can give the organization their undivided attention. But there is no moral or practical reason for regarding this state of affairs as an unqualified evil.

The conventional image of the ideal democratic citizen—the man who is an eager, active member of all the groups to which he belongs—has in fact some dangerous implications. The eighteenth-century philosophers of democracy believed that democracy depended on men who combined a high degree of interest in public affairs with qualities of moderation and balance. Such individuals, in fact, are comparatively few. But the qualities which the eighteenth-century philosophers thought the individual democratic citizen ought to have are fairly well distributed over the population as a whole. There are the very interested, the sometimes interested, and the usually uninterested; and the less interested are apparently necessary in order to inject a quality of restraint into the democratic process. A church could not exist if it consisted only of saints, and the perfectly interested and forever active citizen is not the only kind of citizen that keeps an organization on an even keel.

In short, we cannot describe our present situation in terms appropriate to older oligarchic forms of social organization, nor can we criticize it by the standards that were developed to criticize these older forms. We are dealing with a recurrent problem of liberal reform—the redistribution of power. In its present form, however, the problem does not fit the entrenched categories of most political programs. It is not a struggle between the many and the few, or between "the people" and the ruling class or classes. And in some ways, no doubt, that is regrettable. If the old slogans worked, politics would be simpler and the liberal cause could retain its passion while living on its inherited intellectual capital.

THE RESTORATION OF CONSENT

But after we have cut away spurious issues, the problem of the recovery of government by consent still remains a serious and disturbing one. Men live today not only under the government of the State but under a host of private governments that have great power over them. If this power is not as great as that of the State, it is considerable none the less, and it is felt immediately in the everyday life of the ordinary citizen. Moreover, the voluntary organization is the major channel available to the individual for putting pressure on the State or for acting directly to take charge of his social environment. Yet the avenues to power within the most powerful of these organizations are clogged; with respect to many types of problem, such as neighborhood improvement or the protection of consumers' interests, voluntary organizations are weak or nonexistent; and not least, in both explicit and implicit voluntary associations the relationship between leaders and followers is one between organized and purposeful groups on one side, controlling the channels of communication, and a large mass of scattered and unorganized individuals on the other.

These are the circumstances, I think, in which a good many

of the feelings that mark the contemporary democratic scene have emerged—the sense of alienation and depersonalization, the fear that the individual has been reduced to a state of dependency, the complaint that a trackless maze lies between the ordinary man and the remote authorities, the unnamed judges and invisible bureaus and all-too-visible Big Brothers, who determine his destiny. Such feelings may not be sure guides to the facts, but they have not appeared out of the void. The citizen of a giant modern democracy is immediately and intimately exposed to the effects of decisions and indecisions at the centers of power. He has been taught to think that he can talk back if he wants and that his message will get through. But it is dispiriting to carry on a dialogue with men he cannot reach and sometimes cannot even name.

To be sure, if a man is reasonably well off and relatively well rooted in a stable community, he has available to him a host of smaller associations such as the local church, a parent-teacher association, or a Better Business Bureau. The importance of such small societies can be underestimated. They give many people instruments through which they can take somewhat better charge of their affairs, help them to acquire an identifiable status and sense of usefulness in their communities, and train them in the arts and etiquette of political action. But the reach of such groups, for the most part, is short, and their powers limited. Standing between the individual and "the great society" to which he belongs there are in the main only the big powers—giant associations, visible and invisible, that speak for him and to him, sometimes well and sometimes badly, but in which he has the status at best of a happy conscript. Whatever may be said for or against this state of affairs, it is not the active, energetic condition associated with the idea of self-government.

What can be done about it?

DEMOCRACY WITHIN ASSOCIATIONS

As a very first step, there is the problem of protecting individual rights. Membership in many voluntary organizations is quasi-voluntary at best. Men are governed by the rules of the organizations to which they belong or for which they work, and they must accept these rules whether they wish to or not. The problem of individual rights is today not only a problem of rights against the State—no more than it has ever been. It is a problem of rights within the massive organizations to which the individual normally cannot help but belong. The rights of workers against their employers have been progressively more sharply defined and protected. Equivalent rights of individuals within unions and other organizations need similar definition and protection—for example, the right to speak in opposition to the policies of leadership without being persecuted or harassed, or the right to appeal to an impartial agency against punitive decisions taken by the organization. And while various statutes have now given recognition to the principle that the closed shop has to be complemented by the open union which any man with the requisite qualifications can join, neglected issues such as the right of the individual to transfer his seniority status from one union to another need recognition. Much of this job of defining and enforcing individual rights has already been done, and not infrequently through the independent action of unions or other voluntary organizations. But there is still a long way to go.

The problem of protecting individual rights within organizations, furthermore, is part of an even more troublesome question. This is the more general problem of reasserting democratic processes within large voluntary associations. It is true that a voluntary association may effectively and truly represent the interests of its members in the external democratic competition even though it gives its members little direct control over policy. But the operative word in this statement is "may." There is no guarantee under such conditions that the association's policies are the policies that the membership would favor if it had the chance to express a free opinion. Nor is this the only consequence of the breakdown of democratic procedures within voluntary organizations. Bad leadership cannot be turned out of power. New talents do not have a chance to emerge. And one of the major functions of voluntary organizations on the democratic scene goes by the board. When the government of such organizations is remote and paternalistic, they cannot serve as the training grounds where democratic habits and the democratic ethic of regulated competition are learned. On the contrary, they teach the harsh lesson that democratic rhetoric is different from democratic realities.

Yet paternalism and the monopoly of power are, of course, the dominant pattern. The large democratically controlled voluntary organization is at present the exception rather than the rule. Although the most powerful voluntary organizations usually have democratic constitutions, the majority of them are oligarchies in their actual mode of operation. Two-party systems of government are, of course, rare occurrences in the history of human groups. The kind of political democracy that characterizes the government of the State cannot be taken as a model for the government of organizations like professional associations, labor unions, or veterans' leagues. But enforceable constitutional provisions should exist in such associations that would make it possible for the membership to keep its leaders under surveillance and to discharge them by means of regular and freely contested elections. To insist that an established loyal opposition should always exist would be idle and artificial. But the freedom of dissatisfied individuals to join together in opposition to the policies of their leaders should be protected. When it is possible, for example, for leaders of a union to bring charges against an insurgent group and to appoint their own judges and jury, fundamental principles of due process are denied. Yet this procedure is a not uncommon feature of many union constitutions.

PLANNING FOR SELF-GOVERNMENT

Constitutional protections or interventions by the courts and the legislature, however, touch only the fringes of the problem of recovering government by consent. They may protect the rights of individuals and limit the authority of leadership; but while this is important, it does not in itself produce the conditions that give men a chance to have the active, intimate experience of joining in the government of the groups to which they belong. And unless a voluntary organization contains a reasonable number of men in its rank and file who have had that experience, and who have developed the alliances, skills, confidence, and irritabilities it generates, constitutional provisions for the maintenance of democratic procedures may well add up to so many dead letters. Beyond the enacting of new bills of rights for the members of voluntary associations, these associations need to be reorganized so that a larger number of their members have a chance to take a significant part in processes of self-government and to see the results of their participation close at hand.

This is not to make a fetish of participation for its own sake. It is simply to affirm that participation should be possible for individuals who wish it. Feelings of alienation and helplessness do not grow inside men when they fail to participate actively in the institutions that frame their lives. They grow when men are outraged enough or concerned enough to wish to participate and are nevertheless convinced that they will not be allowed to do so, or will only be permitted to play follow-the-leader if they do. These are the circumstances in which the absence of government by consent is felt immediately and intimately. And the ailment cannot be cured by exhortations to individuals to participate or by the repetition of stale slogans about the opportunities democracy offers each man for such participation. If the opportunities are not there, the exhortations and slogans will only reinforce his cynicism.

Yet providing such opportunities under contemporary conditions is not easy. It requires radical rearrangements in the structure of power within voluntary associations and in the functions they perform. "The greater is the multiplicity of small affairs," Tocqueville observed in arguing for local autonomy in the administration of national decisions, "the more do men, even without knowing it, acquire facility in practicing great undertakings in common." The extensive devolution of authority to smaller units within large voluntary organizations could do much to give men a steadier and livelier experience of government that stands or falls on their active consent.

Even at present, for example, there is a comparatively high degree of participation in the affairs of local unions. But the members of such local units would have more direct control over their immediate environments if these units were given greater autonomy and more important things to do. The local union, to consider just one sort of possibility, could be given a greater part to play in the day-to-day government of the plant community. It is habit, inherited prerogative, and suspicion, not economic necessity, that explains why the local union is often relegated to a plaintiff's role in dealing with such problems as transportation, restaurants, recreational activities, the communication with workers concerning projected innovations, or the provision of facilities for job retraining. Assigning local unions major responsibility for dealing with such problems could encourage the emergence of new leadership, build the informal associations that make for vigorous participation in the processes of self-government, and give individual workers a larger opportunity to try their hand at running their own affairs. There are a number of signs that these or similar programs are beginning to emerge. But their importance in converting the experience of democracy from something vicarious and occasional, like a visit to the polls, into something more constant and intimate has as yet to be fully grasped.

Nor are unions the only voluntary associations to which the principle of the devolution of responsibility applies. The great professional societies, for example, have yet to mount a continuing program of educational activities in local communities. Yet the intervention of such groups at a level where personal give-and-take is possible could do much to control the influence and authority of the massive, shadowy, informal associations like the newspaper syndicates and national communications networks. There are debates about fluoridization in unnumbered local communities; the participation of local doctors and dentists is often by invitation only. There are questions of civil liberty and delay in court procedures; public discussion initiated by lawyers acting as a corporate group in the communities immediately affected is usually *ad hoc*. The administration of welfare services is an issue as intemperately and ignorantly discussed as any on the American scene; yet social workers have made no organized effort at the grass-roots level simply to put the facts and complexities of welfare activities before those who are footing the bill. More will be said in the chapter that follows about the potential function of the organized professions as educational agencies. But one of the important by-products of increased local activities by professional groups would be the reactivation of these groups. There is nothing like exercise to set the juices flowing, in an organization as in a man.

Such concerted programs, however, are unlikely to spring up spontaneously. They have to be stimulated from the center to be parts of a coherent plan. And any such plans are now likely to collide with discouraging physical obstacles. In addition to the reorganization of voluntary associations, the recovery of everyday government by consent requires deliberate attention to the conditions that encourage people to form the friendships and close informal relationships that are the basis for lively cooperative activities. The cities of America are being torn down and rebuilt. In this process there is no single design visible, and there should not be. But the impression that the process has a general direction is nevertheless irresistible, and it seems to consist in the destruction of informal local agencies of government and the creation of great blocks of dormitories with few of the physical facilities or social conditions necessary for the development of a joint communal life.

It should be the objective of urban and suburban planning to produce neighborhoods capable of exercising large grants of local autonomy with regard to local matters like the organization of children's activities, the prevention of delinquency, or the provision of recreational facilities or work for the aged. This does not mean that such neighborhoods should be deprived of professional guidance; it means only the deliberate effort to organize communities so that they are more likely to have the will and the means to form their own voluntary groups and to take a larger part in seeing after their own welfare. It is not cities or urbanization as such that constitutes the problem. It is the characterless, sprawling disorganization of our cities. Variety is inherent in cities; the ugliness and uniformity that kill the interest of the city-dweller in his surroundings is not. Happy anonymity is one of a city's great attractions; the disorientation of the individual is not a necessary consequence.

There are other missed opportunities as well. The use of television and radio mainly as toys is an example. The individual who has some interest he wishes to promote must normally find an organization through which to work. If he cannot find one, he has to form one. In both cases the chance to communicate with others is of the essence. Yet in countless cities and suburbs there are men and women concerned about the conditions in local schools, or zoning, or the disappearance of the trees, who imagine that they are quite alone in these concerns or who do not know where to find their potential allies. There is no law of nature which requires television and radio to be used only by the professionals and only for one-way communication. If the disposition to give social power to individuals is genuine, the facilities of local stations can be employed to encourage communication about local problems among concerned citizens. These facilities can also be made available to other voluntary organizations besides the political parties. We have the technical facilities to rebuild our organizational life. We are not using them.

Cut loose from the stereotypes that surround it, the problem of recovering government by consent is a problem of manageable dimensions. Questions of great scope and technical complexity like military defense, foreign policy, or the control of the business cycle cannot be resolved through the institutions of grass-roots democracy. But such questions are not the questions that invite the individual to take action in his everyday life or that are likely to leave him resentful when decisions are made without directly consulting him. He spends his life at work, in a neighborhood, and inside his home. It is when he feels that he has no voice in the control of the conditions that affect this intimate environment that he is going to feel that he has been disenfranchised.

But such a sense of powerlessness and alienation is not an unavoidable consequence of industrialism or the iron laws of a so-called "mass society." It is the consequence of conditions which it is possible, though not easy, to remedy. The elementary fact about our present condition is that a larger proportion of the members of society than ever before have some opportunity to control the shape of their immediate environments. It is the very growth of this opportunity which explains the widespread and justified complaint that the powers at the disposal of the individual are insufficient. To speak about recovering government by consent is in a sense a mistake. We are still in the process of discovering it.

V

THE DILEMMAS OF AN OPEN SOCIETY

The epidemic spread of the ideal of an open society is one of the fundamental reasons for the revolutions of the twentieth century. In all modern or modernizing societies an unusual project, a project that reverses the normal historical situation, is under way. The project is to make the masses of men feel close to the centers of power by giving them information—or misinformation—about what is going on. "Public relations" is one obvious sign; the extraordinary propaganda efforts that must be made by even the securest totalitarian governments is another. The ideal of an open society has produced a general change in the nature of social authority and in the conditions under which political and economic power can be exercised.

And yet the ideal, now that everyone pays tribute to it, stirs some of our deepest fears and presents us with some of our most acute dilemmas. In abstract theory, the invention of techniques for the quick and universal dissemination of information ought to have been the answer to the liberal tradition's prayers. In actual fact, each new advance in communication is greeted with anxiety and concern that only another instrument has been invented for invading and emptying the minds of millions or for provoking these millions into interfering with the decisions that the few who are saner and wiser must make.

The old phrases still ring—the free market place of ideas, freedom of speech and thought, the right to know, the right to dissent

72

—and what they designate is incorporated in the laws. But the phrases have acquired a hollow sound. The daily drumbeat of sensations and shocks that now passes for the communication of information, the soft-soap and the hard-sell that pass for free debate, the heterogeneous, distracted, and ill-prepared public to whom this carnival of eccentric facts and sodden fictions is offered, the disappearance even of the ability to read as a condition for membership in this public—it is as though a malevolent demon were playing with us, giving us a little less and a little more than we hoped, and turning the ideal of an open society into a caricature of itself. The liberal mind may still applaud Justice Holmes's dictum that freedom of thought means freedom for the thought we hate. But while our heads may insist, our feet inevitably drag when we have to grant this freedom not only to thoughts we hate but to unthoughts.

And our doubts go deeper. If the system worked quite perfectly, if everyone were candid and responsible in the use of the media of communication, we would still be disturbed. For the flow of information is overwhelming. It is debilitating and confusing; when it does not confuse, it narcotizes; when it does not narcotize, it encourages the illusion of understanding. How shall I distribute political knowledge and the political virtues, Hermes asks Zeus in the myth that Protagoras tells in Plato's dialogue. Shall I distribute them as specialized knowledge or skill is distributed, to a few selected groups, or shall I distribute them to all? To all, says Zeus, for cities cannot exist if only a few have the political virtues. But in the democratic society we now inhabit, one cannot help but ask whether perhaps we have a little too much of a good thing.

What has happened to upset the ideal of an open society? The social conditions which the classic democratic ideal of an open society tacitly took for granted have been undermined by the rise of mass media of communication, by the disappearance of a clearly defined educated class that alone speaks for "public opinion," and by fundamental changes in the nature of what men know and communicate. The result has been confusion in our ideas about the nature and purpose of an open society, and the derangement of the institutions that are presumed to embody this ideal. The present condition of communication and political education presents us with another major problem requiring the clarification of democratic theory and the reorganization of existing democratic institutions.

THE IMPACT OF MASS MEDIA OF COMMUNICATION

The ideal of an open society was first engendered in a world in which the primary instrument of communication was the spoken word, and it was possible for listeners to talk back. The assumption on which the idea was based was that communication was normally a direct personal engagement between man and man. The Platonic dialogue was the unspoken model for the democratic debate. This is the first of the assumptions supporting the ideal of an open society which has become progressively untenable. It became partly archaic when printing was invented; the spread of literacy upset it still more; and it has now become almost wholly misleading with the emergence of mass media of communication.

For access to expensive and highly centralized instruments of communication has become a basic factor determining who communicates, what is communicated, and how far the message carries. And the mass media have led to another significant change as well. Communication is today carried on not simply to transmit information, ideas, and feelings, or to promote specific causes. It is also carried on to support the instruments of communication themselves. Lawyers, teachers, professional storytellers, and gossips have always been with us. But they have never dominated the avenues of communication as the professional communicator does today. "The principle of freedom of the press," as Zechariah Chafee has noted, "was laid down when the press was a means of *individual* expression, comment, and criticism. Now it is an industry for profit, using techniques of mass suggestion and possessing great power. . . . Is the old principle of the *Areopagitica* applicable in this new situation?"

The character of what is communicated, furthermore, has been greatly affected as a result. The slanting of news and information is one of the more obvious of the problems that have been aggravated by the rise of mass media; and another problem, whose existence is attested by the results of most national elections during the last thirty years, is that the mass media do not fairly reflect the spectrum of opinions that actually exist in the community. But as the election results also suggest, the power of the mass media to make men hold opinions to which they would otherwise be opposed has been exaggerated. The more important issue is not the direct influence the mass media exert on men's opinions but the influence they exert on the shape and temperature of opinion, on the questions to which it is addressed, the kinds of solution for which it looks, and the atmosphere in which it is formed. The mass media, competing in the market place of commodities, not of ideas, and trying to trap and keep the attention of great numbers of people who have other things on their minds, serve up a special kind of diet. The visceral, the momentary, and the odd take precedence, and bad news is good news because it sells more newspapers. The procession of human affairs is thus cut up into a series of shocks and crises, torn loose from their contexts, with only a brief past behind them and a melodramatic future ahead. The result is to deform men's sense of the public world, to distort events, and to misshape history.

Thinking may not make things so, but thinking plus instantaneous communication often does. The pictures of the world that are created by the mass media react back upon what is pictured. Truth comes to imitate fiction, to be enslaved to the imitation of itself. It is one thing when a quarrel between two citizens of different races, or an exchange of notes between two governments, takes place in private. But these become quite different events if a great many hear about them, and even more different if the news travels fast and the reactions to the news travel back equally fast. The meaning of an event depends at least in part on the theater in which it takes place. Modern communications have enormously expanded the size of that theater, and in doing so they have often diminished the powers of the principal actors to control what takes place.

From Little Rock to Johannesburg, and from Washington to Algiers, the same complaint can be heard: people who are not on the spot cannot be expected to understand "the real problem," yet it is these far-away people who are dictating the answer. The advent of mass communications has not destroyed the politics of smoke-filled rooms. But it has filled these rooms with the smoke and fire that comes from the streets, and the streets may be half-way around the world. An extra dimension has thus been added to most public problems. There is the original problem, and there is the reported image of it, and it is not enough to deal with the original problem in its own terms. Indeed, it frequently loses its own terms. It is not surprising that the suspicion should be grow-ing that our achievement of an open society has simply compli-cated our problems beyond our powers to deal with them.

THE SHATTERING OF THE PUBLIC

Still another change has affected the premises on which the ideal of an open society was based. Whether we think of Athens or the England of John Stuart Mill, the conception of an open society was developed in a stratified social order with a clearly marked ruling class whose powers and privileges were protected from the masses of people below. Liberal democracy, the liberal democracy of Locke, Madison, and Jefferson, tacitly assumed that society would be ruled by a group of educated, civilized, and moderate men who had to quarrel only with their peers and needed to report only to men of their own kind. "Until the middle of the nineteenth century," as Mr. Chafee has pointed out, "most writers wrote for a comparatively small group of well-educated men who formed a coherent body of opinion. . . . The rest of the community did not read much and did not care what was written. Now nearly everybody does read and care, but the standards are variegated."

In the limited open society that once existed the basic liberal virtues—the mutual recognition of individual rights, toleration, fair and moderate methods of argument—could be assumed to be safe because those who did not have these virtues were in fact excluded from active participation in the democratic community. The free market place of ideas in which classic liberals put their faith was a market place circumscribed by a traditional etiquette, crisscrossed by attitudes of social deference, and stabilized by unspoken understandings that allowed men to know who was who and what was up. Nineteenth-century liberals may not have favored such restrictions in principle, but they accepted them as facts. (The ideal of economic *laisser faire* was formulated with the same tacit assumption.) And it is these built-in restraints on the operations of an open society which are no longer present in their traditional form. The rise in the general standard of living, the upsetting of social hierarchies based on inherited rank, the spread of a democratic and egalitarian ethic, and the growth of mass media of communication have all combined to erode or erase them.

It was the presentiment that liberal society was losing its moderating structure, that its internal and informal instruments of self-control were disappearing, that led John Stuart Mill, despite his egalitarian outlook, to emphasize the danger of a tyranny of the majority. And it is the conviction that the conditions that separate an open society from an uncontained society have disappeared which has led a large number of liberal men a century later to share Walter Lippmann's belief that the natural constitutional order of liberal democracy has broken down, and that this is the cause of "the precipitate and catastrophic decline" of Western society. "The people have acquired power which they are incapable of exercising, and the governments they elect have lost powers which they must recover if they are to govern."

For the entity on which the theory of an open society based its hopes is no longer clearly identifiable. That entity was "the public." We now suspect, in the term that Mr. Lippmann used years ago, that it is a phantom public. The old public, whose existence traditional liberals assumed, was composed of individuals who could discuss issues face to face, who had some common values and experiences, and who possessed organizations and resources with which they could move events if they wished. But urbanization, the breakdown of clearly marked social classes with their definite traditions, the emergence of "new men" whose power is based on the possession only of technical and narrow skills—all these have made us doubt that such a public can any longer exist.

The theories that have emerged and that have our ear assert, indeed, that this public has been converted into a "mass." City life is anonymous and impersonal, it is pointed out, so that the sense of community is destroyed. And in addition, the participants in our so-called open society are a mass rather than a public because they do not act and react directly on one another; they react separately to the common stimuli they receive from the centrally controlled mass media. Moreover, if autonomous groups of men do come together as a result of these stimuli and wish to take action, they do not have the means of action at hand. They cannot talk back to a television set, and cannot easily reach the key figures who ultimately control the vast parties, unions, or civic associations to which they may belong. So the open society has become simply an uncontained society, a society that cannot locate authority anywhere.

Is all this true? The question is pertinent and we shall look at it. But whether it is true or not, the source of these ideas is clear. They are responses to the disappearance from the American democratic scene of any clearly identifiable class of men with common traditions and associations who can act, as it were, as the chairmen or moderators of the democratic debate. The old image of a society governed by discussion is out of focus. Another image keeps intruding—the image of an administered and manipulated society listening in on a debate that is factitious.

THE GROWTH OF TECHNICAL KNOWLEDGE

The final assault on the assumptions that supported the belief in an open society has been delivered, however, by the growth of a new kind of knowledge. The advent of science, together with the increase of technical, specialized knowledge in every domain, has fundamentally altered the conditions under which the ideal of an open society has to be pursued. "The 'truths' of the modern scientific world view, though they can be demonstrated in mathematical formulas and proved technologically," Miss Hannah Arendt has said, "will no longer lend themselves to normal expression in speech and thought. . . . The sciences today have been forced to adopt a 'language' of mathematical symbols which, though it was originally meant only as an abbreviation for spoken statements, now contains statements that in no way can be translated back into speech."

It is important to see that the issue has not been created because science has deliberately retreated from public intelligibility. Many social scientists undoubtedly employ a jargon as unnecessary as it is impenetrable, and physical scientists have done less than they can to communicate with those outside their guild. But most social scientists still have lessons to learn in the arts of obscurity from theologians and philosophers. And while it is undeniably true that the language that physicists speak has receded from the common world, so does the language of a man who discovers a new animal and must give it a new name. In fact, the mathematical language of the physical sciences was not originally meant "only as an abbreviation for spoken statements." Its major function is to permit men to order their observations in such a way that they can draw precise inferences from them that they would not otherwise draw, and can have and create experiences that would not otherwise come into their ken. If science merely duplicated what we say and believe in the common world, there would be no point to the scientific enterprise.

But this, of course, is where the trouble begins. Science carries us away from the familiar to the unfamiliar and disturbs us because it does. It breaks up old categories and introduces new standards for determining the truth or falsehood of our opinions. The establishment of scientific institutions and technical expertise represents an assault on deep-seated habits of our culture. The "causation" that physicists explore is not the "causation" we observe in our homely world; the modern scientific philosopher does not answer the questions people ask him but insists on reformulating the questions; the empirical sociologist breaks into the easy flow of our conversations about "human nature," "American conformity," or "the decline of morality," and makes distinctions and asks for evidence. The advent of science, together with the increase of specialized, technical methods of inquiry in every domain, has, in a word, enormously increased the distance between knowledge and conventional opinion. They are different not only in content but in style. And the problem of communication has been fundamentally altered in consequence.

This is why the problem of classified information and governmental secrecy is only a bubble on the surface. The memory of

man does not run to the time when those in power told everything. The present policy of protecting official secrets is new and
disturbing only because it is the open and avowed policy of democratic governments, and because the secrets are matters of life
and death for the race. We are right to be troubled about the
policy of official secrecy. Although the necessity for secrecy about
some matters is plain, knowledge that there are secrets creates
suspicions and doubts, leads responsible men to refrain from having opinions because they think they do not have an adequate
basis for them, and engenders a sense of distance between citizens
and government incompatible with democratic expectations. (It
need hardly be added that the policy of keeping secrets does not
become more palatable because the secrets are badly kept; and
the policy becomes both comic and bitter when, as in the case
of Cuba, information in the public domain would have been a
surer guide to action than information that was not only secret
but wrong.) But the problem of maintaining or creating an open
society is only at its periphery a problem of determining the
proper limits of governmental secrecy. The tidal movement that
has shaken our confidence that the ideal of an open society is
realistic is the emergence of a kind of knowledge which is secret
not by edict but by nature—knowledge that is difficult and specialized and that requires time, training, concentration, and a leap
of the imagination to acquire.

The belief that any educated man could inform himself about
what he ought to know politically was the premise on which men
like Jefferson or Franklin built their social outlook. But the man
who would now understand all the facts that are politically relevant must proceed to acquaint himself with the bottom of the
ocean, the inside of Yoknapatawpha County, and the other side
of the moon. "Modern society," John Plamenatz has written, "is
like a giant building, dimly lit and full of holes and obstacles, in
which no man can move except by groping his way; and even
those (the experts) who have torches find their light put out as
soon as they stray from the corners familiar to them." What must
be known is alien and complicated; knowing it requires the mastery of technical and specialized instruments and symbols; and
unless these instruments and symbols are understood in their own

context, and their powers and limitations taken into account, the reliability and significance of the results they achieve cannot be properly assessed.

Here again is one of the reasons why it is said that a mass society is upon us. The growth of technical problems and technical knowledge seems to have evicted the citizen, to have dispossessed him from the chance to understand the conditions of his life. It has placed him in the hands of a new class of experts— physicists and tax consultants, economists and psychologists, marriage counselors and professional fund-raisers—who stand between him and his experience, interpreting, guiding, and filling in the forms for him. We are acting out, so it seems, a kind of Dantean parable. Our progress in specialized knowledge has banished mystery from more and more separate parts of the physical and human scene. But mystery has reclaimed its rights. It has reappeared in the mystery of the system as a whole, in the inability of anybody to comprehend the nature of that whole or the purpose it serves. We have more knowledge than ever before, and so, strangely enough, the open society has come to seem less possible than ever. The effort to achieve it has led men only to the conviction that they do not and cannot understand the world in which they live.

IS THE IDEAL OF AN OPEN SOCIETY TENABLE?

Do all these changes—the rise of the mass media, the disappearance of the classic, homogeneous public, the rise of science and specialized expertise—mean that the ideal of an open society makes no sense any more? Would it be best simply to admit our mistake, cut our losses, and change our institutions to make them fit the unpleasant but unbending facts? The question is inevitable, and has to be faced. But while the ailments from which our open society is suffering are serious, the question, I think, has an ill-defined conception of the nature and purpose of an open society behind it. The cult and culture of the open society could not be overturned if we wished. And the ideal remains a valid ideal. It presents problems, but it is easy to look at these problems in an unhistorical perspective.

The way to begin, I think, is by noticing a curious fact about the "complexity" of the world we inhabit, a complexity, it is frequently said, which makes the hope futile that men can understand their society sufficiently to have sensible judgments about it. No doubt the twentieth-century social scene is more complicated than the scene which confronted the classic liberals who put forward the ideal of an open society. The scope and pace of events are immeasurably greater; their interrelations are more manifold; the remote is closer to all of us in consciousness and in fact. But in all civilized societies, the social scene has always been "complex." And one reason why we are more aware of the complexity of our own scene is that we have more close and refined knowledge about it. As much as anything else, it is this growth of exact knowledge and controlled human power in more and more areas which has made the ignorance of each of us as individuals more evident.

Indeed, one of the great functions of scientific conclusions is that they open up new questions and make what we do not know clearer and more precise. On the principle that knowing what one does not know is better than cocksureness, this painful situation represents a step ahead in the progress of human intelligence. To be sure, it creates the difficult problem of finding ways in which the specialized knowledge of different men can be brought together and focused on common, practical purposes. But the fact that educated men once found it easier to talk together in a common language has equivocal implications. It may imply that they spoke their common language better than educated men do today. But it may also imply—as, for example, when they discussed the nature of the physical universe—that they thought they knew more than they did.

This observation may help us to look with more perspective on some of the assumptions behind the melancholy doctrine that we live in a "mass society." We inhabit such a society, it is sometimes said, because specialization has replaced general intelligence. Each of us is closed off in his own special niche with its narrow angle of vision; we have been deprived of a vision and view of the whole. In one sense, this is true. The growth of scientific and technical knowledge has undermined the authority of those in religion, philosophy, or politics who claim to know the ultimate purpose and secret of things. The world we inhabit in contemporary liberal democracies is undeniably more complex and confusing because no single authoritative interpretation of the scheme of things entire is accepted. And this is undeniably one consequence of an open society. But is it a virtue or a defect of such a society? The answer we give to this question depends on the answer we give to two other questions. Did traditional monolithic doctrines really give men an understanding of the whole or only the illusion of understanding? And if it was only an illusion, is it this illusion that we wish restored?

A second premise on which the doctrine of a "mass society" has been constructed is similarly questionable. This is the belief that the conditions of modern communication, together with urbanization and the disappearance of the traditional boundaries between the classes, have irreparably shattered what was once a "public" and have converted it into a "mass." It is unquestionable that there is no longer any single homogeneous educated public that holds a monopolistic position as the audience and censor of the public debate. But there are sharply defined ethnic groups, powerful professional societies, trade associations, and workers' organizations. We have many publics, not one. To be sure, we also have many people who belong to a "mass"—mobile people, with few or no fixed ties, little active concern with any voluntary organizations, and dispossessed from ways and means of making their opinions and interests visible. But it is a theoretical error with the gravest practical implications to confuse a pluralistic society in which there are many publics and therefore no single dominant public with a society that has no organized public capable of serving as an independent judge and watchman over the decisions made by ruling groups. If the seeds of a "mass society" are lying around, they are still only seeds, and they are rather scattered.

Similarly, there is no alchemy which turns a society into a mass society simply because it possesses mass media of communication. The members of a radio or television audience are not in physical contact with one another. But then neither are readers of the same book. And even under conditions of so-called urban anonymity, those who shut themselves up to read a book or to watch

a television program are not usually isolated or anonymous individuals. They have families, friends, associations, and jobs. They
communicate with others, and their responses to the object of
mass attention are governed at least in part by the rules, regulations, and expectations of their private milieus. Most studies concerning the formation of public opinion indicate, in fact, that the
mass media do not work directly. Key figures in each community
—the so-called "influentials"—stand between the mass media and
the alleged mass, mediating and directing the responses that
emerge. The term "mass audience" is a name for a large and
heterogeneous audience, but it has still to be proved that it stands
for anything more.

The more apocalyptic of our doubts about the value and possibility of an open society, in short, are the products of doubtful
assumptions and standards of judgment. "The blunt monster, the
still-discordant, wavering multitude," has always been feared,
and the restrictions which democracy places on the powers of
elites have always been mourned. We forget that Milton accused
the aristocrats of his time of being drunk on wine and insolence.
"Imagine," Lord Acton once wrote, "a congress of eminent celebrities such as More, Bacon, Grotius, Pascal, Cromwell, Bossuet,
Montesquieu, Jefferson, Napoleon, Pitt, etc. The result would be
an Encyclopedia of Error. They would assert Slavery, Socialism,
Persecution, Divine Right, Military Despotism, the reign of force,
the supremacy of the executive over legislation and justice, pur-
chase in the magistracy, the abolition of credit, the limitation of
laws to nineteen years, etc."

The point of maintaining an open society is to ensure that those
who make public decisions will be kept steadily aware that there
are, after all, some limitations on their judgment, and that they
are deciding the fate of other interests besides their own. That
there is always some single solution that is surely right, and that
it is known to some elite group, is precisely the assumption for
which there is no justification. Yet it underlies the argument that
the open society is a nuisance. No doubt the members of some
party, or some social scientists, or some "men of light and leading," as Mr. Lippmann argues, will indeed understand matters a

little better than the ordinary run of mankind. But which party, which social scientists, which men of light and leading? If that political question is going to be decided by peaceful discussion, who shall listen in on the discussion? And how is this audience going to be restricted in a society whose distinctive mark is that most men tend not to know their place and would think it dishonorable if they did? These are the pragmatic issues, and the acceptance or rejection of the principle of an open society turns on the answer we give to them.

Indeed, if we think it improper that those who lack specialized training and discipline in the subjects that bear on public policy should have a part in public discussion, we do not merely exclude the many and admit the few. We exclude everybody. All forms of government, whether democratic or dictatorial, suffer from a common and incurable disease. They are composed of men who cannot know all the things which, ideally, they ought to know. The test of a form of government is not whether it can provide rule by omniscient philosophers. The test is whether it can put those who have specialized knowledge to useful work, and whether the generalist at the top of the hierarchy can be kept intelligently informed about the issues that turn up.

It is therefore senseless to reject the ideal of an open society on the ground that it presupposes a kind of omnicompetent citizen who does not exist. The standard is unrealistic. The proper standard for judging the ability to take a significant part in public discussion is simply the capacity to communicate effectively in the existing language for political discussion. There are countries in which large segments of the population do not understand the words they hear, and do not have leaders who can articulate their interests for them. And in any country, no doubt, the language of political discussion is likely to be one that is full of ambiguities and that few use with great precision. But within these limitations, there is no evidence that, in advanced industrial countries, the ability to use the political language effectively is restricted to any particular stratum of the population. In all strata there are some who use that language better than others—for example, journalists, political professionals, union leaders, the heads of voluntary associations. And it is these figures who lead the discussion that takes place and bear the greatest responsibility for its character.

In sum, the suggestion that the ideal of an open society has collapsed into the fact of a mass society combines unguarded generalizations with a kind of eager melancholia. Construed in practical terms, the ideal of an open society does not propose that all individuals should have the knowledge, interest, time, and energy to be competent participants in the debate of every public issue. It proposes only that those who have the responsibility for making decisions be surrounded by groups that are well enough informed and organized to serve as outside critics and to take the debate on public policy out into the open. So conceived, the ideal of an open society is not a quixotic but a quite manageable ideal, and we enjoy an open society not perfectly but approximately.

THE PRACTICAL ISSUES

But we enjoy such a society only very approximately. The present organization of communication and education is not adequate to the task of achieving the goals of an open society even when these goals are realistically defined. The purpose of an open society is to produce groups of competent critics outside the inner circles, and to maintain a relevant and responsible debate on public policy not controlled by the inner circles. A second purpose is to give the members of the larger society that listens to this debate a sound enough understanding of their social environment to allow them to feel that the world they inhabit is not an alien and arbitrary mystery. This is important for its own sake, and it is also important if the debate among the smaller interested groups is to maintain a reasonable level of responsibility. For the debate is a public debate, and the quality of any such debate is affected by the quality of the audience.

From this point of view, there are unmistakable defects in our open society. The debate is inadequately focused and organized. The attention of the bystanders is systematically distracted to irrelevancies. And a quite inadequate understanding exists, even among the best-educated laymen, of the fundamental engine of change in modern society—science. Can anything be done about these defects? There is no simple formula, and no sudden outpouring of good will or new metaphysical vision of man's place and purpose in the universe, that will remedy them. They are likely to be with us for a considerable time to come. But there are three practical lines of approach that might help us to cut these defects down to size.

First of all, there is the problem posed by the disappearance of the classic homogeneous public—the problem of finding the way, our own peculiar contemporary way, to give spine and discipline to the democratic dialogue. In major respects the instruments for dealing with this issue are already at hand. They are the organized professions, the contemporary substitutes for the organized public of the nineteenth century. A considerable expansion of the role which these groups play in the organization of public discussion could do much, I think, to improve its content and quality.

The professions are already strongly represented in this discussion. As the possessors of special information and skills, members of the professions are normally invited to be participants in the decision-making process. And as affected interest groups the professions regularly invite themselves into the proceedings. For there are few public issues, from fluoridization to juvenile delinquency and from foreign economic policy to city planning, that do not touch upon the field of knowledge or interest of one or more of the professions. Yet to act as consultants when called upon, to take part in the public debate through scattered articles in the public press or occasional pronouncements by professional organizations—these are random and *ad hoc* procedures. They have a number of shortcomings. They do not ensure that all the professions that have something relevant to say about an issue will be consulted. They do not give the interested layman the sustained education he needs to grasp the nature of an issue firmly. They do not permit the professions to form the important satellite publics that would serve as agents of communication between the man with specialized knowledge and the ordinary layman. Most important of all, they keep the professions in the position of a respondent rather than an initiator of the public dialogue.

An effectively functioning open society does not require omniscient laymen. But it does require public discussion in which the central issues have been responsibly defined, the essential distinctions made, and the relevant alternatives honestly canvassed. This is the task that the professions might perform, with premeditation and as a regular undertaking. Instruments of mass communication, expanded programs of adult education, and the publication of professional journals for the nonprofessional reader are among the devices that could be employed.

For the professions are the places where knowledge and practice meet. They represent the activities where the first impact of new knowledge on old folkways and inherited folk wisdom are likely to be felt. Public discussion is likely to wrestle with the shadows of the past or with only the superficial symptoms of existing problems so long as it neglects the hidden revolutions that are changing the world most radically—medical developments, for example, that change the balance between the human race and its environment, or the evolution of new concepts of property and justice through the process of judicial decision, or the impact of new technologies on the way we build our cities. Unless the professions take the initiative and serve as the centers for a continuing discussion of such issues, there is not much likelihood that these issues will receive timely public attention. And such an ambitious effort by the professions to address the layman would serve other functions as well. It would indicate to the interested bystander the shape that informed discussion of a given issue takes, and would alert the members of the professions themselves to the larger social implications of their activities.

In the field of penology, for example, new ideas and information in psychology and psychiatry have thrown our practices into even greater doubt than they have been in the past. They have raised in sharper form than ever, indeed, fundamental philosophical questions about the meaning of individual responsibility and the rationale for punishment. And uncertainty about these issues is not restricted to professional circles. It is felt by a very large number of people, and is reflected in the oscillation of opinion between extreme and simplistic positions. Lawyers, doctors, and philosophers have a chance in this domain to work together to create a sophisticated public opinion, aware of the complexity and subtlety of the issues involved. Again, there is hardly any field whose problems are more generally misunderstood, or more frequently torn out of context, than that of social welfare. The transition of social work from an amateur to a professional activity is a symptom of a long-range change in the character of our society. Yet social workers have done little as a profession to acquaint outsiders with the character of the values for which the social-work profession is a trustee.

But perhaps the best example is the role that is available to the scientific community. Scientific discovery and technological innovation are the principal sources of social change. They cannot be slowed down, and the difficulties of forecasting the social consequences of new discoveries and techniques are notorious. But public discussion of the social impact of technological changes usually enters the picture, when it does at all, only after damage that cannot be ignored has been done. The smog over Los Angeles, the overcrowding of American cities, and the condition of creeping uglification from which the American countryside is suffering are all fairly elementary examples. It is this kind of process, caused by a combination of human ingenuity and a refusal to take thought, which has led so many to believe that man is at once making his destiny and that this destiny has slipped out of his control. It is the consequence of a state of affairs in which technological innovations are not normally recognized for what they are—social decisions.

Now new developments in the sciences presage a still more fateful growth in the powers of men to change the human scene: setting military technology aside, these new powers range from automation to control of the weather, and from new organic insecticides to cheaper and quicker methods of transportation. If the benefits of these discoveries are to be maximized and the damaging side effects minimized, the social character of the decisions about their use has to be high-lighted and the attention of the public focused sufficiently in advance on possible consequences and alternative policies. Needless to say, it is neither possible nor desirable to place the final decisions concerning the conditions under which innovations will be introduced in the hands of professional scientists. But it is just for these reasons that such knowledge as we do possess should be more generally broadcast, and that decisions about the uses of our technology should not be made only by those who have a vested interest in ignoring all but a few of the values involved. The scientific community, therefore, cannot restrict itself to giving information when it is asked. It has to raise the questions in its own terms, and to develop an independent role as an educational agency in the community. And if scientific and other professional groups are to play such an educational role, their own education, it should be added, has to be reviewed. Professional education has to be an effort not simply to train a student *in* his profession, but to let him see it from the outside, to make him aware of its place in the spectrum of activities that go on in his society.

If the learned professions are to play a role in the reorganization and revitalization of public discussion, however, they will also need access to instruments of mass communication which are not now available to them except under unusual circumstances. We come to a second and urgent issue. The present distribution of power in the area of mass communications is incompatible with the achievement of basic objectives of an open society. The communication of information is predominantly controlled by the imperatives of the market place. The effect on what is communicated is important, but the effect on the predominant style of communication is even more important. The market-place orientation is responsible for the hit-and-run, shock-and-shiver technique which is used to discuss issues that cannot be adequately understood without sustained attention and cumulative study. The creation—by government, by private action, or by a combination of the two—of powerful noncommercial media of communication to supplement the commercial media is an indispensable means to providing a choice for those who want a choice. No one knows how large or small the audiences for such noncommercial media would eventually turn out to be. But the problem is not a simple matter of numbers. Such new media could help create the interested and sophisticated publics, small or large, which intelligent discussion of public issues requires. And they would make alternative methods for discussing such issues more visible and audible.

But there is a final problem that also has to be met in reconstructing our existing open society, and it cannot be met simply by changes in the political and economic organization of the instruments of communication. It is, once more, an educational problem. The reasonably alert member of any modern society is reminded every day that the world he inhabits is changing at a breakneck pace, and changing not only in its physical or political aspects but in its moral dimensions, in the meaning that people will find in their experience on—and now perhaps off—this planet. Fundamental to all these changes is the scientific enterprise. Yet that enterprise is a closed secret to all but a relatively few men even among the best-educated groups of democratic society. And it is a secret not simply in its content but in its essential character as a discipline of the human mind.

The ordinary uneducated man in the Middle Ages, though he could not build a cathedral himself, could imagine the kind of thinking that a cathedral embodied. Most educated men today do not have as much ability to share imaginatively in the triumphs of their own civilization. And the consequence is a growing sense of alienation, an increasingly pervasive suspicion and hostility towards the basic style and central themes of our society. For many educated moderns science exists as a form of black magic. It looms in their imaginations as something unfamiliar, supernatural, and causeless.

The consequences can be seen in our recurrent bouts of nostalgia for simple solutions and simpler days, in the announcements by the beat and the lost that they have resigned from a world they cannot understand, and in the suspicions of science and reason which exist in the intellectual circles of the most advanced industrial societies. But while there are difficulties in communicating scientific information to educated laymen, it has still to be proved that these difficulties are insuperable. There are risks of superficiality and misunderstanding. At every point the transmission of specialized information to the interested citizen runs the danger of forced analogies, mixed metaphors, and the eager association of unassociated ideas. The task takes time, attention, and art, all of which are in short supply. But without an extensive program of general education in the sciences, the walls between the different publics that compose our open society are bound to become still higher and thicker. And most of the obstacles in the way of such a program would be reduced if its purposes were clearly understood.

That purpose is not to produce more physicists, chemists, doctors, and engineers. To a large extent this would take care of itself if the central purpose of a program of general scientific education at the secondary, collegiate, and adult levels were achieved. This purpose is to give the nonscientist the ability to *imagine* science, to appreciate its character as a discipline of the human mind. To accomplish this purpose, some firsthand exposure to a science, and preferably to more than one science, is surely necessary. But it is not necessary that the individual master a mass of details. The problem is to take him through some representative histories of scientific achievement—to show the gross questions that provoked inquiry, the steps by which the questions were refined, the role played by an organizing theory, the stages by which the theory was confirmed, the difference that the theory makes for the questions men subsequently ask. The object of such a process is to bring out the logic that is in the sciences, the choices that produce a scientific belief, the standards that justify its acceptance. In short, the object is not to provide scientific information as such, but to bring science within the domain of the humanities, to reveal it as a product of the human mind and a mirror through which men can come to a better understanding and assessment of the way that mind works.

Such a program might help dissipate the confusions and exaggerations that now impede the domestication of the scientific enterprise in democratic society. It would help educated men to think of science in natural rather than supernatural terms, and to cease looking upon scientists as either Frankensteins or gods. From the point of view of the long-range prospects of democracy, few issues are more important than the development of a public which has some judgment about both the powers and limits of science.

VI

THE REORGANIZATION OF
WORK AND PLAY

Technology is more than machinery. It is the institutionalization of invention, the adoption of innovation as a way of life. It commits men to a continuing revolution in their relation to their physical environment, and eats away at a culture, at its surfaces and beneath its surface. It means a change in the pace of change itself, in men's relations to one another, in their social systems and forms of government, and in their established convictions about right and wrong and what is most worth seeking in life. The technological innovations that have been taking place at a steadily mounting pace for two hundred years are as responsible as any other single factor for our moral uncertainties and for our political migrations from one god that fails to another.

Machine industry and industrialized agriculture have been introduced in almost no country in the world, in fact, without Draconic measures and cruel repression. It was not the industrialization of contemporary Russia or China but the industrialization of Victorian England that led John Stuart Mill to say that the Industrial Revolution had probably brought more unhappiness than happiness to mankind. And even in our successfully industrialized and rich society the struggles against the machine that were fought a hundred and fifty years ago strike a responsive chord in many of us. In January, 1813, a group of English workers were brought to trial, accused of having committed a capital

crime—destroying the machines that had thrown them out of
work. The prosecuting attorney observed: "It is well known that
. . . there have been various implements of machinery introduced, and wisely introduced, for the purpose of expediting our
manufactures and bringing them into better use. The advantages
to the laborers themselves, if they would have given themselves
the patience to understand the thing, would have convinced them
of the great utility of such machinery; but unfortunately they
took a different course. . . ." "The thing" has now demonstrated
its great utility, but the fear is as strong as ever that we are its
slaves.

For in addition to everything else that technology does to un-
settle us, it contains a paradox, and this paradox is the source of
a special kind of uneasiness that technology provokes in societies
where democratic ideals are established. On the one hand, technology pushes back scarcity. It has provided the economic base
for large-scale democracy. But on the other hand, technology
seems to be the inherent enemy of the autonomous individual.
Together with the advent of the Welfare State, a subject to which
we shall turn in the next chapter, the imperial position we have
given to technology in the organization of our affairs is the principal reason for our present concern about the prospects of the
fundamental democratic ideal of personal liberty and autonomy.
No intellectual and moral dilemma is more insistent in the history
of modern democracy, in fact, than that which has been produced
by democracy's dual commitment to the ideal of personal autonomy on one side and to industrial organization on the other.

For technology and industrial organization consist in part in
fitting the individual to pre-existing standards. They create an
environment for work and for the normal routines of daily life
as inflexible in its own way as the ancient environment of nature
was for the farmer. Despite our astonishment and pleasure in our
technical proficiency, technology is therefore a phenomenon to
which we respond with ambiguous feelings. It is an embracing
department of our lives about whose relation to liberal ideals we
are still uncertain and for which we have still not found a sure
place in our scheme of the virtues. We hold an image of technological society as the affluent society, giving the great mass of

its members a share in the goods of life. We also hold an image of technological society as an air-conditioned nightmare, as a society of men tied down and denatured by a system—by timetables, assembly lines, bureaucratic rules, and the incessant demands of machines. These conflicting images lie in the background of the doubts we now entertain about the soundness of our purposes or the authenticity of the ideals we proclaim. Indeed, America evokes both these images in the imaginations of people elsewhere, and this is a principal reason why the reactions to the United States in the rest of the world are so complicated and equivocal.

The relation of technology and of the basic forms of work and play which it has thrust upon us to the ideal of personal autonomy presents democratic society with a fundamental problem. Can we stand back and look at the issue? What is the place of technology, not in creating material plenty, but in the education of men in autonomy?

THE DISCIPLINE OF THE MACHINE

Begin with the most elementary issue of all—the relation of men to the instruments they use in their work. There is a difference in our relation to a tool and to a machine. A tool—a hammer, an abacus, a flute—is fitted to the shape of our body or brain. We use it at our own pace and the work we do with it carries our stamp. A machine, in contrast, is not shaped to the human body or constructed to the biological human scale. The difference is a matter of degree, and there are exceptions to the rule. But the difference is striking nonetheless. A bicycle must fit the length of our legs; we bend or squeeze our legs into an automobile. In speaking about our relation to a tool, we say that we use it; in speaking about our relation to a machine, we are as likely to say that we tend it or drive it. In working with a machine, it is not we who seem to be using the machine, it is the machine that seems to be using us. The best thing about a machine is also in a way the worst: it does our work for us.

And the work we do with machines is also different. It is different because it changes our relationship to others who are working.

Specialization and the division of labor are as old as agriculture. They are older, going back to the differences between old and young and men and women. But the kind of specialization that makes an industrial system turn has certain distinguishing marks. Once more we are dealing with matters of degree, but they are matters of degree which have repeatedly led observers of the modern scene to say that the basic ideals of liberal society are incompatible with technological organization.

The word "mystery" originally referred to membership in a closed craft guild and to the secret understandings of that guild. But there is a sense in which a technological society seems to multiply mysteries. The British census of 1841 listed 431 occupations. A century later, the Occupational Dictionary compiled by the United States Census Bureau listed 25,000 occupations. The difference does not lie entirely in the heightened propensity of twentieth-century census-takers for nit-picking; and if it does, that also proves the point. Technology produces more specialization, and more refined specialization. Further, it builds opaque walls between specialties, walls of words and walls of different experience. Division of labor and specialization of function existed in the building of cathedrals or in the making of shoes in the traditional cobbler's shop. But the man putting one stone on top of another or trimming heels was nevertheless able to understand what others were doing. That kind of community of language and imagination is undermined by technological specialization. One of the more common experiences of the inhabitant of an industrial society is the sense of helplessness that overcomes him when he is asked by an outsider to explain exactly what it is that he does for a living and precisely why it is important.

But perhaps the most notable feature of technological specialization is that it defines specialized skills in terms of a process or a particular kind of activity rather than in terms of the product created. A man with managerial experience in a textile mill can shift without too much strain to a cannery. A welder does much the same work whether he is working on a ship, an airplane, or a building. A good salesman, as the saying goes, can sell anything. Even teachers, carried along by the momentum of a technological culture, may spend as much time learning how to teach as mastering something substantial to teach. All this suggests an essential characteristic of the organization of work under technology. The worker is a link in the chain; and at the end of the chain, far away from him, the final product emerges. If he does his work badly enough, the result will show up; if he does it well, his contribution fuses and fades with the contribution of everyone else.

The remoteness of the worker from his product, his alienation from the fruits of his labor, is one main theme of Marx. But it has little to do with capitalism or socialism. It has to do with the impact that machine production has had, perhaps unavoidably, perhaps not, on the organization of human work in all social systems. In an industrial society the satisfactions of work seem to be progressively removed from the process of work itself. They reside in the good pay check at the end of the week, in the pleasure of other people's company, perhaps (as we keep telling ourselves) in the secret, inner satisfaction of a job well done. But the circumstances of most men's jobs militate against their working for the purpose intrinsic to work—to produce a piece of work. They must work for what they can get out of it. It is in this context, and not in the context of an alleged decline in moral values, that our repeated complaints that pride in workmanship is dying have to be understood. The conditions that produced the craftsman's special pleasures and ethos have largely disappeared.

Yet this is only one side of the story, and the less important side. Despite the smoke, noise, and ugliness that technology creates, it has not, on balance, added to the tedium of labor or to its sweat and danger. The reverse is true. The skilled craftsmen whom we nostalgically idealize never did the main work of the world. The rake, the hoe, the shovel, the prod, and the whip are not the tools of skilled artisanship. No work has been more tied down to inflexible circumstance and the dull round of routine than the work of the peasant and the shepherd, not to mention the slave. And before the machine came on the scene, such work was usually a life sentence.

We cannot properly estimate the impact of technology on individual autonomy unless we see that it has expanded the range

of choices open to ordinary human beings. Technology has given
an immense impetus to personal mobility, and not only to mobility up (and down) the social ladder but to mobility between
occupations. Whatever its evils, it has given masses of men and
women an opportunity hitherto known only to the members of
privileged classes—the chance to shift and move around, and to
look for better, and, if they wish, more interesting, work.

There is a reason for this, built into the very character of technology itself. Compared with nontechnical skills, a technological
skill tends to have an abstract character. It is normally based on
a principle that can be codified and that can be communicated by
words. Although a technological process may be a mystery to
those who have no experience with it, it is an open mystery. For
the essence of technology lies in its explicitness. Its secrets are
in books and not in the muscles of skilled workmen or the private
understandings of a traditional art or craft. Technology makes
access to work more open, breaks down the protective ramparts
that established occupations build for themselves, and puts the
keeper of professional secrets on the defensive.

Nor does this mean that technology involves the replacement
of skilled work by unskilled work. The difference is more subtle.
In Veblen's words, "In the new era the stress falls rather more
decidedly on general intelligence and information, as contrasted
with detailed mastery of the minutiae of a trade; so that famili-
arity with the commonplace technological knowledge of the time
is rather more imperative a requirement under the machine technology than under that of handicraft." In this sense surely, and
probably in other senses, too, there was incomparably more unskilled work in the pretechnological era than in the industrial
age, as the demise of the institution of slavery under the impact
of industrialism reveals. Far from lowering the need for skilled
work, the general tendency of industrial development is steadily
to increase the proportion of skilled jobs and the amount of special training and education necessary to perform them. And what
is significant about a machine economy is not only that it requires
more people to have training and knowledge, but that the skills
and information they need are more easily teachable and trans-
ferable.

The import of these facts is psychological and moral, not only economic. They mean that despite conventional—and learned—beliefs to the contrary, the era of the assembly line has meant more rather than less variety in the working lives of ordinary men. Andrew Ure was a Scottish manufacturer in the early nineteenth century who had a great many reasons to take delight in the new machinery. It was profitable; a child could produce as much as three or four men had produced before; and besides, the children sang while they were at work. But Ure also saw that the technological division of labor had a different quality from the kind of division of labor that had existed previously. "On the system of decomposing a process into its constituents, and embodying each part in an automatic machine," he observed, "a person of common care and capacity may be intrusted with any of the said elementary parts after a short probation, and may be transferred from one to another, at the discretion of the master. Such translations are utterly at variance with the old practice of the division of labor, which fixed one man to shaping the head of a pin, and another to sharpening its point, with most irksome and spirit-wasting uniformity, for a whole life."

Machinery and the technological organization of work, in a word, have educational implications. Technology, by making it easier for men to move from job to job, has made men more restless, more aware of monotony and more resistant to it. That is the context in which the quest for autonomy, and for interesting work, has become a vital issue. If the discipline of the machine has deprived many men of a sense of personal involvement in their work, it has also trained many men to stand back from their work and to think of changing it. Some of the pain in machinery simply lies in the fact that it has made the work we do more obviously a matter of choice.

THE BUREAUCRATIC DISCIPLINE

But the mixed effects of technology multiply. For we miss the point of industrialism, and particularly of the industrialism of the twentieth century, if we think of it only as a relationship of men to machines. It is a special sort of relation between men and social organizations, and the social organizations themselves are industrial techniques.

Henry Ford's influence on the modern scene, his influence on Russia or India, is as great as Lenin's or Gandhi's. He was neither a political seer nor the inventor of new machines. What he invented was a way of associating men together—the assembly line. Mass production, the great achievement of modern technology, in as much a triumph of social organization and bureaucratic machinery as of physical machinery. And it is an enterprise in the re-education of human beings. Like M. Jourdain, who spoke prose all his life without knowing it, Frederick Taylor, the apostle of scientific management, spoke morals all his life without knowing it. Technology does more than change the physical character of work. It changes the character of work as an organized social process and alters the relation of the individual to the economy and to other men.

Specifically, technology dispossesses the individual from control over the use of his skills. For the man who possesses a skill is ordinarily unable to use it unless he can find a place within an organization. And this is true not only of those who work with machines but of most others who contribute to industrial production. The ideal of autonomy as splendid isolation, as self-sufficiency—the ideal that still speaks in our suspicions of "the organization" and in the suggestion that integrity can be maintained only by resisting and rejecting the organization—that ideal has been subverted not because we have lost the faith of our fathers but because industrialism has largely destroyed the condition to which that faith was applicable.

For the functioning instrument of production is the organization—the factory, office, or laboratory, and all the ancillary organizations like labor unions, commuters' railroads, and public utilities. It is not the individual standing alone. Ownership of land or property, hereditary position, even the possession of a useful skill, does not guarantee the average member of an industrial order his livelihood, status, and sense of usefulness. Neither do they give him his primary point of access to the social order. All these usually depend on his job in an organization. The professional man, the independent doctor, writer, or scientist, is to some extent an exception. He can sell his services directly to those who want them. But even professional men are increasingly subject to the technological imperative. They need access to heavy equipment, to offices, laboratories, libraries, to guaranteed students and readers; and to acquire this access they play a position on a team and fill a role in an organized pattern of work.

In short, work has been bureaucratized. It is his office, his position in an organization, that makes a man's work possible. Between the individual with a skill and the useful deployment of this skill there lies an elaborate social assembly line. His work has to be integrated with the work of others; impersonal rules have to be met to ensure standardized performance; communication between the different individuals working to create a product has to be carefully organized and controlled; administration and management—the art, as Paul Appleby has said, of making a mesh of things—become separate and discriminable functions; a clear hierarchy of authority has to exist.

Even the housewife and the home, in a highly industrialized society, become dependent upon a bureaucratic ordering of things. The automobile, the dishwasher, the lawn mower, and the supermarket are the instruments of work, and, to keep them working, parts have to be rationally distributed, servicemen must be available, and an intricate network of deliveries and communications maintained. Autonomy in the sense of total independence from a social milieu has of course never been possible: even Robinson Crusoe had to bring some tools and acquired knowledge with him. But an industrial order immensely expands the social milieu on which the individual depends. It was Emile Durkheim who stated most succinctly the principle that governs technological society. It is that as the individual becomes more specialized, more clearly individuated in his work, he also becomes just that much more dependent on the social arrangements which determine the demand for his work. And so a slight tremor in the stock market or a minor change in a technique of production can reverberate outwards and cause permanent changes in uncounted lives.

This is the basic context in which our preoccupation with "security" has arisen. Every gathering devoted to considering our

favorite subject, the moral fiber of the nation, asks why there is
so much concern about security. To ask this question is like asking why fishermen think about oilskins or miners about soap. The
shock of the Long Depression has worn off nowhere in the Western world. And it remains, despite our prosperity and affluence,
because prosperity and affluence cannot change the basic circumstance that in a technological society a man's income, status, self-
respect, and chance to use his skills depend on the vicissitudes of
an intricately coordinated social order outside his direct control.

Pre-industrial man could be hit by flood, drought, disease, brig-
andage, and war. Industrial man is less at the mercy of natural
disasters, and despite the overhanging threat of an apocalyptic
war, he is less subject in his everyday life to violence, legal or
illegal. But he is intimately bound to a man-made wheel of fortune, which complicates his misfortunes. His security and insecurity do not have simply economic consequences, but social and
psychological ones. For industrial dislocations have an impact
which a natural cataclysm does not. They create men who appear
to have been told by their society that they are superfluous. As
much as the memory of physical suffering, this is the scar that
is still with us from the Depression, and that aches again with
every report of technological unemployment and of men who find
themselves declared obsolete.

Once more, the Marxian theme of "alienation" is important.
Marx spoke not only of the separation of the worker from his
product, but of his loss of control over the conditions and necessary instruments of his work. The nature of a property system
may affect the degree to which one or another individual suffers
from this situation. But the situation itself is inherent in both
capitalism and socialism. For it is a consequence of the commitment to technology and of the bureaucratic organization of society which that commitment entails. A division between the
ownership and control not only of property but of personal skills
and talents is a consequence of industrialism. The individual may
own his skills and talents; but the enterprise, the union, the price
system and the testing system largely control the use of them.

Yet once again, the picture has to be seen in perspective. The
progressive bureaucratization of human affairs is a characteristic

of all societies that have or want an advanced technology, and no tendency has been more generally blamed for what is wrong with the modern world. The large organization, with its assignment of narrow, specialized tasks and its assembly-line mode of production, has regularly been presented as the paradigm of our condition as we drift irresistibly towards the faceless man and totalitarian tyranny. "The clerks of departments," Balzac wrote, "find themselves sooner or later in the condition of a wheel screwed on to a machine; the only variation in their lot is to be more or less oiled." But it is important to see what bureaucracy has replaced as a major instrument for the government of human beings.

In the main, it has replaced the family and the local community. These are shelters for the individual that are closer and warmer—but they are often just a bit too close and too warm. Far from promoting personal freedom, they have often imposed a stifling authority. A technological society multiplies impersonal bureaucracies, makes men dependent on large organizations, and submits their fate to the arbitrament of external, but man-made, circumstances. But all these conditions are ambiguous in their import. Impersonality in the administration of human affairs means more coldness, but also more equity; the hugeness of organizations means more anonymity for the individual, but also more privacy; and the scope of the individual's involvement in the world means that his mind moves on a larger scale.

Routine work and specialization of function, furthermore, are not creations of bureaucracy. From a historical point of view the major alternative to a bureaucratized system of production has been the division of society into closed classes, each bound to the performance of fixed economic and social roles. And apart from the fact that bureaucratic organization, as much as machinery, is largely responsible for the conditions of economic plenty that seem to be essential for stable democratic institutions on the large scale, the introduction of sharply defined responsibilities, impersonal standards, merit systems, and definite tests of capacity and performance has accelerated the decline of class and family prerogatives and opened up new chances for individuals to compete on their own merits.

Our chronic worries about both the "specialization" and the "impersonality" of bureaucratic arrangements deserve, in short, a second look. The thought that industrial society breeds the alienated man, cut into fragments of himself and deprived of his individual identity because he is dispersed into a series of separate and specialized roles, lies behind the judgment that bureaucratic organization inevitably turns men into robots. But the idea rests on a confusion between the formal standards by which the individual's job is defined and the actual activities in which he engages when he is on the job.

A man is not necessarily cut into a piece of himself because he has been assigned a narrow mission. For better, and not infrequently for worse, he may bring his total personality to that mission. Nor are bureaucracies invariably destructive of the warmth, spontaneity, and "total" human relationships that are commonly thought to mark natural communities of men. Anyone who has ever been involved in an office feud knows better. The main difference between an office feud and a family quarrel is not that one is impersonal and the other personal. It is that it is easier to cut loose from the office feud. The individual, thanks to the separation and dispersal of his roles and to his limited and partial commitment to his office, has greater personal autonomy.

A bureaucratic organization, of course, is not usually established to promote personal relations among its members. (Important exceptions exist even to this generalization. There are organizations, for example, whose overt purpose is to accomplish some external program, but whose latent purpose is simply to bring like-minded people together to draw on one another's warmth. Fringe political groups serve this function.) But whether personal relations are the object of a bureaucracy or not, the description of a bureaucratic organization simply in terms of its formal structure and stated purposes is radically misleading.

A factory or an office is a place where people make friends, where men and women flirt, where cliques are formed, and where the ambitious hustle for position and power. Inside any large formal organization, indeed, there are unofficial associations and shadow systems of authority which those with official authority disregard at their peril. Men get out of line, and when they get out of line, they form new lines and move along them. Not even a prison can be governed except through the systems of authority that exist among the inmates, which are as strong in their own area, if also as officially unrecognized, as the government of Communist China. Studies of organizations in every field show that the effective management of a bureaucracy depends on using these informal organizations and lines of communication within it. There is no surer sign of naïveté in administration than to take an official table of organization at face value. The theory which stresses the formality and artificiality of bureaucratic relations is excessively formal and artificial.

Moreover, complaints about the "impersonality" of bureaucracy mix an ambiguous use of language with an uncertain moral perspective. In one sense bureaucracy is a comparatively impersonal method for governing human work and conduct. Its signs are formal examinations, seniority rights, grievance procedures, established rates of pay for measured amounts of work, I.B.M. machines, the transmission of communications through channels, and rules, rules, rules. And all this, it may seem, produces a world in which the individual has no unique identity but only a place in a filing system, only an identity card. Yet before we give ourselves unthinkingly to the cause of more personal forms of social organization, we should recall that the Nazi bureaucracy, to take only one example, was not impersonal. At its higher echelons it was saturated with the cult of personality. Impersonality is not an invariant trait of all bureaucrats; and more to the point, we often complain when it is not.

When orderly and democratic conditions prevail, bureaucracy does more than give power to officials. It tells those who have to deal with them what the limits of that power are, and defines the rights of individuals within the system. Favoritism and nepotism, no doubt, have their pleasures; and when a man has a reason to complain, there is something to be said for personal government, for having a definite man to complain to or about. But "impersonality," nevertheless, is not an unmixed evil. Impersonal government, government that meets the test of impersonal rules, has in fact been one of the ideals at which liberal societies have aimed. Bureaucracy may subject us to standards not our own, but it also provides a framework for daily life that accustoms men to the idea of rational human arrangements—arrangements that have clearly stated rules that are equally applicable to all. That in itself is a considerable contribution to the education of the race.

THE MORAL SIGNIFICANCE OF TECHNOLOGY
AND BUREAUCRACY

To speak of education is to come to the heart of the matter. In the end the pains of the technological and bureaucratic disciplines are the pains of a process of education. For they unseat attitudes as old as the race; they give a new form and style to social authority, and make it more clearly visible.

The disciplines imposed by the factory system of the late eighteenth and early nineteenth centuries were harsh, incredibly so to the contemporary eye. But it is easy to forget that the traditional family also treated children as instruments of production. Early industrialism did not invent child labor, long hours, or onerous and unhealthy work. What made the disciplines of early industrialism seem so harsh—what made William Blake speak of "the Satanic mill"—was the special social situation in which these disciplines were imposed. Work had been stripped of its intimate associations, and social authority of its traditional costumes and cushions. The factory discipline, whether gentle or brutal, had an alien and external character.

J. L. and Barbara Hammond have caught the essence of the story:

> Scarcely any evil associated with the factory system was entirely a new evil in kind. In many domestic industries the hours were long, the pay was poor, children worked from a tender age, there was overcrowding, and both home and workshop were rendered less desirable from the combination of the two under a single roof. . . . But the home worker at the worst . . . was in many respects his own master. He worked long hours but they were his own hours; his wife and children worked, but they worked beside him, and there was no alien power over their lives; his house was stifling, but he could slip into his gardens; he had spells of unemployment, but he could use them sometimes for cultivating his cabbages. The forces that ruled his fate were in a

sense outside his daily life; they did not overshadow and envelop his home, his family, his movements and habits, his hours for work and his hours for food. . . .

To all the evils from which the domestic worker had suffered, the Industrial Revolution added discipline, and the discipline of a power driven by a competition that seemed as inhuman as the machines that thundered in factory and shed. The workman was summoned by the factory bell; his daily life was arranged by factory hours; he worked under an overseer imposing a method and precision for which the overseer had in turn to answer to some higher authority; if he broke one of a long series of minute regulations he was fined, and behind all this scheme of supervision and control there loomed the great impersonal system.

The moral significance of technology and bureaucracy, their impact on human expectations and attitudes, lies in the fact that they replaced the authority of the home, the church, and the village with a kind of social authority that was explicit and visible: not the village elder and the priest, but the policeman and the teacher; not the parent or the master-craftsman, but the foreman and the poor-law administrator. Technology and bureaucracy do not bring discipline into the world. But the discipline they represent is an exposed discipline, an abrasively present one. Together with the built-in social insecurity of technological society, it is this that explains the resentments and the sense of dislocation which industrialism has brought and still brings with it.

Technology and bureaucracy, in short, are at once consequences and accelerating factors in the longer process which we have already mentioned—the disintegration of traditional forms of social organization and their replacement by formal organizations. A traditional society is a society of small societies. In such a society men do not have careers; they have duties and a destiny. If you know a man's name and the box into which he was born, you can predict the shape of his life. The emergence of the novel as an art form is one of the signs of the decline of this kind of society. The novel, unlike the classic epic, does not portray the actions of men in their recognized positions in life, living out the fate assigned to them. From *Don Quixote* to *Great Expectations,* and from *The Red and the Black* to *The Great Gatsby,* one of its central themes is the theme of the uncertainly placed man, the man who tries to design his own destiny for himself, and sets out from his home to make his name, indeed to make up his name, for himself. And technology on a large scale is another sign of the decline of traditional society and a beneficiary of men's education in formal organization. For a large, deliberate investment in technology requires a society in which the sense is present that the human environment consists of movable parts, that it is there to be rearranged.

If traditional society was breaking up in Europe long before the Industrial Revolution, technology and bureaucracy scattered the pieces. The formal organization—the human association that is deliberately created, that operates through consciously adopted techniques, and that holds men together for clearly stated purposes—is as old as armies, trade, or imperial states and churches. But the triumph of the formal organization is sealed by technology. For technology requires communication and cooperation over great distances, standardized performance, precise and dependable agreements. And after moving men to cities, it brings them together in large units—men who would otherwise be strangers, who cannot depend on old friendships and mutual understandings, and who need to live by explicit rules and uniform procedures if they are to work together without too many mutual frustrations. It is in the dominance of the formal organization and in its progressively greater bureaucratization—the replacement of the family enterprise by the public corporation, of the ward boss and his cronies by a civil service, of the individual philanthropist or patron by the philanthropic foundation—that the long-range social meaning of modern technology can be found. On top of tradition, habit, and manners such a society imposes the discipline of strangers and written regulations, a discipline uncomplicated and unsoftened by personal feelings, cut loose from associations with home and childhood, and serving remote necessities which men may understand but which it is hard for them to take to their heart.

The difficulties which the Communists have experienced with the collectivization of agriculture wherever they have tried it indicates how difficult the transition to such a society is. And although most citizens of our industrialized democracy are habituated to the technological routine, although the horrors of early industrialism have been largely eliminated and those who live with machines have a greater say about the conditions under which they do so, the evidence is imposing that the shock of this transition has not worn off even in countries that have known technology and bureaucracy for a long time. The hankering after more "organic" forms of society; the elevation of Tradition into a thing in itself without specifying which tradition; the sleight-of-hand tricks with the word "freedom," which have made it mean the surrender of the self to the saving Church or Party or Nation; the demands that organizations show us love as well as fairness; the renascent power and popularity of the view that we have given our souls away, that technology and its creators, reason and science, have robbed our civilization of its charm, spontaneity, and compassion: all these testify to the fact that we are still at war with ourselves over the transformations that technology brings and that we are still trying to find the right responses to them.

Yet these are not simply the reactions of primordial human nature against technology and bureaucracy. They are the reactions of men whose attitudes and expectations are the products of a technological scene. A technologically and bureaucratically organized society threatens autonomy. It makes self-sufficiency a more impossible ideal than ever, and wraps the ordinary individual in a network of external organizations and regulations. But it is this kind of society that has also promoted variety of experience and acquainted more people with the freedom and irritations of choice. It is the matrix of the new moral expectations that have made autonomy for the many an issue.

For one reason why men in an industrial society are preternaturally aware of the burdens imposed by external forces is that they live with choice as a steady problem. They must consciously elect a vocation; they must choose the requisite education and pay heavily for their choice or mischoice in years of their lives; they must choose where to live, what organizations to join, what contracts to sign, what authorities to listen to, not infrequently what religion to profess. Under such circumstances, the fact of organization and social discipline, and the fact that it is external to the individual, is bound to be on their minds. When fundamental activities of human life such as work, the care of a neighborhood, the settlement of disputes, and even the play of children are all formally organized, and when the ways of organizing these activities change rapidly, a quasi-instinctive posture of the human mind is altered. Men come to think of social authority not as part of the natural or supernatural environment, but as a load that has been put on their backs. They are bound to be more conscious of its weight.

The pain is evident, but its uses are commonly overlooked. Technology and bureaucracy, with the new visible disciplines they bring, are agencies in the progress of the human mind. For a special kind of social experience is necessary before any considerable number of the members of a society develop the habit of making a distinction between nature and convention, between facts of life that leave them no choice and arrangements that can be altered. Yet this distinction is essential to a reflective morality. Without it, the idea of individual autonomy cannot even be formulated. Technology and industrial organization produce the social experience that pushes this distinction to the attention of more and more individuals. This is their contribution to the liberal education of ordinary men, and it defines their most fundamental contribution to the progress of liberal civilization.

ILLIBERAL TECHNOLOGY

But if an industrial order encourages men to place a special value on autonomy and to complain when they do not achieve it, this does not change the fact that, in the existing industrial order, they have something to complain about. To great numbers of men and women going about their daily business, the disciplines of technology and bureaucracy are not felt simply as external disciplines. They are felt as external impositions. And though a great many others accommodate themselves to these disciplines, and accommodate themselves so well that they are lulled and narcotized by their daily routines, their relation to their work is passive, their activities are prefabricated for them, and the rewards of work are mainly external to the process of work itself.

Privacy is one of the great goods which industrialism and urbanism have made more possible; but privacy ought to be possible without the feeling that nothing that one ever does will be noticed. Fair and equal treatment is one of the consequences of the bureaucratization of human affairs under democratic conditions; but fair and equal treatment ought to be possible without giving the individual the feeling that he is just another cipher, or that he is simply an object for treatment. Fears for the fate of the individual in our gigantic industrial order are not merely the fantasies of chronically malcontented intellectuals. They are justified fears. And they are justified because technological civilization has not yet managed to generate its own animating and guiding ideas of the kind of individual autonomy that it might offer.

From the impact of the automobile on traditional sexual codes to the clash between the scientific outlook and supernatural beliefs, technological civilization has upset our inherited conceptions. But the new moralities and philosophies that are appropriate to a technological era and that might help us to discern the humane possibilities within it have either not emerged or have not been widely accepted. What have gained acceptance instead are philosophies that express the impulse to resist or to soften the choices that have to be made, or else philosophies that tie the awful power of technology to nationalistic passions, class hatreds, and the paying off of old scores.

Meanwhile, our technology remains uninformed by any examined conception of the possibilities it offers, not for the production of material goods, but for the education and liberation of our minds and sensibilities. Still unarticulated are ethical codes that might be adequate substitutes for the ethic of craftsmanship; ideas of personal responsibility that make sense in an age of large organizations; conceptions of the uses of industrial plenty that seek something besides more than plenty; and aesthetic standards that might permit us to control the deadly process of technological uglification.

Not least, no long-range strategies exist for enlarging the amount of personal autonomy enjoyed by ordinary men in their jobs. The construction of a new ethic is a rather largish order. It is also

an elaborate evasion so long as it remains on the metaphysical
heights and ignores the conditions affecting the day-to-day working experience of individuals. A place to begin in thinking about
the civilizing of technology is with a problem to which relatively
little systematic attention has been given—that of increasing the
opportunities for discretion and self-direction that might be enjoyed by ordinary men in their work. The problem has, I think,
three main parts: first, the control of hugeness; second, the reform of the work process; third, the development of a new ideal
of work.

THE CONTROL OF HUGENESS

The massive scale of contemporary organizations is one of the
simplest and soundest reasons for worrying about the chances of
the individual. The economies and advantages of size are unmistakable—up to a point. Beyond that point they are questionable.
For while the bureaucratic organization is often defined as a communications network, an ordered system by which information is
passed from one individual to another, it would be equally accurate to describe a bureaucracy as a system for preventing the flow
of information and for passing on misinformation. And this is particularly the case when an organization is very large. Then the
process of communication generates its own inherent kind of
static.

For a great many messages converge on the man at the top.
An essential function of those below him is to condense and select information, and to stop most communications from reaching
him. Moreover, the larger the organization, the farther information has to travel and the more it is likely to be disfigured and
distorted. Subordinates make mistakes, they like to please their
superiors, and sometimes they need to deceive them. The man at
the top is the heir to all these sins and errors. And the larger his
sphere of authority, the less chance he has, in a quite simple
sense, to know what it is that he is deciding to do, or to control
the specific ways in which his decisions will be executed. Curiously, the greater a man's powers, the higher he is in a giant
organization, the more his decisions come, in one respect, to re-

semble the decisions of the man in the street: his problem reduces to deciding whose advice to take and whom to trust.

There are other considerations that also bear against hugeness. Ambition is not a universal human trait, but some people suffer from it, and the number of sufferers is usually larger in a democratic society. Small organizations are desirable from this point of view. They give a larger number of ambitious people a chance to be at the top or close to the top of an organization. Hugeness, in contrast, has an enervating effect or worse. The ambitious man who sees no room at the top for himself, or who feels that he might as well be invisible for all the difference that his presence makes, is quite often the source of factionalism and disloyalty. He puts himself at the top of shadow organizations, of cliques and coteries, and cuts the great organization down to size. Sometimes this contributes to efficiency, sometimes not; but in any case it puts ambition and individuality on the outside looking in. The danger of hugeness is that it can turn the exercise of initiative into an underground operation.

Yet there are some protections against these dangers if they are deliberately borne in mind. Guaranteeing the rights of individuals against the organization is one protection. Another and even more important protection is the maintenance of the individual's opportunity to choose among organizations. This is a principal reason for preserving a decentralized economic system; it is also the reason why the maintenance of full employment bears not only on the issue of economic security but on the issue of personal freedom. A man has greater freedom to say No to an organization when he can find equivalent employment elsewhere. And, in addition, the structure of many of our organizations can be redesigned. Large organizations are indispensable in managing the instruments and dealing with the problems of modern society. But smaller organizations can also exist in the interstices between the large ones, or they can be established as independent, separately visible organizations doing work for large organizations on a contractual basis.

Within large organizations, furthermore, smaller units can be given greater grants of independence in the performance of the job and in the selection, assignment, and supervision of individual

workers. Once more, the difficulty goes back to the word "centralization." It is an ambiguous term. Centralization is necessary to
secure coordination, the advantages of expertise, and the precise
fixing of responsibility. But the process of centralization can consist in the establishment of general rules within which subordinates exercise discretion, or it can consist in taking decisions out
of the hands of subordinates. Moreover, there are alternative
strategies for keeping matters under centralized control. Direction by central authority can aim at catching the errors of subordinates; it can aim at preventing errors by multiplying rules
and regulations; or it can seek to discover where the subordinates'
own knowledge and resources can be strengthened so that they
can be counted on to avoid major errors on their own. The last
process leads to decentralization, although it requires centralized
direction if it is to be maintained successfully.

The reasons for decentralization do not lie simply in the fact
that it reduces the costs of maintaining elaborate communications
systems and avoids the disadvantages of having overworked people in central positions making decisions that their subordinates,
closer to the scene of action, might make more sensibly. Another
reason lies in the character of human work itself. The individual
worker's relation to his work is not simply a relation to a machine or job. It is a relation to a social group. In the famous
"Hawthorne Study" conducted at the Western Electric Company
in Chicago thirty years ago, two groups of workers were selected
to serve as the subject of an experiment on the effect of lighting
conditions on efficiency. One group was subjected to variations
in lighting conditions, and the other, the control group, was not.
Yet efficiency kept rising in the experimental group whether the
lighting was improved or, as the Irish say, disimproved. And
efficiency also rose steadily in the control group, which experienced no changes in lighting at all. The most notable result of
this experiment was the "discovery" that people are likely to work
better when they feel that attention is being paid to them and
that they are the members of an identified group that has been
given a significant task to perform. Indeed, a man's mere knowledge that he is engaging in an experiment seems to have a certain
inspiriting effect.

The individual's autonomy in an industrial order is not, therefore, just a matter of struggling against the inhuman demands of a machine. It is also—and mainly—a matter of attaining a measure of autonomy in the relation to other human beings. A man is a member of a community when he is on the job: the community consists of all those whose work or whose decisions (or whose malingering and indecisions) affect the work he does, and the pains, satisfactions, rebuffs, and rewards he gets out of his work. In a modern industrial society this community is large and indistinct, fading off beyond the individual's horizons. What counts is the degree of definiteness it can be given for the individual. His relation to the key figures whose actions most heavily and directly affect his own is the key to his relation to his work. If these individuals are remote from him, if he is unknown to them, he has the status of a replaceable part in the system. But if the individuals who make the major decisions about his status and job are close to him, if he is seen by them and sees them, if he can reach them and try to influence them directly, he has an identity on the job and has taken the first step towards some personal autonomy.

THE REFORM OF THE WORK PROCESS

These considerations take us to a second issue affecting the autonomy of the individual in a technological and bureaucratic era. This is the reform of the process of work itself. The issue is anything but academic. The struggle over work rules has moved to the center of industrial conflicts. And the repeated controversies it provokes offer the simplest evidence that higher pay, scientific management, and "human relations" techniques are not enough, and that the question of providing the worker with a larger measure of autonomy while he is at work is a realistic economic and political issue. It is a source of some of the major chronic frictions of industrial society.

The controls that the men who work exercise over the character of work are already much greater than we normally recognize. To those who still harbor the unvarnished image of the individual worker squeezed by the inexorable machine, it is salutary to recall that there are standard names like "rate-buster" for those who break the unwritten laws of work. The men on the job create rules for themselves, rules that have coercive force, and the existence of these rules is a major element in understanding the actual nature of industrial work. They break into the individual worker's freedom of action; but they reflect the autonomy which the group has managed to retain or steal from the official authority of the organization. It is in this context, for example, that the recurrent issue of featherbedding arises.

The insistence by workers' organizations on maintaining established jobs, rules, and privileges is one of the major impediments, as is well known, to the introduction of technological innovations which are otherwise desirable. Yet featherbedding is a more complicated issue than is generally suggested. To the man who pays the bill, and usually to the outsider, featherbedding seems, quite simply, an arrangement to pay people for not working or for doing unnecessary work. To the worker himself, however, it represents an effort to preserve his investment in a job and the equity he has established in the way in which it is performed. And costly though featherbedding is, the alternatives may be more costly. In a society in which workers have democratic expectations, a refusal to recognize that the worker accumulates an equity in his job and a legitimate interest in the work rules appropriate to it is not likely to produce good performance from him.

The struggle over featherbedding is a symptom of a larger problem—the disorganization of work routines caused by technological change and the threat to the security and autonomy of the worker implicit in such changes. Featherbedding is like a hand-made dam built to contain a flooding stream. It comes into being at least in part because more fundamental and permanent arrangements are missing. "Just as men for centuries neglected the problems of soil erosion," Robert Merton has observed, "in part because they were unaware that erosion constituted a significant problem, so they are still neglecting the social erosion ascribable to present methods of introducing rapid technological changes."

The neglect of this overhanging issue is probably as responsible as anything else for the popular feeling that technology is a threat and that technological changes are introduced by men who are aware of its benefits but not its price in men's working lives—in short, that those who control "the thing" have not given themselves the patience to understand it either. This is the atmosphere in which resistance to technological change and tensions over work rules lead to major battles. A coordinated investigation of a major social problem is necessary. What are the consequences of technological changes for the nature and social conditions of work? What are the ways of distributing the risks and costs of such changes so that they do not fall inequitably on one stratum of the population? Inquiry into these questions has been scattered and unorganized, and what inquiry there has been has usually taken place under conditions that cast doubt on its objectivity. Such inquiry should be jointly sponsored by labor and management. It would offer an instance of a cooperative approach to the problems of technological change that would in itself help to clear the air.

But what is required besides empirical inquiry is a re-examination of only half-conscious notions about work and its significance that now dominate the industrial process. Frederick Taylor, the founding father of scientific management, once wrote: "One of the very first requirements for a man who is fit to handle pig iron as a regular occupation is that he shall be so stupid and so phlegmatic that he more nearly resembles an ox than any other type." The assumptions about the way to organize industrial work that lie behind this remark are still with us. To prepare an efficient program for a process of technological production, it is undoubtedly necessary to break the process down on paper into the simple, separate operations that compose it. But it does not follow, as is so often assumed, that each individual worker must then be assigned one and only one of these simple operations.

To organize work on the basis of this unexamined inference is questionable on grounds of simple efficiency. For the narrower the job of the individual worker, the more elaborate the system must be for coordinating his contribution with that of others. As Herbert Simon has pointed out, the devices we now possess for coordinating the work of large numbers of individuals are ingenious and powerful, but their effectiveness is in no way comparable to the coordinating power of the individual human nervous system. The most subtly organized and delicately responsive "instrument" in the productive process is still the human animal. And a centralized plan for the division of labor, which is based on the analysis of a mechanical process into its minute segments and which asks the individual to cut himself down to the size of one of these segments, leaves the individual's capacities to coordinate and judge idle and unused.

More, indeed, than the "coordinative capacity" of human beings is involved. What is also involved is their psychological relationship towards their work, the meaning they can ascribe to it in their scheme of values. "Taylorism" belongs to an attitude towards work inappropriate to an age of abundance and of machines that can free men not only from back-breaking labor but from an increasing number of purely routine tasks. It connects work with grim necessity and unavoidable pain—with man's punishment for the sin of Adam. To the extent that it finds any virtues in work itself, they are simply the virtues of endurance and fidelity. In this respect Taylorism is of a piece with many popular efforts to improve the conditions of industrial work. By and large, social reformers have focused on wages, hours, the strengthening of labor organizations, and the repair of the economic and legal context for work. And contemporary "human relations" techniques have concentrated on the external issues that affect the individual's relation to his job, treating a worker's discontents with his job as due, in the main, to discontents displaced from his personal life. One cannot resist the suspicion that, like coffee breaks, piped music, and company picnics, these techniques are attempts to make work agreeable by inviting the worker to think about something else. Like Taylorism, they accept a traditional philosophy of work which conceives it as a brute necessity, a path to money or prestige, a purgative for the soul, perhaps a divine assignment—as anything but a process, in short, whose rewards lie in the process itself and in its immediate product.

To be sure, the labor of thousands in mass-production plants cannot be effectively coordinated without hierarchical organization and centralized direction. And it is doubtful that work can ever be an unbroken pleasure for anybody, much less for everybody. It is understandable that the conception of work as a means rather than an end has prevailed. Nevertheless, it is now a growing anachronism. Technology, which has accepted and exploited this conception of work, is on the way to making it outmoded for an increasing number. It is creating a steadily larger number of jobs requiring not only highly developed skills but a highly developed sense of personal responsibility and commitment. If that kind of work is to be done well, its rewards cannot be entirely external to the performance itself.

There is no certainty about what automation will bring. But it surely need not mean the still further development of those tendencies in modern work processes which have made work a standard and routine performance and have made the worker's relation to his work impersonal and external. It can mean not only a significant rise in the ratio of skilled workers to unskilled workers, but also an increase in the opportunities workers have to exercise discretion, to leave their own individual stamp on the work they do, and to feel like distinguishable and significant parts of a common enterprise. Enlarging the scope and extending the cycle of individual jobs; organizing workers in teams in which they regularly exchange assignments within the framework of the total job for which the team is responsible; the redesigning of work routines so that the rhythms of human beings rather than the rhythms of machines are controlling; the systematic effort to give more discretion to the individual: these are not only technical questions or economic questions. Perhaps they will add to efficiencies and evoke more effort from the individual; their more important aspect, however, is that they would symbolize and encourage the development of a new relationship between men and the activity that is at the center of their lives.

Needless to say, there are social and psychological obstacles to the development of such programs. Many workers at least initially resist technological and organizational changes that require more personal discretion and responsibility from them, and apparently prefer work they can do passively, dreamily, and without paying close attention to it. But a certain number of such jobs are going to exist in any case. The problem is to provide, for the increasing number of jobs that will require high skills and care, conditions that will invite the worker to feel an emotional stake in his work. Probably a much larger degree of self-government on the job is one of the prerequisites. In the past a small portion of mankind—artists, scholars, public men, and some professional sinners and saints—have been able to put their hearts into their work for the pleasure of the work itself. In a period in which it is possible to speak of a thirty-hour week or retirement in the fifties, it is also possible—and it is necessary—to think differently about work itself and to seek to introduce arrangements that might bring the work of larger numbers closer to the kind of work that a privileged few have enjoyed in the past.

WORK AND PLAY

To do so, however, requires the development of new conceptions of work and play, and of their place among other activities. Behind the great majority of man's social visions in the past there has been the dream of a Garden of Eden—a world, here or hereafter, free from the necessities of toil, the complications of sex, the difficulties of thought, a world in which men are as tame, placid, and cooperative as domestic animals. For we usually come by our social visions simply by eliminating in imagination the pains that plague us. But if the Garden of Eden has not lost all its appeal, some of its charm has begun to wear off. And technology is the culprit. It has produced problems with which we can deal only by reversing habits of imagination and judgment that have been produced by the main experience of the race.

Some of these problems are becoming increasingly evident. Our economic thinking, as Mr. Galbraith has pointed out, is still bound to goals that make sense only for an age of scarcity. But it is when we turn to our inherited notions of work and play that the need to reformulate our ideas is particularly sharp. We make a sharp disjunction between work and play. It is a disjunction that is rooted in ancient philosophic and religious distinctions between the means of life and its ends, matter and spirit, discipline and freedom from discipline, the realm of ordinary experience and the realm of higher values—distinctions that are themselves, in part, the reflections of men's social experience in aristocratically and clerically governed societies. Nor would it have made sense for men, through the ages, to think anything else but that work is undesirable and leisure desirable. But democracy, technology, the progressive reduction of hours of work, and a consumer-oriented society have made this sharp disjunction misleading.

All work, of course, has its dull and wearying aspects. In any occupation, including the most individualistic, men employ ways of doing things that represent the habits of their trade. Housekeeping details and moments of pure routine dominate the most romantic callings. And no matter how absorbing his work may be, the normal man wants a break, a change, and a chance to do something else or nothing at all. The characteristics of the kind of work that carries its own intrinsic delights, however, are clear.

Ideal work is felt not as an external discipline but as a self-discipline. It is not a response to problems all neatly defined in advance, and it does not consist in the mechanical application of ready-made solutions. Secondly, ideal work gives a man a sense of accumulating knowledge and mastery. It is not simply repetitious. It affords the chance to make discoveries, to develop new skills, to learn freshly what one is capable of doing. Finally, ideal work is meaningful. It is concerned with what men think is important and it allows them to feel engaged and committed, to believe that they are giving to their work what they think important about themselves. That kind of work has become available to an increasing number of professional people and executives, and the fact that they now compose the class with the least amount of leisure is instructive. One need not deny that money has its charms to see that the right kind of work can also be a motivation for work.

Technological progress, indeed, seems to have overturned a classic social pattern. It is the working and middling classes who increasingly compose the new leisure class. And when we turn to the leisure provided and manufactured by contemporary industrial society, we find a problem that is the twin of the problem of work. Work and play have been placed at opposite poles, but the characteristics of industrial work that make it demeaning and meaningless are also the characteristics of industrial leisure which make that leisure demeaning and meaningless. Leisure is also devoted to what is ready-made. It is taken passively. And it is an epiphenomenon—an occasion, in Richard Hoggart's phrase, for "sensation without commitment," a series of experiences without a connection to the past or to the future in the individual's personal development. It is one thing to say that there are limits to what can be done to make work in an industrial society approach the ideal of work that has been described. It is quite another thing to say that leisure under technology is condemned to be only the slack image in reverse of work at its worst.

The question of the uses of leisure is not one which it is easy to discuss. It has become surrounded with tendentious slogans and immoderate polemics about "mass culture"—a term which, despite the growth of leisure, no one has taken the time to define very exactly. Only sentimentality or callousness, I think, can lead observers to overlook what technology, democracy, and affluence have done to enhance the average quality of human experience.

In Ernest Nagel's words:

> It is not possible to deny the charge that, despite improvements in the material conditions of life for an increasing fraction of the populace, much of our energy is directed toward the realization of shoddy ideals, and that relatively few men lead lives of creative self-fulfillment and high satisfaction. . . . Nevertheless, the failings noted are not unique to our own culture. . . . In view of the size and the heterogeneous character of the American population, and of the fact that adequate leisure and training for developing and pursuing rational ideals are a fairly recent acquisition for most of its members, it is perhaps remarkable how rapid has been the growth of sensitivity in our society to the great works of literary, scientific, and artistic imagination. It is simply not the case that the mechanisms of our alleged mass culture are all geared to enforcing meretricious standards of excellence, or that there is today a decreasing number of opportunities for men to cultivate their individual talents.

Sound as this verdict is, however, the largest amounts of money and effort have been spent in trying to keep men alternating between a state of shock and a state of oblivion. It is effrontery to present the slicked-up and cut-down culture being mass produced for our new leisure class in the terms in which those who profit from it usually present it—that is to say, as a great achievement, a demonstration of the promise of democracy. And it is not only the content of this culture that is at fault. It is its character as a passive culture, as a series of events to be consumed and thrown away.

What counts in leisure is what counts in work—the opportunity to think of it as part of a career, as a series of tests to be met and goals to be achieved. There are plenty of commonplace examples of leisure so conceived—whether it is the man working at his chess game or the woman seeing how far she can go in dress designing—and there are also an increasing number of facilities for such leisure. But the extraordinary resources of the mass media of communication have not been used, on the whole, to advance this kind of activity, but rather to distract people away from it. And even the honest efforts that have been made by television and other agencies to improve their offerings have been infected by a conception of leisure time as a procession of discontinuous experiences. A series of programs on public affairs will be a series of engagements with separate ideas. And the approach is similar in town halls and discussion groups. The possibility of moving from the simple to the complex, of introducing a progressive process of work-in-play, is ignored or feared.

Nor is the problem of leisure simply the problem of providing more facilities, or better conceived ones, for the cultivation of personal skills and tastes. The shortening of the work week and the lowering of the retirement age have made forced leisure, unwanted leisure, an increasingly characteristic feature of democratic society. Yet we do not have enough teachers or enough people to do the work of local civic organizations. The organization of communities in such a way as to give occupation and status to qualified people who have the leisure for such work is a new kind of problem. Compared to the problems of overwork or of dependent old people that have existed in the past it is an agreeable problem. But it is also an urgent one.

There are still some unsettled issues of social welfare left over from previous generations. But together with the reform of work, the problem of leisure is in all probability the next great welfare issue with which liberal political and social programs will have to be concerned. It will call for the reform of television and radio, and for reconceived and far more ambitious programs of adult education by colleges, universities, and voluntary organizations. And it will require the reform of anachronistic institutions that now relegate those condemned to leisure to the outskirts of most communities. The problem of compulsory leisure, of leisure without direction or fruits, is not an easy problem to solve. The traditional large family, which was not a consciously contrived piece of social engineering, was the principal agency in the past for giving the old and the young an identifiable and useful place and function in society. There is no immediately obvious substitute for it on our urban and suburban landscape. The same objective can be achieved only by deliberately planned labor policies and educational programs, and by the creation of communities where those who want to work can find work that needs to be done.

A society gives men a strange education in the uses of themselves when its main anodyne for the insignificance of their work is the promise of release to other forms of insignificance. The problem of leisure has become a central and permanent problem of our society. It is in what we can do to make leisure—and work —occasions for self-discovery that the meaning of contemporary democracy for personal autonomy will ultimately be tested and revealed.

VII

THE WELFARE STATE:
POSTSCRIPT AND PRELUDE

A hundred and thirty years ago Tocqueville suggested that the greatest danger to democracy was the possibility that it might produce an immense tutelary power, laboring for the happiness of the people, but acting as the sole agent and arbiter of that happiness.

It provides for their security, foresees and supplies their necessities, facilitates their pleasures, manages their principal concerns, directs their industry, regulates the descent of property, and subdivides their inheritances; what remains, but to spare them all the care of thinking and all the trouble of living? Thus it every day renders the exercise of the free agency of man less useful and less frequent; it circumscribes the will within a narrower range and gradually robs a man of all the uses of himself. The principle of equality has prepared men for these things; it has predisposed men to endure them and often to look on them as benefits. After having thus successively taken each member of the community in its powerful grasp and fashioned him at will, the supreme power then extends its arm over the whole community. It covers the surface of society with a network of small complicated rules, minute and uniform, through which the most original minds and the most energetic characters cannot penetrate, to rise above the crowd. The will of man is not shattered, but softened, bent, and guided. . . . Such a power . . . does not tyrannize, but it compresses, enervates, extinguishes, and stupefies a people, till each nation is reduced to nothing better than a flock of timid and industrious animals, of which the government is the shepherd.

These are the words of one of democracy's coolest and most sympathetic critics. Does it describe the prospect towards which the modern Welfare State is carrying us? Democracy, its partisans have felt, gives individuals a more generous chance to make uncoerced choices, and to make them in terms of standards that fit their own independent ideals of personal fulfillment. But there has always been the fear as well that democracy is inimical to personal autonomy. Its busyness, its warm gregarious interest in the state of each man's soul, its egalitarianism and its alleged tendency to elevate the average into an ideal, have all been said to be at odds with the aristocratic ideal of autonomy. And the advent of the Welfare State has raised all these old questions in a new and aggravated form. No institution has been said to challenge the ideal of autonomy more fundamentally than the Welfare State. None raises more partisan passions. What is the place of the Welfare State in the historical career of liberal democratic ideals? What questions does it raise for the prospects of personal autonomy?

THE WELFARE STATE: POSTSCRIPT TO EMERGENCY

Politics is not the place where words are used exactly. To discuss the Welfare State temperately, it is necessary at the very beginning to see that the phrase "the Welfare State" is an inflated way of describing rather modest facts. The dictionary defines "welfare" as a "state of faring, or doing well; especially, condition of health, happiness, prosperity, etc.; negatively, exemption from evil or calamity." But despite the magnitude of the activities in which the contemporary Welfare State engages, it does not in fact try to guarantee to anyone that he will fare or do well, or that he will be healthy, happy, or prosperous. Still less does it—or could it—exempt any man from evil or calamity. What we know as the Welfare State is simply a State that undertakes to guarantee all its citizens certain minimal decencies of life. Whatever we may think of this objective, to which all modernized States are now formally committed, it is considerably less ambitious than the word "welfare" suggests.

But more important than the question of words is the convention that has been accepted as the premise for most discussions of the Welfare State. This is the convention that the Welfare State is the product of a systematic point of view, a philosophy. This is at best a half truth. In the United States, at any rate, the Welfare State is not a unitary thing, and still less the expression of any general and organized commitment to social planning. It is a postscript to emergency, the heritage that has been left with us by the disasters of depression and war. Most of the programs that are now established were adopted under the spur of necessity, and some at the spur of the moment. A very large proportion of the welfare activities of the modern State are in fact not even the consequences of past depressions. They are tied to past wars and to the need for national defense. Pensions, medical care for veterans, G.I. educational benefits, are obvious examples; but the steeply graduated income tax and federal aid to science, research, and education also belong in this category.

But we must extend our perspective. From a longer point of view, the Welfare State is not simply the product of the immediate emergencies of the last thirty years. It is the product of the chronic emergency that has been with us since the moment, whenever it was, that Western society cast its fate irreversibly with machinery, cities, productivity, and economic growth.

What is the chronic emergency that is faced by an industrial society? On one side, such a society cuts into the lives of individuals, leaving them exposed to technological change, to fluctuations in the market, to mass wars, and to shattering events in remote places. On the other side, industrial society reduces the size and social radius of primary groups like the family, the parish, and the local community, making it more difficult for them adequately to fulfill their traditional functions as forms of social insurance. The family has been progressively reduced to its nucleus—man, wife, and children—and has lost its close associations with an extended clan. The individual's ties to his immediate community have become more impermanent, depending on his job and income rather than on any attachment to birthplace or old friends. Under these circumstances neither the family nor the local community are equipped to provide sufficient assurance of protection against the whims of fortune. Moreover, these are not merely unfortunate results of industrial progress. A vigorous, growing industrial economy requires a mobile population that is ready to move from job to job and place to place. In countries where large sections of the population lack this readiness to pick up and move, the pace of industrial development has invariably been slower.

Within this context the Welfare State serves indispensable functions. It cushions the shocks of industrialism where the old cushions will not work, and it provides services that are necessary if industrial development is to move ahead. A growing and innovating industrial society cannot be composed of individuals so dependent on family and local associations that movement will cut them loose from all their social moorings. Forms of social insurance and guarantees of assistance that are regional and national in scope are required. This is what the Welfare State provides. It is the direct, though unintended, consequence of the assault on traditional forms of human association which was demanded and sanctioned by nineteenth-century liberalism and capitalism.

Indeed, while the Welfare State is obviously guilty of frequent waste and inefficiency, its policies can be construed as responses to the need for economizing public resources. Grant only two assumptions, and most of the major programs of the Welfare State automatically unfold. The first is that the community cannot turn its back on those who are in trouble. This is in accord with elementary principles of Western morality, and is also a matter of simple prudence. The second assumption is that there will be a number of people in trouble who have not had the resources or the will or the foresight to make provision for such contingencies in advance. Given these assumptions, it is clear that, on one side, somebody is going to have to pay, and, on the other side, that it is sober sense to distribute the costs. The principle that individuals should be legally required to insure themselves against becoming public charges follows automatically. In most respects social security legislation can be justified on the same grounds as compulsory automobile insurance against damage to third parties.

In fact, the Welfare State is a profoundly conservative institution. It helps to preserve two habits of mind, and, through them, two institutions that have long been thought to be at the very center of Western civilization. They are institutions that have been peculiarly weakened by the growth of industrialism. The first is the family; the second, property. The Welfare State helps us to maintain a vivid and personal sense of both. In contrast with older forms of social assistance such as poorhouses, the activities of the Welfare State are framed mainly for the family setting and are generally aimed at the maintenance of family units that might otherwise be pressed out of existence. In liberal democratic Welfare States the so-called "social services" are distinctly family services.

The relationship of the Welfare State to the institution of private property is equally significant. The history of industrial development is the history of the depersonalization of the institution of private property. Individual ownership and family capitalism have been replaced by corporate ownership and professional management, and the distinction between ownership and management has become increasingly sharp. The psychological link between the individual and his property, therefore, has been greatly weakened. As Joseph Schumpeter has pointed out, "The capitalist process, by substituting a mere parcel of shares for the walls of and the machines in a factory, takes the life out of the idea of property. . . . And this evaporation of what we may term the material substance of property—its visible and touchable reality—affects not only the attitude of holders but also that of the workmen and of the public in general. Dematerialized, defunctionalized and absentee ownership does not impress and call forth moral allegiance as the vital form of property did."

The Welfare State has not, of course, restored property in its more vital form. But it is incontestable, I think, that the Welfare State has given countless numbers of men and women an experience they would not otherwise have had. This is the experience of knowing that something tangible is theirs, personally and by right—something they can fall back on as individuals in a world in which they are steadily exposed to injury from impersonal sources.

One of the most important arguments that was offered on behalf of private property during the nineteenth century was that it provided the security of resources and the protected area of privacy necessary to the development of individual personality. The argument has much to be said for it: some guarantee of minimal material security, independent of all judgments by political or social authority concerning the individual's worth or deserts, is generally necessary if men are to have the courage or the means to resist the pressures of the group, the government, or the more powerful. But in its nineteenth-century version the argument had a fatal flaw. It was used to justify an economy in which a very large number of people had no property at all, and no guarantee that they would have the minimal material resources necessary to personal autonomy.

The Welfare State has substantially altered that state of affairs. It has given men the sense that they own something, whether it is the equity in a job guaranteed by labor-management agreements or insured protection against absolute penury when they are unemployed. Many may collect such insurance with guilt or hesitation. But whether they do or not, they are enjoying in a small way the same position as that of the man of independent means—a phrase which we choose to use to describe a man who is dependent on an elaborate system of law and public protection so that he can enjoy resources that have been bestowed on him through no doing of his own. The case against welfare benefits is also a case against the inheritance of private property. For in its own way the Welfare State simply represents the extension to our corporate economy of the eighteenth-century principle that all men have a right to property.

THE WELFARE STATE AND DEMOCRATIC EQUALITY

However, there are special imperatives, peculiar to democracy, to which the Welfare State is also plainly a response. "No doubt my distaste for democracy as a political theory," Mencken once wrote, "is, like every other human prejudice, due to an inner lack. . . . In this case it is very probably my incapacity for envy. . . . In the face of another man's good fortune I am as inert as a curb broker before Johann Sebastian Bach." One of the gods in the pantheon of modern liberals, Justice Holmes, held a similar sentiment. "I have no respect for the passion for equality," he wrote, "which seems to me merely idealizing envy."

The Welfare State is of course not simply a response to the imperatives of industrial growth. It is a response shaped and impelled in large part by the democratic ethic of equality. Does it simply rationalize envy and produce what Plato thought to be the essence and absurdity of democracy—a form of government that dispenses a sort of equality to equals and unequals alike?

It is well to look at this question in terms of political realities before examining the moral issue it raises. The Welfare State is undoubtedly a product of democratic pressures. The problem of the distribution of wealth is a central problem in all political systems. Since those who have less inevitably outnumber those who have more, the democratic extension of the suffrage and of political rights to ever larger sections of the community is bound to increase pressures for the redistribution of wealth. In addition, the democratic competition for votes obviously invites office seekers to promise the expansion of existing welfare programs whether or not such an expansion endangers other and more important purposes. This is unquestionably one of the dangers of the democratic Welfare State, and particularly so if the community is accustomed to think of "welfare" in terms of individual packages of benefits rather than in terms of social goods such as parks, livable cities, public support for the arts, or scientific research.

Yet these pressures—to continue to discuss them without praising them—must be seen in perspective. The redistributive Welfare State is not simply a mindless response to democratic pressures; it is a necessary condition of democratic stability, and its importance grows the closer a democratic society approaches its ideal of careers open to the talents. For precisely to the extent that a democracy opens opportunities to all comers and succeeds in making individual character, ability, and performance the key to social position and power, it makes life steadily harder for the underdog. Despite comforting illusions to the contrary, it is gen-

erally easier for men to bear defeat when they think they have
been beaten unfairly. The sense that the world is unjust, like the
belief in heaven, is enormously consoling. It allows men to keep
their self-respect and to live in hope, and is probably a necessary
condition for psychological survival.

In consequence, if a successful democracy is to endure its good
fortune, it must find ways of easing the exacerbated feelings of
those who find themselves at the bottom of the pile. It cannot
allow the differences in the abilities of men to be excessively
accentuated by violent differences in wealth. It must probably
not ask for too steady or ostentatious a show of deference to those
on top. And it must guarantee basic securities to those on the
bottom, so that the lash of envy is not joined to the lash of need.
If we take the bleakest point of view, and conceive the passion
for equality to be only envy under an assumed name, the redistributive Welfare State makes a kind of practical sense that political realists should adore.

And there is, of course, more to the issue. If the sense of injustice is a condition for psychological survival, we need not worry
too much that it will disappear. There are usually substantial
objective reasons to support it. The Welfare State has eliminated
gross and irrational inequalities whose existence threatened the
survival of the democratic system. To be sure, many economic
anomalies remain, and some special oddities have also been produced by the Welfare State. By and large, its redistributive policies favor those who have organized representation; those who
are unorganized and those who are on fixed incomes have not
benefited nearly so much, if they have benefited at all. It is odd
that the linotypist who puts a book together should often make
more than the author who has written it, and it is not only odd but
socially mischievous that teachers, journalists, or government officials should have incomes substantially below those available in
other and presumably less useful occupations.

But in considering what the Welfare State does in eliminating
old inequalities or creating new ones, it is useful to notice what
is frequently overlooked when the ideal of social equality is
discussed. There is no general case either for egalitarianism or
against it. For it makes no sense and conveys no information

whatsoever to say that men are either equal or unequal unless we say in what specific respects they are equal or unequal. If we call Tweedledee and Tweedledum equal, we tacitly imply that they are equal in intelligence, or strength, or as powerful bores, or in the possession, say, of the right to vote. Without this tacit implication, our statement would be entirely opaque. And when we say that men are equal or unequal in one respect, we do not necessarily say that they are equal or unequal in any other respect. An equal right to apply for a job does not imply equal ability to perform the job; an equal chance for an education does not imply equal ability to profit from the education, nor does it imply—though some partisans of equality of educational opportunity seem to forget it—that all children should have the same education.

The argument between egalitarians and their opponents, therefore, is generally an argument with a suppressed premise. The argument is not about whether men are really equal or not. It is about the standards that are employed and the particular characteristics of individuals that are singled out as the basis for calling them equal or unequal. Sensibly construed, egalitarianism is not an effort to eliminate the distinctions between people. In fact, it manufactures new distinctions in the very process of destroying old ones. If we remove racial or religious distinctions in selecting applicants for professional positions, for example, we have to substitute other standards such as the ability to do well on written examinations. This may be a good criterion or a bad one, but it divides people into different classes. In practice, egalitarianism is simply an effort, in other words, to eliminate distinctions that seem arbitrary, unreasonable, or purposeless. And in each case the specific distinctions under attack by the egalitarian, and the new distinctions with which he would replace them, have to be examined.

From this point of view, the general question to be raised about the "egalitarianism" of the Welfare State is not whether its programs are compatible with the recognition of excellence. Any system of distributing wealth and opportunity encourages some forms of excellence—if only the excellence of a hereditary leisure class that can concentrate on the arts of consumption—and dis-

courages others. The crucial question is whether the Welfare
State encourages the kinds of excellence that we wish encouraged and discourages the kinds we wish discouraged—or rather,
whether (since its effects are bound to be mixed) the excellences
encouraged are worth the cost. To this there is no wholesale answer. There are only specific problems, each of which has to be
answered, in fear and trembling, as it arises.

But it can at least be said that the Welfare State's social services and redistributive policies do not in fact dispense economic
equality to equals and unequals alike. The man who receives help
from a welfare agency is usually (though not always) enabled to
live at a level of minimal decency. But it is a very minimal level,
as anyone who doubts can discover by trying it himself. Nor is
there strong evidence to support the apparently widespread fear
that a guarantee of basic economic securities eats away at the
industriousness and self-reliance of a population. That some individuals will regard such a guarantee as an invitation to take
things easy is undeniable: the behavior of many rich people ver-
ifies this proposition. By and large, however, if an economy is
prospering, if opportunities are plentiful, and if the ethic of success and achievement is in the air, the incentive to work is also
present. "The notion that economic insecurity is essential for efficiency and economic advance," as Mr. Galbraith has noted, "was
a major miscalculation—perhaps the greatest in the history of
economic ideas. . . . The most impressive increases in output in
the history of both the United States and other western countries
have occurred since men began to concern themselves with reducing the risks of the competitive system." The psychological
theory that men will work only if the threat of starvation is at
their backs says something about the kind of work that is offered
them. But it has little objective support otherwise.

THE MORAL ORIGINALITY OF THE WELFARE STATE

Why, then, has the Welfare State aroused the fears it has? If
these fears are based on myths, why do these myths have the
currency they do? One obvious reason is that some men have
been hit where it hurts—in their incomes and social influence.

But another reason is that the Welfare State has shaken up and rearranged some of our traditional moral notions. The Welfare State is not in the main a product of a deliberate philosophy, but in its practice it has developed and expressed certain tacit assumptions, and it is in these assumptions that the moral originality of the Welfare State is revealed. They represent its contributions to the education—or miseducation—of our generation.

First of all, the Welfare State has carried into practice the principle that ideas like "minimal decency" and "human welfare" are variable notions. Their meaning depends on place, time, cultural predispositions, and the general level of wealth attained by a society. "Minimal decency" for an American in 1860 is not "minimal decency" for an American a century later. And the difference does not lie only in the cost of living. It lies in the different levels of expectation and the different conceptions of what is possible that prevail. There is more to such a principle than just a recognition that standards of material well-being are historically determined. What is also involved is the adoption of the rule that a life of "minimal decency" has a psychological component.

A man who lives in a particular society, who is moved by certain aspirations, who takes an attitude towards himself that is at least in part a reflection of (or a reaction to) reigning attitudes, cannot be said to be living decently simply because he can keep body and soul together. He has to be able to do so under conditions that allow him to retain some self-respect. By adopting this principle, the Welfare State has helped expand our working conception of minimally decent living conditions. This is one source of the feeling that welfare policies have gone too far. For the policy of helping others while allowing them to retain their self-respect has not been the usual policy in human affairs.

Moreover, the policies of social assistance followed by the Welfare State have introduced a new context for helping others. The help is given to individuals who have a legal right to be helped. That is the second moral innovation for which the Welfare State is responsible. It has partially subverted the conditions in which one of Western civilization's more cherished moral virtues—the virtue of charity—has flourished. There is, presumably, less occasion for charity in the Welfare State—at any rate, for material charity. Even more to the point, the assumption on which charity is based has been called into question. In what has been taken to be its noblest form, charity is a free gift, a form of assistance to others who have no right to such assistance. This is undoubtedly why it has been thought that it is more blessed to give than to receive: it is more agreeable to the ego. But in the Welfare State all citizens enjoy certain basic guarantees of assistance. Such assistance is their right, and not simply their benefactor's moral duty.

What are the justifications for this principle? There are many. But surely one is the ideal of a liberal society. A liberal society is committed to more than the improvement in the material condition of mankind. It seeks a kind of society that is composed of autonomous individuals with their own rights and powers, people who do not have to depend on the good will of their masters to enjoy minimal securities and freedoms. If the phrase "human dignity" has any meaning, this is presumably a good part of what it means. The Welfare State is in this sense a peculiarly liberal institution.

THE TUTELARY POWERS OF THE WELFARE STATE

But the most substantial reason for the fears that the Welfare State has aroused lies in the simple and justified suspicion that the liberal tradition has always entertained towards the State. Writing almost forty years ago, and in a book favoring a form of socialism, Bertrand Russell observed: "The purposes of the State are mainly evil, and anything which makes it harder for the State to obtain money is a boon." It is sometimes said by passionate democrats that it is impossible for a democratic welfare government to endanger freedom since this government, after all, is "all of us." To take this unction to our soul is tempting. But the concern of "all of us" for liberty has not been demonstrated; and in any case the statement is a transparent myth. A government may be freely chosen, but it is still not all of us. It is some men vested with authority over other men. And in a Welfare State a very large part of this authority is inevitably exercised by officials vested with administrative authority by a bureaucratic hierarchy.

The question of personal liberty in a democratic Welfare State is raised most sharply when we turn to this issue.

The power of administrative officials is very great for a number of reasons. To begin with, in a crowded society it is increasingly necessary to have them. And to the power which the performance of a necessary function gives, the administrative official brings other powers. He is closer to the problem and more directly engaged in the actual conduct of policy than the elected official who may be above him. He can give his job, including the building of his little empire, his full-time attention. Moreover, he is relatively hidden from public view, and is not competing for public favor as the politician, the businessman, or the leaders of voluntary organizations are.

Not least, he enjoys a grant of discretion in the exercise of his powers. Discretion is unavoidable in any field where judgment is involved, but the exercise of discretion is the essence of the administrator's task. It is why we need him and not a computing machine. An official in a welfare agency, for example, may be required by the orders given him to deny certain forms of assistance to individuals who are voluntarily unemployed. He may be provided with the further specification that any individual who is out of work because he has voluntarily quit his job and moved to another locality shall be regarded as voluntarily unemployed. But the letter of this rule will kill if the administrator applies it to a man who has changed his residence because his wife is ill and requires a sunnier climate. The attempt to dot every *i* and cross every *t* when framing policies or writing legislation only prevents those who must administer these policies and laws from behaving intelligently. The sensible exercise of foresight obviously involves making allowances for the circumstance that not everything can be foreseen.

Yet in granting discretion to the administrator, he is also given more freedom to act stupidly, capriciously, or tyrannically. And the normal methods by which we control those with authority are not so easily available in his case. The elected official has to return to the electorate for its judgment. The judge has to make his decisions in the open, under the eye of a watchful legal profession, and with a view to the relationship of his decision to past precedents and future decisions. Such pressures, if they affect the administrative official at all, do not do so to nearly the same extent. In any society that seeks to live under the rule of law this raises grave issues. If contemporary democracy is to continue to be a recognizable shelter for personal liberty, the increasing power of administrative agencies presents problems that have to be managed in some way.

The accepted techniques of political supervision and legislative investigation can do much, but it is doubtful that they are enough. They can curtail larger tyrannies and injustices, but they are unlikely to find the petty tyrannies and stupidities that hurt anonymous individuals. And it is these small evils that are usually the most debilitating; they are the everyday evils, and they are likely to fall on those least able to stand up to them or to fight back. Between the individual and the agencies of the Welfare State there needs to be constructed a layer of protective groups and associations. Special voluntary associations need to be developed that are peculiarly concerned with the protection of the rights of individuals in their dealings with administrative authorities.

Whether these groups should be new groups or whether existing groups like legal aid societies and civil liberties unions are adequate to the task is not so important as that the function should be performed. And in areas especially dependent on public welfare services, groups like the neighborhood association and the settlement house have particularly important functions. Those who need help most, as Helen Hall has remarked, need it close. In addition to government agencies they need something more personal than government agencies, and they also need groups to whom they can turn for help if they want to put the officials of public agencies under pressure. Plans for urban renewal and public housing which omit these considerations are plans conceived in a vacuum.

THE INADEQUACIES OF THE WELFARE STATE

Yet the question with which we began remains. The multiplication of rules and regulations in a complex society may be unavoidable; the support and help of the State may be essential.

But is public concern for personal liberty bound to be diminished, and is the individual will bound to be weakened, by these tendencies? It takes considerable hardihood to venture a prophecy about these matters, although there are apparently plenty of hardy souls around. No one can be sure that the democratic despotism of which Tocqueville spoke does not lie around the corner. But if what is wanted is not prophecy but a policy for fending off this fate, then the suggestion can be offered that the Welfare State may indeed go too far if it does not go far enough. It does too much, strangely enough, when it also does too little.

The Welfare State is a postscript to emergency and bears the marks of its origins. In the main, it is a set of arrangements for dealing with problems which are conceived to be problems of a certain sort—namely, residual problems. For the problems that a society faces are in general of two kinds. A problem is "residual" when it is the consequence of the occasional inevitable lapse of a social system from its normal mode of operation; it is also "residual" if it is a problem that would arise under any conceivable social arrangements because it is part of the irreducible imperfection of man's condition. Thus, for a long period during the nineteenth century, economists had no word for unemployment. The word was "overpopulation." Poverty was conceived as a residual problem of all societies. On the other hand, a problem is an "institutional" problem if it is the product, not of inevitable human failings, but of the particular way in which a society orders its affairs. It is an institutional problem, indeed, if it is the consequence of social arrangements that are working as it is generally expected and desired that they should. "War is the health of the State," said Randolph Bourne, thereby proclaiming that war was an institutional, not a residual, problem in human affairs.

The central issue with regard to the Welfare State is whether the problems with which it is concerned are in the main residual or institutional. The prospects of personal autonomy under the Welfare State depend on the answer we give to this question. For up to this point most of the facilities provided by the Welfare State have been like the arrangements we make against the possible breakdown of our automobile. They are preparations essentially against what are conceived to be accidents.

Because we have had a number of such "accidents" and because our foresight has grown, our preparations against such contingencies have multiplied a thousandfold. But it is at least possible that we would need fewer detailed regulations, fewer bureaus, committees, and meddlesome interventions by the State, if the Welfare State adopted a systematic institutional approach to the problems it faces. Planning, as Gunnar Myrdal has pointed out, is often confused with direct and detailed regulations by the State. "The opposite, however, is true; there is still such a large measure of intervention because the measures are not ideally co-ordinated and planned." For to a considerable extent the problems with which the contemporary Welfare State is attempting to deal are in fact regular and normal problems of an industrialized democracy. They are problems that emerge because the system is working as it should.

The urgent problem of technological change offers the most obvious illustration. If many men have the feeling today that their independence and personal autonomy are being undermined, one reason is that their skills, jobs, and daily lives are dependent upon impersonal processes of technological change. Technological change, furthermore, creates more than technological unemployment. It changes the working environment, disturbs established and sometimes hard-earned positions, and affects the mental interest that men bring to their work. Not least, the introduction of technological innovations by superior authority without sufficient advance notice produces a general atmosphere of insecurity. Featherbedding, the insistence on seniority privileges, and other practices of unions which express resistance to technological change have to be understood in this context. The problems provoked by automation are only the most recent and dramatic examples. Citing the economic benefits of technological progress does not change the fact that some men pay a heavy price in their pocketbooks and pride for this progress.

Yet technological unemployment and displacement are not residual but institutional problems. They are signs that our system is working well. For technological innovation is a structural feature of our system, and one of its central justifications. To adopt purely remedial and *ad hoc* programs for dealing with the problems it creates is analogous to creating systems of traffic control based on the assumption that men use automobiles only in emergencies. To be sure, the attempt to control the pace of invention or the direction of scientific research is as a rule undesirable. Nor does the present state of our social knowledge permit us to foretell the long-range consequences of most technological changes. Yet despite the imperial range of our ignorance, it is still possible to act prospectively rather than retrospectively with regard to many problems created by technological change.

The importance, for example, of providing regular facilities for retraining workers in advance of their technological displacement has recently begun to receive belated recognition. But recognition of the principle is not enough. The facilities provided need to be built on the assumption that the vocational re-education of adult citizens will be as permanent a part of our society as elementary schools for children. Similarly, the problem of recovering our cities from their present ugliness and disorder has to be seen in the same context. For in the long view, the problems American cities face are not accidental but integral features of industrial growth. Such growth has always depended, for one thing, on the movement of people with rural backgrounds to the urban environment. One difference between a town and a city, indeed, is that a city is a permanent center for floating populations. The doctrine that welfare services can catch up with the attendant problems if we simply provide them with more money and greater public support is a doctrine of despair, although more money and support would of course help. The need is to transform existing services, which are therapeutic in their orientation, into services based on the recognition of permanent facts of life in industrial society.

The army assumes that it is not an accident but rather in the nature of the case that new recruits from civilian life should need a period of preliminary training and adjustment to military routines. It makes regular provision for this problem instead of waiting to send those who falter to the guardhouse or the hospital. But the transition of a rural Puerto Rican family to New York is likely to be at least as violent. As one example of what could be done, provided we adopted a philosophy of social action different from that which presently governs the Welfare State, reception centers for the orientation and advising of new arrivals to our cities could be provided. Far from adding to existing welfare and police costs, such facilities would probably prove to be an economy. In a democratic society, of course, new arrivals could not be required to reside in such centers. But it is hard to believe that they would not be more attractive than the facilities that are now provided. And they would reduce the need for many of the programs we now employ in order to pick up the pieces after the damage has been done.

Other fundamental welfare problems fall into place when it is seen that they, too, are institutional problems. In dealing with old age, the momentum of the past carries us along at right angles to the actual issues we confront. Men have hoped for an old age free from toil and material worries. For the overwhelming majority of Americans the hope is realizable. But at the same time the progress of medicine has enormously lengthened life expectancy, and has produced people who take much longer to grow old. Notwithstanding these changes, the policies of labor, business, and government continue to push the normal age of retirement steadily downward, as though there were some mysterious virtue in making men feel old at a steadily earlier period in their lives. The problem of retirement, as a result, is coming to be the problem of what to do with retirement.

At the other end of the spectrum, the so-called "youth problem" is also an institutional problem. "Youth" is not just a biological category; it is a sociological category. It designates that period of life during which people who are physically mature are kept by social conventions or regulations in a dependent and apprentice status. That period has been enormously extended. Prosperity, restrictions against the entrance of young people in the labor market, and the lengthening of the average period of time spent in schools have all conspired to this end. Yet people grow up biologically at the same old pace, and there is some evidence that better diets and the stimulations of the mass media may even speed up the process. The phenomenon of the adolescent and the teen-ager is intelligible only if we take this gap and tension between biological maturity and socially recognized maturity into account.

We can of course try to deal with the problem by treating it individual case by individual case. Unless the social context in which it arises is considered, however, we shall probably have a steadily increasing amount of business on our hands. For it is one thing to mount a program for youth as a preventive measure against juvenile delinquency, or to create a scholarship system in order to advance the objectives of national defense. It is quite another thing to mount a program based on the recognition that a society with conventions and institutions like ours creates certain permanent needs, and has to provide facilities that will make it possible for different and predictable kinds of young people to come into their own. For some of them, schools are the answer, for some, schools are not; for some, financial support while at school is not necessary, for others, it is both necessary and desirable. The difference is between a residual and an institutional approach to the issue. The difference would show up in the character, though probably not the expensiveness, of what we tried to do. For while tension between the generations is a residual issue in all moving societies, the forced juvenilization of a portion of the population is not.

The issue, in brief, is whether the Welfare State can be converted from an instrument for dealing with problems perceived as residual into an instrument for dealing with problems perceived in institutional terms. Allowing for gradations in between the extremes, when a problem is perceived as the consequence of social arrangements that are working as they are expected to work, one of two responses is invited. The first is to decide that the institution creating the problem is worth preserving just the same, and to create, accordingly, supplementary institutions to deal with problems deliberately accepted as permanent. The second is to decide that the institution creating the problem is not worth preserving unchanged at that price, and to proceed to reform or replace it. In either case, however, an explicit decision about means and ends, about social goals and their costs, has been made. In short, a measure of rational planning has been introduced. The disagreeableness of planning, in fact, is not that it inevitably leads to more regulation and inhibition of human energy. The inherent disagreeableness of genuine planning—and the virtue of planning—is that it brings a society's operating values out into the open and forces a deliberate choice among them. Such a choice is undoubtedly more painful than a choice that is made without knowing it, but it is also more responsible and its consequences can be examined and controlled.

It is unexamined habits of thought that tie us to our present condition. It is generally assumed that "centralization" is incompatible with "decentralization." On the contrary, the drift towards centralization can be arrested only by coherent policies and leadership at the center. For agencies and regulations multiply when general policies are missing and when there are no regularly established facilities for dealing systematically and in advance with the normal dangers of life in a developed economy. The opponents of centralization, indeed, are their own worst enemies. They encourage the policy of too little and too late, which produces the very conditions they wish to avoid. And similarly, it is assumed that "social planning" is inherently inimical to free individual choice and personal autonomy. But this depends on the kind of planning that is introduced and the purposes by which it is guided. It can complicate or simplify, cut down the alternatives available to individuals or add to their number and interest.

If the Welfare State could break loose from its origins in emergency, it could become a prelude to a society in which the interventions by centralized authority in personal life and in local and regional affairs would be fewer rather than more numerous. Certainly nothing is more consonant with the liberal ideal than to try to free ordinary citizens from the enervating interference and regulation of officials in far-away places. But even if the Welfare State is as bad in this respect as its opponents say, it is worth asking why this is the case. And the answer may be that it does too much because it does too little.

VIII

THE RESPONSIBLE SOCIETY

We have now looked at some of the changes in our circumstances which challenge the ideals of government by consent, an open society, and the autonomous individual. But a problem that affects all the others remains, the problem of redeeming ourselves from the growing sense that it is not we but things that are in the saddle. For the big decisions seem to be anonymous, bureaucratic, purely technical, while the fundamental choices, the decisions concerning principles and values, are not made: our purposes are simply dictated to us, things simply happen.

One of the most distinctive phenomena of our time, the phenomenon behind existentialism, the protests of the beat, and the anxieties about organization men and lonely crowds, is the spread of the debilitating feeling that the moral intelligence cannot take hold of a world organized as ours is organized, that the moral conscience has no field of action. Science and bureaucracy have demonstrated the capacity of men to coordinate human intelligence and to apply it to the organization of human affairs. Yet they seem to have created a world in which moral vision, social imagination, and even the political controversy that enlivens the democratic scene have become anachronisms, futile ripples on a stream of events which they are powerless to affect. The ideal of responsible government has become difficult even to define.

THE NOSTALGIC ANSWERS

What are the sources of this widespread feeling? The nostalgic answers will not do. It is said that we have forgotten our roots. But if we look back upon our past, we will find in it ideas that we cannot now believe and practices that would repel us although they did not repel our ancestors. We need principles of selection to disentangle our past and to disentangle ourselves from parts of it. It is said that our troubles are due to the fact that we have given up our faith in absolute standards of right and wrong. But the faith in absolutes carries its own troubles, and in any case millions of ordinary men and women, and not a few of the high and mighty, continue to hold their moral and religious beliefs as articles of an absolute creed. In practical political terms, the statement that we have abandoned a faith in absolutes means only that modern secular democracies do not credit any man or group with infallible authority in regard to morals and the proper organization of society. And this will continue to be the case so long as we try to define responsibility in the government of our affairs in democratic terms.

Nor is there much intellectual mileage in the sweeping, and increasingly popular, proposition that we have given ourselves away to false gods, to science, technology, and impersonal organization, and that now man is alienated from himself. If he is, he will not recover his wholeness and integrity by cursing the elements in which he is going to have to live, move, and find his being. Although the higher metaphysical interpretations of the current crisis in liberal society are intended to be protests against our irresponsibility, they are in fact endorsements of that irresponsibility. They assume an incurable conflict between humane purposes and the conditions for action available to us, and build the separation between our powers and our ideals into the unalterable nature of things. They merely add to the overhanging feeling that there is nothing that can be done.

The presence and popularity of these explanations simply reveal one of the principal causes for our present sense of disorientation. Behind the mounting body of opinion that our power and prosperity are bad for us there lies the unresolved paradox of too much rationality and intelligence in the creation of techniques and instruments, and too little rationality and humanity in the determination of our purposes and standards. No general understanding, much less agreement, exists in our society concerning the relation of scientific methods to the reconstruction of our moral and social values. The nature of social reason—the characteristics, possibilities, and limits of a deliberate effort by human beings to use their knowledge to remake their institutions—is still in fundamental dispute.

And it is likely to remain in dispute for a considerable time. An approach to the problem of making social decisions more responsible cannot wait and had better not wait until this question is settled. A hundred or five hundred years from now, if the race survives, I suspect that men will still be mourning the fact that human knowledge and power are so much greater than human wisdom. At the immediate moment there are two points at which our uncertainty about the meaning of responsibility and our difficulties in asserting and enforcing it are felt most deeply. And it is at these two points that the problem must be approached.

The first is in the area of professional morality. A new breed of man—the scientist, the technician, the specialized official in public and private bureaucracies—has emerged and is exercising a mounting power over our affairs. But the conditions of his power are new, and the codes by which he carries on his work elude our commonplace categories. We are still at sea concerning the ethic that is appropriate to the expert, the responsibilities that should go with his new position.

In the second place, the organization of the decision-making process is giving us trouble. It is highly organized. It assigns the individual his role precisely and tells him what is wanted of him and how far he can go. Yet responsibility for decisions concerning fundamental values is hard to fix. It seems to fall through the mesh of all our organization and to be lost in a no-man's land. We seem to have allowed to grow up around us a decision-making process in which those who make key decisions are invisible, and in their invisibility do not themselves know that they are making such decisions. The result is a kind of organized irresponsibility built out of the decisions and actions of countless disciplined and responsible men dutifully ignoring what they are told it is their

business to ignore. No definite human beings are accountable—
only society, only "the system."

Let us turn first to the question of ethics.

THE SPECIALIZED JOB AND THE UNSPECIALIZED CONSCIENCE

The problem of the moral responsibilities of the expert or the
official is the peculiar moral problem of our time. It is the problem, writ large, of most men who are social actors and who have
some freedom of choice in an age in which, on one side, social
assignments are specialized and precise, and, on the other, the
individual conscience is held to be sovereign and to have the
whole world as its potential domain.

For the present era, despite its bureaucratic arrangements and
its departmentalization of learning, is not the first to assign each
man his special limited role in the social scheme. But it is the
first to do so and at the same time to remove the encircling and
sheltering authority at the top that defined the purpose of the
whole. It is the first to tell each man that in addition to all his
particular responsibilities he has the general responsibility of deciding for himself what is right and wrong. In our intricately
organized society an individual's job, once he has chosen it, is
no longer his own to define. It has its own independent rules and
conditions, and the consequences which his work will have are
not for the individual alone to control. Yet his conscience is on
its own, and it is he who must decide whether these consequences
are acceptable, and what he owes to himself and his community
as a specialist and what he owes as a citizen and man.

What should a business executive do if he knows that he will
leave a community high and dry by moving his plant to a more
profitable location? And has he the same choice to make when
he owns the plant and is risking his own money, and when he is
a hired professional manager and is risking other people's money?
Again, should the economist advising a government how to raise
money for roads recommend that it would be better to raise
money for schools? Or to take the most obvious example, should
the nuclear physicist refuse to do any work that might contribute
to the making of nuclear weapons? Should he do so even if this

means—as it probably does—that he must give up research in his chosen field? The problem of the expert is that he appears to be irresponsible when he refuses to raise questions about the significance of what he is doing, but that he also appears to be irresponsible when he does. For he then steps out of the domain where he is clearly competent and where he is charged with a definite mission and takes it upon himself to intrude his judgment where it has not been asked and where it has no special authority. Is there any set of principles which can help conscientious men in this situation?

Let us try to answer this question by looking at the principle which underlies the present organization of bureaucracies and existing codes of professional conduct. The principle, I think, is a sound one. But misinterpretations of it are responsible for our uncertainties about the meaning of professional responsibility.

The fundamental principle supporting both the organization of bureaucracies and prevailing codes of professional conduct is a distinction between factual knowledge and value judgments, between statements about what is or will be and decisions concerning what ought to be. So far as official principle goes, the organization or the client decides the goals for which the expert's or the professional's skills will be used. He has the right and obligation to refuse to lend his skills to purposes that are illegal. But within these broad confines, the technical specialist's job is simply to say whether the goals that are proposed are attainable and what it will cost to pursue them. His responsibility is to put his talents honestly at the disposal of those for whom he works, and not to allow personal inclination or preference to affect his performance. For statements about the facts are one thing. There a specialist can claim some authority, and impersonal standards exist by which his authority can be measured. But expressions of moral preference are quite another thing. Here standards vary, and a specialist can claim no more authority than anyone else.

It is easy to see why this distinction between facts and values should raise objections. A long line of thinkers, beginning with Plato, have attacked it on the ground that it provides the intellectual rationale for allowing knowledge to be used in the service of any wild flag that waves. It seems to say that knowledge and expertise are important only where instrumentalities are concerned, but that the ends and purposes of a society must be determined by caprice or by fiat. And yet, although many subtle issues are involved, the distinction, in its fundamental aspects, cannot be avoided.

The very essence of moral responsibility is to use the knowledge we have in order to assess the actual conditions and consequences of the goals we pursue, and to realign these goals when we find that they are not what we thought or hoped they were. But we cannot use our knowledge to examine our ideals objectively if we deny that a distinction can be made between our knowledge and our ideals. And it is only by making such a distinction, furthermore, that we can formulate rules for controlling the expert. For unless we can separate statements of fact from statements of preference, we cannot tell when the expert is talking through his professional hat and when he is talking through the same hat that the rest of us talk through. The distinction between facts and values is essential to orderly inquiry and to the very idea of professional responsibility.

Accordingly, the first part of the morality that is appropriate to the expert in modern society is that he make the distinction, explicitly and regularly, between his special competence and his special preferences. The authority enjoyed by the expert as an expert frequently spills over and lends a specious authority to the opinions he has in other fields. As a man among men he is entitled to such opinions, but then he ought to draw the line publicly between what he knows and what he opines. Admittedly, that is not always easy to do. At the edges the expert's beliefs about the facts will fade into his moral preferences, just as they do with most men. But it is his professional duty to try to keep the two apart.

The biologist who holds forth on the population problem, the psychoanalyst who writes on problems of war and peace, the theologians and philosophers who enjoy a kind of generalized mandate to be wise—all these are performing as intellectuals and not merely as specialists when they use their disciplines to comment on public affairs. They are dealing with issues that are not purely biological, psychological, religious, or philosophical. Thus, to consider obvious examples, Professors Teller and Pauling are operating partly as scientists but mainly as citizens when they advise us to continue or to stop nuclear tests. Their expertise is relevant to the question whether the military objectives of nuclear tests justify the risks of fall-out. It is a question that cannot be answered responsibly without scientific information. But it is not a scientific question, for the answer to it depends on the values we assign to one set of risks as opposed to the other. It is a moral and political question.

To the extent that he can, therefore, it is incumbent on the expert who discusses such questions to make it plain just when he crosses the line and enters this new domain. Far from encouraging irresponsibility, the adoption of such a policy would add immeasurably to the responsibility of the decision-making processes in which scientists and experts now play so large a part. On the one side, it would help prevent idolatry of the scientist and expert. On the other side, it would help remove some of the fears and resistance which their power provokes. For there are many who suspect that scientists and experts do not quite know what they are doing, and who cannot forgive them for thinking that they do.

THE NEED FOR PROFESSIONAL OBEDIENCE

Moreover, there are fundamental practical reasons for insisting on the distinction between professional knowledge and moral judgments. It is an essential distinction if the professional man is to know his place, and in a democratic society it is essential that he know his place. There is an inconvenient consequence to the common assumption that a man's duty to think as a citizen always takes priority, and that his unspecialized conscience should always prevail over his specialized responsibilities. It is an assumption that disenfranchises the ordinary citizen.

For my only chance as a citizen to exercise some control over the decisions that affect my destiny lies in being able to put my finger on the men who are responsible for these decisions. But I cannot reasonably assign responsibility to those who are in charge of an organization if the principle is accepted that the experts and officials who advise them should only do their jobs, or do them well, when they approve of the policies that have been instituted. This applies particularly to the ethic proper for officials and consultants working for democratic governments. The citizen has not chosen these men to be the agents of his conscience. And while they are admittedly the keepers of their own consciences, they also have an obligation to the democratic citizen, who has a right to be governed by those he has elected to office.

Indeed, our current preoccupation with the phenomenon of the organization man, the man who is subservient to the organization and loses his conscience in it, is in some ways rather strange. For the phenomenon of bureaucratic obstruction is one of the most serious problems now confronting us in making democracy work. Such obstruction is not usually the work of officials with slack moral principles. It is usually the work of conscientious and morally committed men who oppose the policies adopted by their organization. A problem of mounting difficulty for contemporary democratic governments is that of seeing to it that the politically chosen officials, who are theoretically responsible for policy, are also in genuine control of the bureaucratic machinery. And this requires an established code of professional obedience. One runs the risk of nonconformity in seeming to say a good word for conformity, but a society that seeks responsible government must contain disciplined men, in both the public and private sectors, who normally do what their organizations ask them to do.

Of course, there are limits. "When you think of the long and gloomy history of man," C. P. Snow has remarked, "you will find far more, and far more hideous crimes, have been committed in the name of obedience than in the name of rebellion. . . . Yet the duty to question is not much of a support when you are living in the middle of an organized society. I speak with feeling here. I was an official for twenty years. . . . I think I know the virtues, which are very great, of the men who live that disciplined life. I also know what for me was the moral trap. I, too, had got onto an escalator. I can put the result in a sentence: I was coming to hide behind the institution. I was losing the power to say 'no.'" And surely the man who has lost the power to say No has lost as much as any man can lose.

And yet you cannot applaud a man simply for following the dictates of his conscience. It all depends on the contents of that conscience. We applaud General de Gaulle for disobeying the orders of his superiors in World War II. We do not applaud the Algerian generals for disobeying General de Gaulle. The problem is analogous to the ancient problem of determining when civil disobedience is morally legitimate. It is always legitimate—provided the provocation is extreme and one shares the moral principles of the man who disobeys. There is a difference between policy and occasional justified exceptions to it, and no organized social group can act on the principle that disobedience to its official decisions is either permissible or laudable.

These considerations apply to the moral problems faced by officials and specialists. Short of civil disobedience, there are other alternatives open to conscientious men when the organizations for which they work outrage their moral sensibilities. In a society that gives them some freedom of choice, they can protest or strike or resign. And they may be right to do so even if they oppose decisions that have been reached by democratic procedures. Such procedures are not a magic sacrament that convert folly into wisdom and evil into good. Where matters of conscience are concerned, every man, as John Locke observed, must in the end "judge for himself whether he should appeal to the supreme judge, as Jephtha did." But when he makes such an appeal, the issues ought not to be oversimplified. Noncooperation does not become a virtue just because it is conscientious noncooperation. And in an official it is a vice unless very strong reasons can be brought forward to justify it. To suggest that the individual can keep his moral integrity simply by resisting the lures and pressures of his official position is akin to the ancient belief that men could remain tame and pure if only they learned to resist the lures and pressures of women. Both notions forget that the lures and pressures in question serve a useful purpose.

THE ILLUSION OF SPECIALIZATION

Yet a willingness to draw a line between his professional skills and his private values is not all that is required to make the expert a responsible wielder of power. Unless supplemented by an additional principle, the code of professional obedience would be a legitimation of irresponsibility. For while the distinction between facts and values, between specialized knowledge and the unspecialized conscience, is a sound and necessary one, it is open to an easy misinterpretation. It states an ideal, a regulative principle by which men ought to try to guide their behavior. It does not describe anybody's possible behavior in any context in which social decisions are being made. The failure to recognize this has been a source of considerable confusion. It is the confusion inherent in any failure to distinguish between ideal goals and the practical strategy for pursuing them.

In his essay "Science as a Vocation" Max Weber, the great theorist of modern bureaucracy, wrote: "The true teacher will beware of imposing from the platform any political position upon the student, whether it is expressed or suggested." No true teacher in the social studies or humanities and few in the natural sciences could live up to this maxim. The teacher who promises that he will not even suggest his preferences is making a promise he cannot keep. And in misleading his students and himself, he is making it harder for everyone to disentangle the facts and the values, the opinions and the opinionation, in what he has to say. And this applies equally to the specialist who serves or advises an organization and contributes his professional knowledge to its decision-making processes. It is one thing to say that there is an intellectual distinction between facts and values. It is another thing to say that any man can always be sure in which domain he is.

For when a man works for an organization, he is in a political context. He may wish only to do his professional job, letting the chips fall where they may, but the chips fall where they may, upsetting established positions here, reversing past judgments and policies there. No one but a fool can advise his superiors or instruct his inferiors in an organization without realizing that they are going to like or dislike what he says, and are going to look for reasons to exploit, dilute, or reject his message. In circumstances in which decisions are being made, the communication of neutral information is an inevitably partisan act, and the man who wants the information he conveys to receive the attention it deserves has got to care about what is done with it and the purposes for which it is used.

Moreover, in almost any situation in which social decisions are being made, a large part of the specialist's job is to communicate his specialized knowledge to the nonspecialist. This requires him to select, to choose the right words in the ordinary and not quite exact language of everyday life, and to indicate the degree of reliability and importance that should be attached to different parts of his story. It is not easy to separate such activities from evaluative ones. And all these difficulties are enhanced the higher the specialist goes in the bureaucratic hierarchy. The higher he goes, the more he becomes a generalist, the more he has to make judgments about matters that do not fall precisely in his own field of competence. Without the support of his own discipline, the hard-won capacity to distinguish between knowledge and preference tends to fade.

In short, the reason for making the distinction between factual judgments and value judgments is not that it neatly and comfortably compartmentalizes moral responsibility, making some men specialists in value judgments while allowing others to concentrate entirely on questions of fact. The reason for making the distinction is that it highlights the different responsibilities the same individual has. The expert has a professional duty to put his knowledge and skill at the disposal of the community. But he has an equal responsibility to discover what his own values are, and to examine and express them. Sound moral and social decisions cannot be made if the best professional knowledge we have about the facts is ignored. Neither can they be made if a mistaken conception of the division of labor and responsibility prevails, and the expert imagines that decisions about the moral imponderables are none of his business.

The formation of public policy with regard to fallout shelters is an example. It is possible, though difficult, to estimate the probable destruction if big bombs are dropped, or medium ones, or what are now called, with a sensitive regard for our feelings, small ones. It is also possible, though harder, to judge the effect of a major program of fallout shelters on the temperature of international affairs. But there are other questions, too. What will be the effects of such a program on the psychology of children? On the feeling-tone of daily life? On the general health of democratic institutions and habits of mind? These are not easy questions to answer, but they are part of the issue. And the expert who never raises them, who restricts himself to giving his best answers to the specialized questions he is asked, is retreating to a false conception of professional responsibility. He is allowing the questions to be artificially formulated so that they remain questions that fall neatly into his own professional basket.

The consequences of this policy of studied neglect of the imponderables are evident in many places. The tax policies drawn up by financial experts have had a plain, though as yet unmeasured, effect on the expense-account morality and aesthetic that have invaded American life. The decisions of prudent and responsible investment counselors who have no desire to damage the United States' position abroad have made and unmade Latin-American governments. Such decisions are like that of the drunkard who lost his wallet in Central Park and looked for it in Times Square because the light was better there. The notion that the only questions that must be asked or answered are the questions on which men can have assured opinions is the modern bureaucratized intellectual's comforting substitute for the certitudes of moral absolutism.

There are no experts in morals. But to think that this means that the expert oversteps the bounds when he states his moral views is, quite literally, to demoralize the decision-making process. All that follows from the fact that there are no experts in morals is that morals are everybody's business. Specialization of function does not release the technician from playing an inevitable part in the making of moral decisions. Nothing can. And responsibility in decision-making can be achieved only if those who are most influential in the process do their work while recognizing its larger implications, stating these implications as they see them, and accepting responsibility for the consequences.

THE SOCIAL ORGANIZATION OF RESPONSIBILITY

But the question of responsibility in the control of our affairs cannot be discussed in purely individual terms. Responsible government is not simply a matter of decision-making by responsible men. It depends on the presence of social institutions with certain characteristics. And the emergence of bureaucracy and specialized expertise illustrate this principle. They have not deprived us of responsible men, but they have affected the conditions for responsible government.

For on the one side, bureaucracy tends to concentrate the authority to make important social decisions in central but often invisible positions. On the other side, it often dilutes responsibility, making it collective and impersonal, and encouraging men to pass the buck. In individuals it tends to produce a kind of occupational myopia, a trained incapacity, in Veblen's phrase, to see any problems but the problems they are told to see. In organizations it frequently produces an irresistible motion without meaning, a sort of institutional fanaticism in which sober men redouble their efforts after having forgotten their aims. And not least, the special genius of bureaucracy, as it were, lies in manufacturing problems of mixed responsibility. For part of what we mean by bureaucracy is a process by which some men are given definite assignments as the trustees of other men's interests. And so long as they accept this trusteeship, such men no longer have souls that they can quite call their own.

The replacement of the owner by the professional manager in the modern corporation, the substitution of the foundation for the individual philanthropist, the growth of pension funds and mutual investment companies whose directors have extraordinary influence on the economy although they have no property—these are instances and products of bureaucratization. And those to whom this process gives the authority to make decisions are faced by special problems that do not affect the man who has to choose only between his own personal interests and what he takes to be the social interest. Such men have to choose between different obligations, all of which are legitimate and compelling. This is a structural feature of a bureaucratic age; and this is why the characteristic moral problem of such an age is the problem of the man who does not have the right to do what, as a lonely individual, he might think it right to do. It is the problem that made Stoics of so many of those other bureaucrats, the Romans.

Nor is Stoicism appropriate only to those who work inside bureaucracies. The first rule of Stoicism is to recognize that there are things that are in one's power and things that are not: it is an admirable maxim for those who have to stand and wait to be served by bureaucracy. For it is a form of organization that tends to deprive the public of some of its most effective instruments of control. In politics, for example, one may vote for a different party if one is dissatisfied. But that vote will have only an indirect influence on the individuals in the great departments and bureaus who, if they cannot make policy, can usually torpedo it.

The practical social conditions for responsible government, in short, have been enormously changed as a result of modern bureaucracy and science. Government has not become the private business of despots. In a thousand ways, furthermore, science and bureaucracy have made human action more responsible—more considered, more precisely governed by exact principles, more responsive to the problems not simply of tomorrow but of the day after tomorrow. Yet the structure of responsibility within which social decisions are made is somehow disjointed and ill defined.

What is it to speak, in social terms, of responsible government? In the final analysis, responsible government is accountable government. It is government by men who can be asked questions about what they are doing, and who have to respond satisfactorily to the questions they are asked. In seeking responsible government, therefore, it is necessary to have one's mind on more than the individuals who are making the decisions. Social arrangements have to exist which give eyes and teeth to the process of holding them accountable for what they do.

First of all, the major activities of the government in question —whether it is the government of the State, or a business, or a voluntary organization—have to be out in the open. Institutions for inquiry and publicity have to exist, and they cannot be subject to manipulation by those whose behavior is under examination. Second, those who make the decisions have to be visible and identifiable individuals. A great many others may contribute to these decisions. But responsibility for the decisions has to be specifically assigned and accepted, and there has to be a general understanding about where this responsibility lies.

Third, the men or groups who conduct the examination of the government in question have to be competent groups. They have to know the right questions to ask, and they also have to be able to tell a good answer from a bad one. Moreover, they must have sanctions at their disposal. They must have the power to punish or reward the decision-makers, and most important of all, they must be able to take their business elsewhere if they do not like the answers they receive.

Fourth, there must be effective communication between those who perform and those who judge the performance. On the one side, the standards of judgment employed by the critics must have some relation to the realities of the performers' tasks. On the other side, the government must be aware of the demands of its constituency and the critics who ask the questions must be reasonably representative of all sections of that constituency. The constituency of the board of directors of a large corporation, for example, is only in part its stockholders. It also includes the corporation's customers, its employees, and all the other individuals in the community who are affected by the smoke or traffic congestion or housing problems its activities create. The organization of a critical public so that it includes the genuine constituency of the decision-makers under surveillance is frequently a problem of organizing interests that are scattered and inarticulate and do not have effective sanctions at their command. It is in itself a major problem of democratic government.

These, in outline, are the social conditions for responsible government. They apply not only to the relationship of citizens to the State, but also to their relations with the myriad centers of private power whose decisions affect the shape of neighborhoods, the character of work and leisure, the communication of information, the distribution of the national wealth, the impact of our economy abroad, and the purposes for which our resources and energies are used. And to state these conditions is to suggest the

questions that should be raised in examining our existing structure of responsibility, and the directions in which we should look
if we wish to repair our current arrangements for holding our
rulers responsible.

Something can be done, to begin with, by reorganizing the
processes through which bureaucracies make their decisions. The
decision-makers can be made more visible by attacking tendencies within bureaucracies—like the excessive use of the committee
system—which dilute and hide individual responsibility. And
much can also be accomplished through techniques of administrative devolution and decentralization. It is easier to experiment
when the stakes are small, and it is easier to affect a policy when
an entire massive system does not have to be bucked. And the
devolution and decentralization of authority also make individuals more sharply aware of the implications of what they are
doing, and make it harder for them to shift responsibility to
others.

Indeed, a systematic effort to establish arrangements in every
domain that would require men far down the line to make decisions that would show where they stand would be a major
contribution to the strengthening of an ethic of personal responsibility. "Whenever the sphere of action of human beings is
artificially circumscribed," John Stuart Mill observed, "their sentiments are narrowed and dwarfed in the same proportion. The
food of feeling is action: even domestic affection lives upon voluntary good offices. Let a person have nothing to do for his country, and he will not care for it." The same maxim applies to social
units that are smaller. Bureaucracy is educational in its impact.
When it is so organized that it deprives the individual of the
chance to exercise his discretion, when it does not permit him to
be personally responsible for the consequences of what he does,
it trains him in irresponsibility.

But the greatest weaknesses in the existing structure of responsibility cannot be repaired by changing the internal organization
of bureaucracies. The accountability of decision-makers is hard
to assert and enforce for two principal reasons. The first is the
absence of alerted publics that know the questions to ask and

that can judge the answers they get. The second is the absence of effective sanctions in the hands of such publics.

EXEMPLARY PLANNING

To deal with these problems, the principle that defines a pluralistic society has to be grasped and extended. The existence of social alternatives, the struggle between antagonistic influences, is more than a condition for freedom. It is a condition for a responsible society, a society that makes its decisions in the light of purposes it has examined and consciously chosen. And in our existing social order, with its thrust towards standardization and its proliferating powers and techniques that seem to dictate our purposes to us, there has to be deliberate planning to provide alternatives. What we need, and do not have enough of, is the conscious canvassing of new possibilities and the concrete testing and demonstration of social ideas in deliberate action. We need to invigorate existing agencies and to create new ones whose function is to be the thorn in the side of existing bureaucracies— agencies that bear witness to what might be, that animate, enlarge, and discipline the public imagination. Such agencies could give the public a better chance to choose what it wants and, indeed, to discover what it wants.

The man who wants to build a house is at the mercy of his architect unless certain conditions are present. If he has a friend whose problem was much like his own, and if he likes the job his friend's architect did, he has a model which allows him to judge his own architect better. In practical matters we do not have to be experts in order to judge experts; we can base our judgment on the results of their work. But to judge the results intelligently, we need to be aware of other possibilities. And the better the alternative models we possess, the better judges we are likely to be. A public that can ask government officials the right questions about slum clearance or real-estate developers the right questions about suburban planning needs to have examples of different approaches at hand. It can begin to learn what it really likes only when it has had some education in what else is possible.

Moreover, it is only when a public can take its business else-where that it can exert the most effective kind of pressure on decision-making. The creation of compact cars by American auto-mobile manufacturers was undertaken largely as a result of rising competition from small foreign automobiles. Similarly, the his-tory of public universities in the United States is intelligible only if we understand the countervailing influences exerted by a well-developed system of private higher education; and the influence of public institutions on the private colleges and universities is equally noteworthy. It is not enough, indeed, that there be com-petition. The most stimulating competition is likely to come when the contestants are operating in contexts in which quite different considerations and pressures are present.

This is why a competitive economic system does not provide by itself a sufficient guarantee of useful social competition. The standard argument that such a system provides the public with an adequate choice between alternatives overlooks the standard-ized character of the competition that takes place. In major areas —as ·the amount of money spent on advertising suggests—the choices are largely factitious. Whether we think of mass-produced housing, or of the offerings of different broadcasting networks, or of popular priced cigarettes, the differences are superficial. For the basic context of operation is the same. To be sure, it is not very important that a different kind of competition in the manufacture, say, of whiskies be introduced. But it is a matter of the greatest importance for the quality of our experience in a democratic society that a different kind of competition be intro-duced where such issues as our work, play, or participation in the dialogue of an open society are concerned.

Unless agencies exist that bear witness to other possibilities, the publics to whom existing agencies are theoretically account-able are unlikely to ask the questions they might, and cannot take their business elsewhere even if they ask the questions and dislike the answers. The men who now make decisions—in com-munications, in urban and suburban development, in the auto-mation of plants or the organization of bureaucracies—are making social decisions. They make these decisions within a context in which technical and narrowly economic considerations predominate, and in which larger social costs and consequences (including economic costs and consequences) can be passed off for others to worry about. The character of such decisions could be highlighted and their implications dramatized if we joined to our competitive economic system a system of exemplary planning. This would be a system in which special social agencies were enabled and encouraged to venture into social experimentation and to project new models and standards of achievement.

The basis of such a system already exists. The task of exemplary planning belongs in the main to the many powerful organizations our society possesses that are free to act outside the pressures of the market place. The federal government is one of these agencies, but only one. It can engage in the task directly, as it did with the TVA. But a major part of its role lies in what it might do, through new provisions in the tax laws or through other devices, to enable other agencies to engage in the business of setting examples. Labor unions might experiment, for example, by establishing their own pilot plants in which new ideas for the organization of work routines and the government of the work community could be tested. The philanthropic foundation could venture into the field of mass communications. Universities could lead the way in the development of educational television, and in new ventures in neighborhood planning and in continuing education for adults. The American land-grant college was the organizing and inspiriting center in the successful development of the American countryside. A similar role in the reorganization of our cities awaits the urban universities that are willing to engage in affirmative experiments in community planning.

But this is not the place to multiply such specific suggestions. Much of what has been suggested is already going on. The point is to see the point, to catch the ideal that these practices prefigure and to do on principle what is now done by accident or necessity. For there are special reasons, reasons peculiar to our position in history, why we cannot leave the exploration of alternative social policies to mere chance. As Robert Heilbroner has observed, "The price of an economy of abundance is the replacement of the traditional economic control mechanism with new kinds of social controls. The central problem of the new society will be to find means of assuring its own discipline in place of the disappearing force of economic pressure." The discriminating use of our powers and wealth requires a systematic program of social education —a program of social experimentation, that is to say, which would embody and dramatize alternative uses to which we might put our powers and wealth.

For science and technology do not merely satisfy existing needs. They have become what Shelley thought poetry was—the unacknowledged legislators of the race. For they create new needs and demands, remaking "human nature" as they go. Nobody missed a telephone, after all, until it was invented, and the desire to live in Utopia Heights could not arise until Henry Ford produced a cheap automobile. And science and technology are not only remaking our desires. They are also removing the grim imperatives of scarcity which once served to regulate society's allocation of its resources. In the past a great price was paid in unheeded moral and social consequences in order to allow technology and economic progress to do their work of eliminating scarcity. We have now grown too rich to afford this luxury. The clearest tests by which men in the past were able to measure the usefulness of what they were doing are no longer available to us. We need new tests, not simply the negative test of unmet needs, but positive tests which will help us to determine what we should desire and what purposes we should adopt.

The theologians make a distinction between the morality appropriate to a state of sin and the morality appropriate to a state of grace. There are rules that men should follow when they are struggling against evil and temptation. But they need other guides when their task is to make the most out of a state of grace. Something like a shift from sin to grace has happened to American democratic society. For all the ills that are still with us, the easily dramatizable conflicts, the clear moral confrontations, have for the most part receded. It is a new situation in the history of liberal reform and, indeed, in the history of politics. The problem of liberal reform has become that of dramatizing, for an increasingly comfortable people, the existence of problems that are not immediately visible and which it takes an exercise of imagination to recognize. It is the problem of projecting an animating vision of what such a people might do. Our present malaise reflects our feeling that we are becalmed, that we are surrounded by possibilities we have not managed to define or seize. The reiteration of old truisms about democracy will not remove this malaise, and neither will new ideas so long as they remain abstractions. The visible rehearsal of these ideas is also necessary.

Something else, finally, is also desirable. It is the engendering of an open debate about social priorities. The relative distribution of our wealth and energies—in a defense establishment, in consumers' goods, in advertising, in education, in scientific research, in relieving the desperate scarcities beyond the American shores —has been affected by political decisions at every turn. But the debate on social priorities is still half suppressed. It has not been raised to the level of a debate on principles. The occurrence of such a debate would do more than anything else to restore the conviction that we are living in a society that is consciously choosing the direction in which it wishes to move.

A monolithic ideology can give a society standards and a sense of purpose. It does so at the price of declaring these standards infallible and of foreclosing the choices the society will make. A democratic society cannot provide either such comforts or such illusions. It exists to recognize that men may change their minds and shift their values. But then its problem is to provide the conditions that will give men the chance for disciplined change, for change that is guided by a discriminate examination of ends and goals. In a modern democracy it is not a preordained and fixed design, and not even an abstract statement of national goals on which everyone agrees, that can give men a sense of purpose. It is the active exploration of purposes, the practical demonstration of ideas. To maintain and extend the conditions for such a process is to build a responsible society.

IX

EPILOGUE: WHY CHOOSE DEMOCRACY?

We have been overexposed to ideologies and political abstractions in this century, and have seen how much men are willing to sacrifice for the sake of ideological certainty. It is not surprising that sensitive men have developed something close to an ideology of uncertainty, and should look with a jaundiced eye on all questions about the justification of political systems. Why choose democracy? Trained in a hard school that has taught us the perils of belief, can we say anything more than that fanaticism is odious and that democracy should be chosen because it asks us to believe in very little?

On the contrary, it asks us to believe in a great deal. I do not believe we can show that the inside truth about the universe, human history, or the human psyche commands us to adopt democratic ideals. Choosing a political ideal is not like demonstrating the truth of a theorem in some geometry, and those who think that democracy needs that kind of justification are indirectly responsible for the uncertainty about it. Despite the semantic inflation from which the current discussion of political ideals suffers, the reasons for choosing democracy are neither mysterious nor difficult. But they are unsettling reasons, and they ask those who accept them to bet a great deal on their capacity to live with what they have chosen.

166

THE SIGNIFICANCE OF THE DEMOCRATIC POLITICAL METHOD

In an area so full of grandiose claims, it is safest to begin by using the word "democracy" in its narrowest sense. So conceived, democracy is the method of choosing a government through competitive elections in which people who are not members of the governing groups participate. Whatever may be said for or against democracy so conceived, it is surely not a supreme ideal of life. It is doubtful that anyone has ever treated the right to cast a ballot once every year or so as an end in itself. A society in which the democratic political method has been consolidated, to be sure, has a tremendous source of reassurance. It possesses a peaceful method for determining who shall hold power and for effecting changes in the structure of power. Yet even peace is only one value among others. It is worth something to have security and order, but how much it is worth depends on the kind of security and order it is. The importance of the democratic political method lies mainly in its nonpolitical by-products. It is important because a society in which it is well established will probably be different in at least four respects—in the conditions that protect its liberties, in the kind of consensus that prevails, in the character of the conflicts that go on within it, and in the manner in which it educates its rulers and citizens.

First, liberties. Construed strictly as a method for choosing governments, democracy does not guarantee the citizen's personal liberties. Democratic governments have attacked personal liberties, as in colonial New England, and undemocratic governments have often protected them, as in Vienna before World War I. Yet competitive elections have their points, and it is only one of their points that they allow a society to choose its government. For in order to maintain competitive elections, it is necessary to have an opposition, the opposition must have some independent rights and powers of its own, the good opinion of some people outside government must be sought, and at least some members of the society must have protections against the vengefulness of the powers that be. And this carries a whole train of institutions behind it—courts, a press not wholly devoted to promoting the interests of those in power, and independent agencies for social inquiry and criticism.

It is these necessitating conditions for elections that give elections their long-range significance. So far as political democracy is concerned, these conditions are only means to ends: they make competitive elections possible. But it is because a system of competitive elections requires and fosters such conditions that it justifies itself. The conditions required for maintaining an honest electoral system are the best reasons for wishing to maintain it. Indeed, a man might value such a system even though he thought all elections frivolous and foolish. He would have as good a reason to do so, and perhaps a better reason, than the man who always finds himself voting happily for the winning side. The outsider and the loser are the peculiar beneficiaries of a political system that creates institutions with a vested interest in liberty.

The democratic political method, furthermore, helps to foster a different kind of social consensus. There have been many kinds of political arrangement that have allowed men to feel that the government under which they live is *their* government. There is no clear evidence that democracy is necessarily superior to other systems in promoting a sense of oneness between rulers and ruled. But the special virtue of a democratic political system is that it permits men to feel at home within it who do not regard their political leaders as their own kind, and who would lose their self-respect, indeed, if they gave their unprovisional loyalty to any human institution. Despite all that is said about democratic pressures towards conformity—and a little of what is said is true—the democratic political system ceremonializes the fact of disagreement and the virtue of independent judgment. If it is to work, it requires an extraordinarily sophisticated human attitude—loyal opposition. The mark of a civilized man, in Justice Holmes' famous maxim, is that he can act with conviction while questioning his first principles. The ultimate claim of a democratic government to authority is that it permits dissent and survives it. In this respect, it dwells on the same moral landscape as the civilized man.

The democratic political method also changes the character of the conflicts that take place in a society. The perennial problem of politics is to manage conflict. And what happens in a conflict depends in part on who the onlookers are, how they react, and what powers they have. A significant fact about political democracy is that it immensely expands the audience that looks on and that feels itself affected and involved. This is why democratic citizens so often find democracy tiring and feel that their societies are peculiarly fragile. Hobbes, who said that he and fear were born as twins, recommended despotism in the interests of psychological security as well as physical safety.

But to say that democracy expands the scope of a conflict is also to say that democracy is a technique for the socialization of conflict. It brings a wider variety of pressures to bear on those who are quarreling and extends public control over private fights and private arrangements. And it does so whether these private fights are inside the government or outside. The association of democracy with the conception of private enterprise has something paradoxical about it. In one sense, there is more important enterprise that is private—free from outside discussion and surveillance —in totalitarian systems than in democratic systems. The persistent problem in a democratic system, indeed, is to know where to draw the line, where to say that outside surveillance is out of place. That line is drawn very firmly by those who make the important decisions in totalitarian societies.

But the final contribution that the democratic political method makes to the character of the society in which it is practiced is its contribution to education. Begin with the impact of political democracy on its leaders. The democratic method, like any other political method, is a system of rules for governing political competition. And such rules have both a selective and an educational force. They favor certain kinds of men, and make certain kinds of virtue more profitable and certain kinds of vice more possible. From this point of view, the significant characteristic of democratic rules of competition is that the loser is allowed to lose with honor, and permitted to live and try again if he wants. The stakes are heavy but limited. Such a system of competition gives men with sporting moral instincts a somewhat better chance to succeed. Even its typical kind of corruption has something to be said in its favor. The greased palm is bad but it is preferable to the mailed fist.

The democratic political method, furthermore, rests on methods of mutual consultation between leaders and followers. There are various ways in which support for the policies of political leaders is obtained in a democracy, but one of the most important is that of giving men the sense that they have been asked for their opinions and that their views have been taken into account. This makes leadership in a democracy a nerve-racking affair. One of the great dangers in a democratic political system, in fact, is simply that leaders will not have the privacy and quiet necessary for serene long-range decisions. But this is the defect of a virtue. In general, power insulates. The democratic system is a calculated effort to break in on such insulation. The conditions under which democratic leaders hold power are conditions for educating them in the complexity and subtlety of the problems for which they are responsible.

And the coin has its other side. "We Athenians," said Pericles, "are able to judge policy even if we cannot originate it, and instead of looking on discussion as a stumbling-block in the way of action, we think it an indispensable preliminary to any wise action at all." But the fruits of free discussion do not show themselves only in public policy. They show themselves in the attitudes and capacities of the discussants. Democratic political arrangements are among the factors that have produced one of the painful and more promising characteristics of modern existence—men's sense that their education is inadequate, men's assertion that they have a right to be educated. And democratic politics help to promote a classic conception of education—it must be social as well as technical, general as well as special, free and not doctrinaire. We can reverse the classic conception of the relation of education to democracy and not be any further from the truth: education is not simply a prerequisite for democracy; democracy is a contribution to education.

USES OF DEMOCRACY

But enough of political systems. In any liberal view of men's business, politics is a subordinate enterprise. It has its soul-testing challenges and pleasures, and its great work to do. But like the work of commerce and industry, the work of politics is essentially servile labor. The State is not the place to turn if you want a free commentary on human experience, and governments do not produce science, philosophy, music, literature, or children—or at any rate they do not produce very convincing specimens of any of these things. Politics may achieve its own forms of excellence, but the more important human excellences are achieved elsewhere. And it is from this point of view, I think, that democracy should in the end be considered.

For the democratic idea is based on the assumption that the important ends of life are defined by private individuals in their own voluntary pursuits. Politics, for liberal democracy, is only one aspect of a civilization, a condition for civilization but not its total environment. That is probably why the air seems lighter as one travels from controlled societies to free ones. One receives an impression of vitality, the vitality of people who are going about their own business and generating their own momentum. They may be going off in more different directions than the members of a centrally organized society, but the directions are their own. The best reasons for choosing democracy lie in the qualities it is capable of bringing to our daily lives, in the ways in which it can furnish our minds, imaginations, and consciences. These qualities, I would say, are freedom, variety, self-consciousness, and the democratic attitude itself.

That democracy is hostile to distinction and prefers mediocrity is not a recent view. And there is an obvious sense in which it is true that democracy makes for homogeneity. Democracy erodes the clear distinctions between classes. It destroys ready-made status-symbols so rapidly that the manufacture of new ones becomes the occupation of a major industry. Most obvious of all, democracy increases the demand for a great many good things, from shoes to education. By increasing the demand, it also puts itself under pressure to cheapen the supply.

Yet certain pertinent facts must be set against these tendencies. First, more good things *are* more generally available in democracies. Second, egalitarianism's twin is the morality of achievement. There is a tension between the democratic suspicion of the man who sets himself apart and the democratic admiration for the man who stands out, but the egalitarian hostility towards osten-

tatious social distinctions is normally rooted in the belief that
each man should be given a chance on his own to show what he
can do. And finally, pressures towards uniformity are great in all
societies. Is suspicion of the eccentric in egalitarian metropolitan
America greater than in an eighteenth-century village? It is difficult to think so. "The fallacy of the aristocrat," Bertrand Russell
has remarked, "consists in judging a society by the kind of life
it affords a privileged few." Standing alone takes courage anywhere. Usually it also takes money; almost invariably it requires
the guarantee that the individual will still retain his basic rights.
In these respects modern liberal democracy, despite all the complaints about conformity, has made it easier for the ordinary un-
privileged man to stand alone, if he has the will to do so, than
any other kind of society known in history.

For however ambiguous some of the facts may be, the official
commitment of liberal democracy is to the view that each man
has his idiosyncrasies, that these idiosyncrasies deserve respect,
and that if the individual does not know what is good for him,
it is highly unlikely that a self-perpetuating elite will know better.
And this is not just an official commitment. The institutions of
liberal democracy go very far in giving it concrete embodiment.
Assuming that the members of a democratic society have minimal
economic securities, there is a flexibility in their situation which
not many ordinary men have enjoyed in the past. If they fall out
of favor with one set of authorities, they have a chance to turn
around and look elsewhere.

It is unquestionable that there are great constellations of concentrated power in contemporary democratic societies; it is
equally unquestionable that there is some freedom in any society.
For in dealing with power, bright men learn how to work the
angles. But in a democratic society there are more angles to
work. Individual freedom of choice is not an absolute value. Any
society must limit it; indeed, one man's freedom often rests on
restricting the next man's. But while freedom of choice is not an
absolute value, the democratic doctrine that each man has certain fundamental rights assigns an intrinsic value to his freedom
of choice. If it has to be limited, it is recognized that something
of value has been sacrificed. Social planning in a democracy is

for this reason fundamentally different from social planning in undemocratic environments. The vague phrase "social utility," in a democratic setting, implicitly includes as one of its elements the value of freedom of choice.

What difference does this make? One difference is that variety is promoted; a second is that individuals are educated in self-consciousness. Needless to say, variety, too, has its limits. We do not have to protect dope peddlers in its name. But the full import of variety, of the mere existence of differences and alternatives, is frequently overlooked. It does not merely give us more choices, or offer us a break in the routine. It affects the immediate quality of our experience; it changes our relation to whatever it is that we choose to have or do or be. This is what is forgotten when freedom is defined simply as the absence of felt frustrations, or when it is said that if a man has just what he wants, it makes little difference whether he has any choice or not. A good that is voluntarily chosen, a good which a man is always free to reconsider, belongs to him in a way that a passively accepted good does not. It is his responsibility.

And this means that democratic variety has another use as well. No one can say with assurance that democracy makes people wiser or more virtuous. But political democracy invites men to think that there may be alternatives to the way they are governed. And social democracy, in reducing the barriers of class, caste, and inherited privilege that stand between men, adds to the variety of people and occasions the individual meets and puts greater pressure on his capacity to adapt to the new and different. Political democracy and a socially mobile society thus invite the individual to a greater degree of consciousness about the relativity of his own ways and a greater degree of self-consciousness in the choice of the standards by which he lives. These are conditions for intensified personal experience. The role of democracy in the extension of these attitudes represents one of its principal contributions to the progress of liberal civilization.

The extension of such attitudes, to be sure, has its risks, which explains much of our uneasiness about what the democratic revolution means. Fads and fashions engage and distract larger groups in modern democratic societies. And social mobility,

though it gives breadth and variety to men's experience, may
well foreshorten their sense of time. Cut loose from fixed ranks
and stations, each with its legends, rationale, and sense of historic
vocation, the citizens of a modern democracy face a peculiar
temptation to live experimentally, with the help of the latest
book, as though no one had ever lived before. But these are the
risks not simply of democracy but of modernity, and they can be
controlled. The courts, the organized professions, the churches,
and the universities are storehouses of funded experience. In a
society in which they are given independence from the political
urgencies of the moment, they can serve as protections against
the dictatorship of the specious present. Modernity implies a revolution in human consciousness. Democratic social arrangements
reflect that revolution and accept it; but they also provide instruments for guiding and controlling it. None of democracy's contemporary rivals possess these two qualities to the same extent.

In the end, indeed, the risks of democracy are simply the risks
implicit in suggesting to men that the answers are not all in. Democracy gives political form to the principle that also regulates
the scientific community—the principle that inquiry must be kept
open, that there are no sacred books, that no conclusion that men
have ever reached can be taken to be the necessary final word.
Cant, obscurantism, and lies are of course a good part of the diet
of most democracies. Man is a truth-fearing animal, and it would
be a miracle if any social system could quickly change this fact.
But the institutions of liberal democracy are unique in that they
require men to hold no irreversible beliefs in anything except in
the method of free criticism and peaceful change itself, and in
the ethic on which this method rests. Such a social system permits
men to give their highest loyalty, not to temporary human beliefs
or institutions, but to the continuing pursuit after the truth, whatever it may be. The intellectual rationale of democracy is precisely that it does not need to make the foolish and arrogant
claim that it rests on infallible truths. Men can believe in it and
still believe that the truth is larger than anything they may think
they know.

Yet the question that probably gnaws at us most deeply still
remains. Freedom, variety, self-consciousness, a sane awareness

of human fallibility, and loyalty to the principle that inquiry must be kept open—obviously, these have much in their favor. But they are refined values. Has liberal democracy priced itself out of the competition? Does it have anything to say, not to those who already know and enjoy it, but to the many more who must come to want it if human liberties are to be a little more secure in the world than they now are?

One of the debilitating illusions of many Western liberals is that the values of liberal culture are only our own values, that they have little point for those who look at the world differently, and no point at all for those whose lives are poor, mean, brutish, and short. Although colonialists used this view for different purposes, they shared it, and it betrays an inexact understanding of the nature of liberal values. Freedom, variety, self-consciousness, and the chance to seek the truth are all taxing experiences. Their virtues may be hard to conceive by those who have never enjoyed them. Yet in spite of the discomforts these values bring, the evidence indicates, I think, that most men would be happy to have them, and would think their lives enhanced. The difficulty with the most characteristic liberal values is not that they are parochial values. The difficulty is that men have other more imperious wants, like the need for medicines, schooling, bread, release from usurers, or a chance to get out from under corrupt and exploitative regimes. Illiberal programs promise these substantial material improvements and frequently deliver. And liberal programs, if they speak of freedom and leave out the usury and corruption, do not generally bring freedom either.

But let us assume, as there is every reason to assume, that liberal programs, if they are willing to recognize that they, too, must make a revolution, can also improve men's material condition. What can be said to the young man or the young—or old—nation in a hurry? What good reasons can we give, reasons that take account of their present condition and justified impatience, when we try to explain to them—and to ourselves—why the liberal path, despite its meanderings, is preferable to the authoritarian path?

One thing that can be said, quite simply, is that the authoritarian path closes up behind the traveler as he moves. The virtue of liberal democracy is that it permits second thoughts. To choose an authoritarian regime is to bet everything on a single throw of the dice; if the bet is bad, there is no way out save through violence, and not much hope in that direction. To choose a liberal approach, while it does not guarantee against errors, guarantees against the error so fatal that there is no peaceful way out or back. But there is another reason as well. The reason for choosing democracy is that it makes democrats.

Imagine a regime wholly committed to the welfare of those it rules. Imagine, against all the practical difficulties, that it is intelligent, honest, courageous, and that it does not have to enter into any deals with any of the international blocs that dominate the modern scene. And imagine, too, that this regime aims, in the end, to bring democracy and liberal values to the country it rules. But assume only that it claims, for the present, to be the one true spokesman for the public interest, the only group in the society that knows what truth and justice mean. What is the consequence? The consequence is that a democratic attitude is impossible. That attitude has been described in various ways—as a love for liberty, equality, and fraternity, as respect for the dignity of the individual, as a consistent regard for individual rights. The descriptions are not wrong, but they overintellectualize the attitude. At bottom, the democratic attitude is simply an attitude of good faith plus a working belief in the probable rationality of others. And that is what political authoritarianism destroys. Once a society is governed by the doctrine that some one group monopolizes all wisdom, it is divided into the Enlightened and the Unenlightened, and the Enlightened determine who shall be accorded membership in the club. In a modern State this makes almost impossible the growth of that mutual trust between opposing groups which is a fundamental condition for the growth of a strong political community that is also free.

The competition that takes place in a democracy is an instance of cooperative competition. It is a struggle in which both sides work to maintain the conditions necessary for a decent struggle. Accordingly, it rests on the assumption that there are no irreconcilable conflicts, that differences can be negotiated or compromised, if men have good will. Such a system requires men to deal with one another honestly, to make a serious effort to reach agreements, and to keep them after they have been made. It requires them to recognize, therefore, that the other side has its interests and to be prepared to make concessions to these interests when such concessions are not inconsistent with fundamental principles. A democratic ethic does not ask men to be fools. They do not have to assume that their opponents have put all their cards on the table. But democratic competition is impossible if the parties to the competition cannot assume that their opponents will recognize their victory if they win and will cooperate with them afterwards. The intention to annihilate the opposition or to win at all costs destroys the possibility of a regulated struggle. In this sense democracy is an exercise in the ethic of good faith. It is a system that makes it possible for men, not to love their enemies, but at least to live without fearing them. That kind of mutual trust between enemies is what authoritarianism destroys.

No doubt, such an argument may seem pathetically beside the point to men who live in societies that have been torn by distrust for centuries and that have known government only as a name for cruelty and dishonesty. If such men succeed in installing democratic regimes in their countries, they will do so by recognizing their enemies and distrusting them. But the harshness that goes with any deep social revolution is one thing if it is recognized as a bitter and dangerous necessity and is kept within limits. It is another if the violence is doctrinal, and the assumption is made that men can never cooperate unless they have the same interests and ideas. Such an assumption, as all the evidence suggests, encourages the adoption of terror as an official policy and condemns a society to an indefinite period in which power will be monopolistically controlled. In a diversified modern society, indeed in any society that has even begun the movement towards modernity, the doctrine of governmental infallibility trains men in suspiciousness and conspiracy. Perhaps other objectives will be achieved, but under such circumstances their taste will be sour.

Nor does the doctrine of infallibility destroy only good faith. It is also incompatible with a belief in the probable rationality of others. To hold a democratic attitude is to proceed on the as-

sumption that other men may have their own persuasive reasons
for thinking as they do. If they disagree with you, this does not
necessarily make them candidates for correction and cure. This
is the homely meaning of the oft-repeated assertion that democracy has faith in the reasonableness and equality of human beings. The faith does not assert that all men are in fact reasonable,
or that they are equal in the capacity to think well or live sensibly. The faith is pragmatic: it expresses a policy. And the policy
is simply to credit others with minds of their own, and to hold
them responsible for their actions, until there are strong and quite
specific reasons for thinking otherwise. Such a policy allows room
for the idiosyncrasies of men and permits the varieties of human
intelligence to be recognized and used.

In the end, the man who asks himself why he should choose
democracy is asking himself to decide with which of two policies
he would rather live. One is the policy of normally thinking that
his fellows are dangerous to him and to themselves. The other is
the policy of thinking that they are reasonable until they show
themselves dangerous. To act on either policy has its risks. Why
should a man choose one rather than the other? One reason can
be found if he asks himself about the consequences the policy
he adopts will have for the elementary feelings he will entertain
towards his fellows, not in some transfigured world to come, but
here and now. The point of the democratic policy is that it makes
for democratic feelings. Those who do not wish to see human
society divided into exploiters and exploited, those who wish to
see each man come into his own free estate, believe that in that
ultimate condition men will treat each other with the respect and
fellow-feeling that equals show to equals. It is in the name of
such moral attitudes that they seek democracy. The final reason
for choosing the democratic method is that it provides a training
ground, here and now, in just these attitudes.

THE DEMOCRATIC PROSPECT

But arguments have their limits. It is not through disputation
that men become convinced of the worth of a social system. It is
through its capacity to exemplify a vision of human possibility
and to move towards that vision. In the past the United States

was a contagion. Its distinction, the quality that set it apart, was that it was a society moved by its prospect. The sense that American democracy has a prospect—that its future does not consist simply in rolling with the punches of its adversaries or in expanding its present sort of affluence still further—is most obviously absent from the present scene.

More than arguments about the advantages of democracy in comparison with other systems is required to restore that sense. At the end of his great book, Tocqueville wrote: "Let us, then, look forward to the future with that salutary fear which makes men keep watch and ward for freedom, not with that faint and idle terror which depresses and enervates the heart." The faint and idle terrors that depress and enervate us today are in part self-induced: they are not justified by a circumspect estimate of the resources of American democracy. But neither can such an estimate explain our spotty and undiscriminating affluence, or the bewilderment, scorn, and violence that lie a millimeter below the surface in the slums of our deteriorating cities, or the advancing bulldozed ugliness of our countryside, or the present condition of the public welfare, voluntary associations, the media of communication, and our work and play.

Like any social system, democracy must give men something in which to believe. They have to discern in what they are doing the intimation of a civic order that has beauty and design. That end cannot be accomplished by the currently fashionable technique of filling the air with words and filling words with air. Not even courage, good will, intelligence, and resolute action are enough. The action has to add up to a scheme of action; it has to be action lit by purposes that are visible, concrete, coherent, and deliberately chosen.

For in the modern world it is motion with a meaning, change in an identifiable and desired direction, which is the basic generator of belief in a social system. And the point about democracy, the point to it, is that it rests on the assumption that men have some choice about that direction, that it is not given to them or prearranged for them, but that, within limits, they can define it for themselves. When they do, when they use the chance for choice that makes democratic arrangements precious, the question "Why choose democracy?" becomes redundant.

ACKNOWLEDGMENTS

The public acknowledgment of private debts may well be more embarrassing to the creditors than to the debtor. Those who have helped me in the writing of this book, I hasten to say, have no responsibility for what it contains. But I cannot forgo the pleasure of thanking them just the same.

During most of the period in which this book was written, I have also been collaborating on a variety of projects with Pendleton Herring and James Perkins. For an even longer number of years, my colleague Ernest Nagel has stimulated me with his ideas and helped me to clarify my own. And by giving me his ear he has also helped me to continue to think that it is not entirely inappropriate for a contemporary philosopher to interest himself in some of the substantive problems in the world around him. I am in the debt of these men for ideas I have shamelessly stolen from them, and for the support and pleasure of comradeship with them.

I have gained a great deal as well from association with many colleagues at Columbia. To name only a few is invidious, but I cannot forbear mentioning John Cooley, James Gutmann, Albert Hofstadter, Alfred Kahn, Sidney Morgenbesser, and Meyer Schapiro. Paul Lazarsfeld, Robert Merton, and Richard Neustadt have also taught me more than they know. Others outside Columbia who have helped me by listening tolerantly and talking back firmly include John Fischer, John Gardner, August Heckscher, and John Honey. Cass Canfield, Jr., Roger Klein, and Evan Thomas, of Harper & Row, have also given me encouragement and valuable advice.

My greatest debt, however, is once more to my family. My daughter and son have adjusted themselves uncomplainingly to the tendency of their father to disappear into a brown study, and my wife's editorial assistance has come close to complicity in the crime. The combination of patience and impatience with which she has read the successive drafts through which the manuscript has gone is testimony to her staying powers and the principal cause of my own. The dedication of this book to her bespeaks this debt, and others as well.

In 1959–60 the Carnegie Corporation of New York granted me a Reflective Year Fellowship, which permitted me to take up concentrated work on this book. I am extremely grateful for this encouragement and assistance, and for the understanding and imagination displayed by the officers of the Carnegie Corporation in the administration of this grant. I am also grateful to my University, Columbia, for its cooperation in giving me a special leave of absence so that I could accept the fellowship.

Early in the winter of 1959–60, shortly after I had begun the writing of this book, the Special Studies Project of the Rockefeller Brothers Fund asked me to serve as the principal author of the final study in the series of Rockefeller Panel Reports on American democracy. This study was published under the title *The Power of the Democratic Idea*, and was subsequently included in the volume *Prospect for America*. Since a writer cannot cut himself in half, there are some occasional similarities between sentences in *The Power of the Democratic Idea* and sentences in this book, particularly in the earlier chapters. The similarities, however, are very occasional, and, in any case, they are more apparent than real. The Rockefeller Panel Report represented the consensus of a group of citizens of differing social and political views, and the ideas it contained were not pointed towards the problems examined in this book. What I say in this book is wholly individual, and I take note of the one or two duplications that exist only to absolve the members of the Rockefeller Panel from any connection with its contents.

Thanks are due to the following publishers for permission to quote from books issued under their imprint: The Free Press; Random House; Houghton Mifflin Company; McGraw-Hill Book Company; George Allen & Unwin; Penguin Books, Ltd.; Harper & Row; The Beacon Press; Harvard University Press; Columbia University Press; The Macmillan Company; Longmans, Green Ltd.; Alfred A. Knopf; The University of Chicago Press; Little, Brown and Company. An earlier draft of Chapter VII was delivered as a public lecture at the University of Buffalo and subsequently published by its School of Social Work. Chapter VIII borrows here and there from a paper read to the Public Affairs Seminar of the Brookings Institution. Two or three paragraphs lean on an address delivered to the National Conference on Social Welfare in 1961, and published in *The Social Welfare Forum*, 1961.

                                                                    C. F.

NOTES

CHAPTER I: THE POLITICS OF MALAISE

p. 6: ". . . respected and influential observers . . . have reinforced this new self-image."

The well-known American books which have contributed to the belief in mass society include David Riesman's *The Lonely Crowd;* W. H. Whyte's *The Organization Man;* Walter Lippmann's *The Public Philosophy,* and, earlier, his *Public Opinion;* C. Wright Mills' *White Collar* and *The Power Elite;* Joseph Wood Krutch's *Man the Measure;* and Erich Fromm's *Escape from Freedom* and *The Sane Society.* An especially ambitious and learned statement is Hannah Arendt's *The Human Condition,* Chicago: University of Chicago Press, 1958. For critical examinations of mass-society theories, see Daniel Bell, *The End of Ideology,* Glencoe: The Free Press, 1960, and William Kornhauser, *The Politics of Mass Society,* Glencoe: The Free Press, 1959. Seymour M. Lipset's essay, "Trends in American Society," in Lyman Bryson, ed., *An Outline of Man's Knowledge of the Modern World,* New York: McGraw-Hill Book Co., 1960, is a lucid brief statement of some skeptical doubts.

p. 6: ". . . Mollie Panter-Downes reported . . ."
The New Yorker, May 28, 1960, p. 103.

p. 6: ". . . the fear that . . . in this century only the simulacrum . . . of freedom is likely to be retained . . ."

A representative and reasonably tempered statement is E. H. Carr's: "Mass democracy is a new phenomenon—a creation of the last half-century—which it is inappropriate and misleading to consider in terms of the philosophy of Locke or of the liberal democracy of the

183

nineteenth century. . . . To speak today of the defence of democracy as if we were defending something which we knew and had possessed for many decades or many centuries is self-deception and sham." (*The New Society*, Boston: Beacon Press, 1957, pp. 75–6.)

p. 7: Quotations from Tocqueville.
Democracy in America, edited by Phillips Bradley, New York: Alfred A. Knopf, 1945, Vol. II, p. 319.

CHAPTER II: THE NATURAL HISTORY OF DEMOCRACY

Among the books which have provided general illumination in the writing of this chapter and of Chapter III are the following: Gabriel Almond and James Coleman, eds., *The Politics of the Developing Areas*, Princeton: Princeton University Press, 1960; Robert A. Dahl, *A Preface to Democratic Theory*, Chicago: University of Chicago Press, 1956; Pendleton Herring, *The Politics of Democracy*, New York: Rinehart & Co., 1940; Daniel Lerner, *The Passing of Traditional Society*, Glencoe: The Free Press, 1958; Seymour M. Lipset, *Political Man*, Garden City: Doubleday & Co., 1960; David M. Potter, *People of Plenty*, Chicago: University of Chicago Press, 1954; Joseph A. Schumpeter, *Capitalism, Socialism, and Democracy*, New York: Harper & Brothers, 1950; David Truman, *The Governmental Process*, New York: Alfred A. Knopf, 1951; and John Plamenatz's essay in *Democracy in a World of Tensions*, edited by Richard McKeon, Chicago: University of Chicago Press, 1951.

p. 11: "Politics . . . is an indicator of disequilibrium . . ."
Alexander Leighton's book on the wartime relocation center for Japanese and Japanese-Americans at Poston, Arizona, is an excellent case study in the breakdown of settled expectations and the emergence of new instruments of government in compensation. (*The Governing of Men*, Princeton: Princeton University Press, 1945.)

p. 13: ". . . government is constantly engaged in a struggle for men's allegiance . . ."
Arthur Bentley's *The Process of Government* is probably the classic statement of this thesis.

p. 15: "In America, Tocqueville reported, . . . you meet a politician where you expected to meet a priest."
Democracy in America, Vol. I, pp. 305–7.

p. 15: Quotation from Keynes.

General Theory, p. 150. Quoted by W. W. Rostow, *The Stages of Economic Growth*, Cambridge: Cambridge University Press, 1960, p. 3.

p. 16: "The censors of the city of Geneva condemned Rousseau's Social Contract . . ."

Conclusions de M. le procureur général Henri-Robert Tronchin . . . , in E. Dreyfus-Brisac, ed., *Du Contrat Social*, Paris, 1896, appendix XI, p. 422.

p. 17: Reference to the Turkish shepherd.

See David Riesman's introduction to Lerner's *The Passing of Traditional Society*, and also chapters I and II.

p. 17: "A modern society . . . is an experiment in dissatisfaction . . ."

But while this explains the nostalgia of many sophisticated moderns for a simpler age, it does not justify that nostalgia. Lerner, for example, has this to say about those undergoing modernization: "A deep problem of values is imbedded in the life-histories of these men-in-motion. The moral issues of modernization often are reduced to this: *Should* they want what they want? . . . Western responses to this question usually reflect only our own value-dilemmas. Rather more relevant is the judgment of Middle Easterners on what they have and what they want. . . . A very powerful finding of our study is that Middle Easterners who are modernizing consider themselves happier than do those who remain within traditional lifeways. This is in striking contrast with the impressions conveyed by some observers, often from highly modern settings themselves, who feel that the undermining of traditional ways by new desires must be a net loss. Among such observers the passing of cherished images of passive peasantry, noble nomads, brave Beduin evokes regrets. But these regrets are not felt by the modernizing peasants, nomads, Beduin themselves, or felt less disapprovingly by them than by the moderns who study them and love the familiar way they used to be." (*The Passing of Traditional Society*, pp. 73–4.)

p. 17: "Modernity . . . has its inherent dilemmas."

In Joseph Conrad's *The Nigger of the Narcissus*, the crew of the *Narcissus* is subverted by the arrival of Donkin, a modern man. "Our little world went on its curved and unswerving path carrying a discontented and aspiring population. They found comfort of a gloomy kind in an interminable and conscientious analysis of their unappreciated worth; and inspired by Donkin's hopeful doctrines they dreamed enthusiastically of the time when every lonely ship would travel over a serene sea, manned by a wealthy and well-fed crew of satisfied skippers."

p. 18: ". . . modernity . . . can produce a . . . tension between means and ends."

Robert Merton's discussion of "anomie" emphasizes this issue. "The culture may be such as to lead individuals to center their emotional convictions about the complex of culturally acclaimed ends, with far less emotional support for prescribed methods of reaching out for these ends. With such differential emphases upon goals and institutional procedures, the latter may be so vitiated by the stress on goals as to have the behavior of many individuals limited only by considerations of technical expediency. . . . As this process of attenuation continues, the society becomes unstable and there develops what Durkheim called 'anomie' (or normlessness). . . . Contemporary American culture appears to approximate the polar type in which great emphasis upon certain success-goals occurs without equivalent emphasis upon institutional means." (Robert K. Merton, *Social Theory and Social Structure*, Glencoe: The Free Press, 1949, pp. 128–9.)

p. 19: "Economic abundance is . . . a general condition for democratic stability."

This theme is extensively explored by David Potter in his *People of Plenty*. Potter stresses, among other points, the effects of poverty and of basic physical conditions—such as the number of people who must share a room—on methods of child-rearing, the formation of personality, and the development of the psychological attitudes necessary to make democratic processes of mutual accommodation work. Another study of the same theme is Seymour M. Lipset's chapter, "Working-Class Authoritarianism," in his *Political Man*. Oscar Lewis's *The Children of Sánchez*, New York: Random House, 1961, provides a case study in depth of the culture of poverty.

p. 20: "As Walter Bagehot pointed out . . ."

In his *The English Constitution*.

p. 20: ". . . a form of government can be relatively efficient and still not have the staying power it needs."

For an elaboration of this point, see Seymour M. Lipset's essay,

"Political Sociology," in R. K. Merton, L. Broom, and L. S. Cottrell, Jr., eds., *Sociology Today*, New York: Basic Books, 1959.

p. 21: Quotation from Joseph Schumpeter.
    Capitalism, Socialism, and Democracy, p. 137. The quotation has been slightly rewritten. In making the remark, Schumpeter was referring specifically to capitalism rather than to democracy.

p. 23: ". . . a social order which offers the individual a broad spectrum of . . . groups among which he can choose."
    An illustrative contrast is offered by Edward Banfield. "A single issue of the weekly newspaper published in St. George, Utah (population 4,562), reports a variety of public-spirited undertakings. The Red Cross is conducting a membership drive. The Business and Professional Women's Club is raising funds to build an additional dormitory for the local junior college. . . . The Future Farmers of America . . . are holding a father-son banquet. A local business firm has given an encyclopedia to the school district. The Chamber of Commerce is discussing the feasibility of building an all-weather road between two nearby towns. 'Skywatch' volunteers are being signed up. A local church has collected $1,393.11 in pennies for a children's hospital 350 miles away. The County Farm Bureau is flying one of its members to Washington, 2,000 miles away, to participate in discussions of farm policy. Meetings of the Parent Teachers Associations are being held in the schools. . . .
    "Montegrano, a commune of 3,400 persons, most of them poor farmers and laborers, in the province of Potenza in southern Italy, presents a striking contrast. . . . No newspaper is published in Montegrano or in any of the thirteen other towns lying within view on nearby hilltops. . . . Twenty-five upper class men constitute a 'circle' and maintain a clubroom where members play cards and chat. Theirs is the only association. . . . There are no organized voluntary charities in Montegrano. . . . There are two churches. . . . The churches do not carry on charitable or welfare activities, and they play no part at all in the secular life of the community." (Edward Banfield, *The Moral Basis of a Backward Society*, Glencoe: The Free Press, 1958, pp. 15–16.)

p. 23: ". . . the existence of such groups . . . provides . . . avenues into . . . the general stream of social life."
    The classic statement is probably Emile Durkheim's: "Where the State is the only environment in which men can live communal

lives they inevitably lose contacts, become detached, and society disintegrates. A nation can be maintained only if, between the State and the individual, there is intercalated a whole series of secondary groups near enough to individuals to attract them strongly in their sphere of action and drag them in this way into the general torrent of social life." (Emile Durkheim, *The Division of Labor,* Glencoe: The Free Press, 1947, p. 28.) See also Robert A. Nisbet, *The Quest for Community,* New York: Oxford University Press, 1953.

p. 25: ". . . the basic consensus . . . consists in a shared allegiance to the rules of the democratic game."

These rules, of course, have a penumbra of vagueness around them. When we say that our political opponents are forgetful of the great traditions of the nation, we follow standard democratic practice. When we say that they are traitors, we do not. Somewhere in between two such statements a line has to be drawn, but it takes a developed taste to know where to draw that line. Nor can this kind of vagueness be avoided: it is a characteristic of any moral code that represents a serious effort to regulate human behavior. Such a code cannot be so flexible that it can be accommodated to anything that men wish to do, but neither can it be so rigid that it condemns them to inevitable failure by leaving no room for new and different circumstances. And the necessity for a measure of vagueness is all the greater in a public or political code. As Spinoza observed, we cannot expect that the public business will invariably be conducted in accordance with the rules of piety that are binding on individuals in their personal lives. Mr. Dooley made the same point more briefly when he remarked, "Politics isn't beanbag."

But when the gap between personal and political morality becomes too great, personal morality is undermined and the moral authority of the political system is affected. This may be one of the simplest reasons in favor of democratic political procedures: making such procedures work does not require as radical a break with principles of personal morality as do other political methods.

p. 27: "According to Walter Lippmann . . ."

Mr. Lippmann writes: "It was only in the fine Victorian weather, before the storm clouds of the great wars began to gather, that the liberal democratic policy of public agnosticism and practical neutrality in ultimate issues was possible." (Walter Lippmann, *The Public Philosophy,* New York: New American Library, 1956, p. 79.)

But is "agnosticism" the proper word to describe the policy of taking no official position at all?

p. 27: "*. . . a Party, a Church, or a Committee on Ultimate Truths . . .*"

The practical political implications of the view that all correct political judgments must start with the One True Metaphysics have been spelled out by a Polish philosopher, looking back on the Stalinist period in Poland: "The point is that the term 'Marxism' did not designate a doctrine with a specific content. It meant a doctrine defined only formally, its content being, in each case, supplied by the Infallible Institution. . . . The word 'Marxist' does not describe a man who believes in a world view defined by a given content. It refers to a man with a mental attitude characterized by his willingness to accept institutionally approved opinions. From this point of view the content of Marxism at a given moment does not matter. A man is a Marxist if he is always ready to accept as the content of the doctrine that which is recommended by the 'Office.'" (Leszek Kolakowski, "Permanent and Transitory Aspects of Marxism," in Pawel Mayewski, ed., *The Broken Mirror*, New York: Random House, 1958, pp. 158–9.)

The same point applies to any other doctrine around which an ultimate consensus is sought. Mr. Lippmann argues that it was a mistake for the liberal democracies to adopt the policy that the individual's beliefs about first and last things fall outside the sphere of the public interest. Yet the majority of those who take this position and who plead for a return to "Natural Law," including Mr. Lippmann, do not propose an "Office" and want none. The difficulty, therefore, is to make out what it is they do propose. For without an "Office," an ultimate philosophical consensus will not yield the practical consensus they seek.

p. 27: "*. . . the air is thin in the land of higher generalities.*"

What are "the higher generalities" which, according to Mr. Lippmann, are the indispensable guides we need? He answers: "They are the laws of a rational order of human society—in the sense that all men, when they are sincerely and lucidly rational, will regard them as self-evident. The rational order consists of the terms that must be met in order to fulfill men's capacity for the good life in this world. They are the terms of the widest consensus of rational men in a plural society. They are the propositions to which all men concerned, if they are sincerely and lucidly rational, can be expected to converge." (*The Public Philosophy*, p. 95.) If Mr. Lippmann were asked his advice on an issue in foreign policy and answered in such language, he would be put down as an unresponsive witness.

There is no mystery about the continuing refusal of those Mr. Lippmann calls "men of light and leading" to accept the philosophy of Natural Law. The advocates of Natural Law have still to produce a single example of a higher generality which can help men in any concrete context in which they have to make decisions. For these generalities are systematically evasive. Consider, for example, a man who is asked his opinion of teetotalism and responds with the generalization that "pleasure is the purpose of life." The normal inference would be that he takes a dim view of life without alcohol. But suppose he goes on to tell us that he does not wish to take a position with which any rational man might possibly disagree, that he is seeking "the broadest consensus of rational men in a plural society," and that when he speaks of "pleasure," accordingly, he means the pleasures of abstention as well as the pleasures of drink. In that case he would leave us as ignorant about his opinion as we were originally, although our ignorance, no doubt, is now at a higher level of generality. This is also the nature of arguments that invoke "Natural Law." The classic defenders of both capitalism and socialism, for example, based their arguments on the common premise that the individual is owed the full fruits of his labor. Today, the widely shared belief in the sanctity of life exists side by side with strong disagreements about capital punishment, euthanasia, or the justifiability of war. In sum, the easier it is for everyone to accept a so-called self-evident truth, the less content it has.

p. 28: "The abstract formula has to be filled in, and at this point individual judgment and personal preference reappear."

Faced by dissenting members of his army as convinced as he that they spoke for God, Oliver Cromwell was moved to exclaim: "I cannot but think that in most that have spoken there have been some things of God made known to us and yet there hath been several contradictions in what hath been spoken. But certainly God is not the author of contradictions."

p. 28: "The insistence on the necessity of an ultimate philosophical consensus . . . does not cement a democracy together, it breaks it apart."

Mr. Lippmann writes: "Originally [freedom] was founded on the postulate that there was a universal order on which all reasonable men were agreed: within that public agreement on the fundamentals and on the ultimates, it was safe to permit and it would be desirable to encourage, dissent and dispute. But with the disappearance of the public philosophy—and of a consensus on the first and last things—there was opened up a great vacuum in the public mind, yawning to be filled. As long as it worked, there was an obvious practical advantage in treating the struggle for the ultimate allegiance of men as not within the sphere of the public interest. It was a way of not having to open the Pandora's box of theological, moral and ideological issues which divide the Western society. But in this century, when the hard decisions have had to be made, this rule of prudence has ceased to work. The expedient worked only as long as the general mass of the people were not seriously dissatisfied with things as they were." (*The Public Philosophy*, pp. 78–9.)

But it seems strange to describe the century of Dickens, Carlyle, Marx, and the Abolitionists, a century in which there were Chartist riots in London, a Commune in Paris, and a Civil War in the United States, as one in which no hard decisions had to be made and the general mass of the people were not seriously dissatisfied. And are we to infer that the function of Natural Law is to make the mass of the people satisfied with the status quo? Most important of all, if hard decisions now have to be made, there seems no point in making them harder by opening "the Pandora's box of theological, moral and ideological issues which divide the Western society." The Western consensus, developed after the Hundred Years' War, which almost destroyed Western society, is that this box had better remain closed. Mr. Lippmann, to be sure, seeks a wholly uncoerced consensus, one based on hard inquiry and rational persuasion. But agreement on the issues on which he seeks consensus has not been found after twenty-five hundred years of argument. To assert that the cause of liberal democracy is lost unless an ultimate philosophical consensus is now reached is not to propose a remedy for existing ills. It is to offer a counsel of despair, and one for which a justification is utterly lacking.

The argument achieves what plausibility it has, in fact, only from an ambiguity in the word "philosophy." In everyday affairs, we speak of a man's "philosophy" when we wish to designate the values to which he consistently holds, or the settled views of his relation to his fellows or his place in the world which appear to be reflected in his behavior. And in this sense, the citizens of a democracy must share a common "philosophy" at least to some extent if their political arrangements are to be reasonably manageable. But we are not speaking here of argued opinions or organized doctrines; we are talking about attitudes, feelings, and practical beliefs. "Philosophy" in its professional sense, however, stands for the attempt to analyze the logic of our beliefs and disbeliefs, to clarify the types of reasoning appropriate to different departments of human thought and action, and to offer rationally defended views about the basic constitution of the universe. When Mr. Lippmann deplores the existing philosophic dissensus, he is speaking of philosophy in the second, professional sense; but the practical political question with which he is dealing is that of a consensus in the first, everyday meaning of "philosophy." Accordingly, when he writes, "There is not much doubt how the struggle [between liberal democracy and its opponents] is likely to end if it lies between those who, believing, care very much—and those who, lacking belief, cannot care very much," his view, though widely shared, is based on a fundamental error. Men may believe and care very much even if they have no philosophy at all in the professional sense of the word; and even the philosophical skeptic, after all, may believe very strongly in his skepticism, care very much about it, and cherish the political liberties that permit him to expound it.

p. 28: ". . . when we hear the language of ultimates . . . we are listening to the overture to the democratic political performance and not to the performance itself."

"The 'invention' of parliamentary government has had the effect of purging the major parties of doctrinaire radicalism or conservatism, as they have had to take their turn in ruling the country and the empire and in confronting practical problems not susceptible of doctrinaire solution." (Adams Ulam, *Philosophical Foundations of English Socialism,* Cambridge: Harvard University Press, 1951, p. 124.)

CHAPTER III: IDEALS AND IDOLS OF DEMOCRACY

p. 30: ". . . there are many definitions of democracy . . ."

But this does not mean that any definition will do. Although it has become a commonplace to say that there are two different conceptions of democracy abroad in the world—the totalitarian conception and the liberal conception—the meaning of the word "democracy" is not to be found in the abstract definitions of the term that men offer but in the way they actually use it. And in its actual use, everyone seems to have in mind, at the very least, a government freely chosen by the governed and responsible to the governed. When Marxists say that "bourgeois democracy" is not "real democracy," they mean to say that elections and the competition between parties, as they occur in the West, are a masquerade, and that the governed are not offered a genuine choice; and when liberal democrats denounce the "democracy" that prevails in Eastern Europe, they mean to say the same thing. The disagreement is not about the use of the word, but about the facts.

Marx himself used the word "democracy" in its ordinary sense. Speaking of the Paris Commune, he wrote: "The Commune was formed of the municipal councillors chosen by universal suffrage in various wards of the town, responsible and revocable at short terms. . . . Instead of continuing to be the agents of the central government, the police were at once stripped of their political attributes, and turned into the responsible and at all times revocable agents of the Commune. So were the officials of all other branches of the administration." (*The Civil War in France*, p. 40.) For a lucid discussion of this entire issue, see John Plamenatz's essay in Richard McKeon, ed., *Democracy in a World of Tensions*. The quotation from Marx is taken from this essay.

p. 32: ". . . there are two democratic traditions, not one."

The best brief statement is by George H. Sabine, "The Two Democratic Traditions," *The Philosophical Review* [October, 1952], Vol. LXI, No. 4.

p. 34: "Coercion is implicit in all forms of government . . ."

This is what gives a continuing air of paradox to the phrase "government by consent." "In politics," Lord Lindsay has said, "government by consent is strictly a contradiction in terms." For if men consented to each decision of their leaders, there would be no need for taxes, penal sanctions, and all the rest of the machinery of government; at most there would only be a need for administrative coordination. Indeed, we cannot even say that a government rests on the consent of the governed simply because the people like what their government is doing. That can happen in a rigidly authoritarian system. If this is what is meant by "consent," then it might be said that liberal democracy, which accepts the inevitability of discontent and disagreement, is based on the principle that government by consent is impossible.

The attempt to define "consent" as the absence of coercion is one theme in Rousseau's conception of "the general will," and is a principal theme in anarchist ideas of political freedom and Marxist hopes for the withering away of the State.

p. 35: ". . . if there is a sizable imbalance of power . . . then the settlement that is reached is an imposed settlement . . ."

But this does not mean, of course, that every interest in the community either can or should have equal power with every other interest. It is good to be able to impose settlements on gangsters.

p. 37: ". . . the ideal of individual autonomy."
"In 1790 a French conservative, Sénac de Meilhan . . . remarked that 'the French Revolution seems to be a revolution of the human mind.' The main idea, if we must single one out, seems to have been a demand for self-determination, a sense of autonomy of the personality, a refusal to accept norms laid down outside the self . . ." (R. R. Palmer, "The World Revolution of the West: 1763–1801," *Political Science Quarterly* [March, 1954], Vol. LXIX, No. 1, pp. 4–5.)

p. 37: ". . . this pipe-dream, this fantasy of self-creation . . ."
Emerson wrote in his essay "Politics": "The wise man is the State. He needs no army, fort, or navy,—he loves men too well; no bribe, or feast, or palace, to draw friends to him; no vantage ground, no favorable circumstance. He needs no library, for he has not done thinking; no church, for he is a prophet; no statute-book, for he is the lawgiver; no money, for he is value; no road, for he is at home where he is; no experience, for the life of the creator shoots through him. . . . He has no personal friends . . ."
Tocqueville took a bleaker view of the same ideal. "Aristocracy," he wrote, "had made a chain of all the members of the community, from the peasant to the king; democracy breaks that chain and severs every link of it. . . . Thus not only does democracy make every man forget his ancestors, but it hides his descendants and separates his contemporaries from him; it throws him back forever upon himself alone and threatens in the end to confine him entirely within the solitude of his own heart." (See John W. Ward, "Individualism Today," *The Yale Review* [Spring, 1960], pp. 380–92.) The word "individualism" was first used by Henry Reeve in translating Tocqueville's *Democracy in America;* and, as Tocqueville emphasized, the other side of democratic individualism is the need and penchant for voluntary association.

p. 38: Quotation from H. D. F. Kitto.
H. D. F. Kitto, *The Greeks,* Harmondsworth: Penguin Books, 1951, p. 9.

p. 39: ". . . the rule of law and . . . the fundamental rights of individuals."

The largest sin of omission in the treatment of democracy in this book is the absence of any systematic treatment of the ideas and institutions associated with these phrases. But this would necessitate an extended and complex digression.

p. 39: ". . . in a liberal society . . . private governments . . . exist as a matter of policy."

This should not be taken to imply that socialism is by definition incompatible with democracy. For free elections to take place, voters must be independent of government control, which means they must not be at the mercy of the government for their jobs and livelihood. But this can be guaranteed, in principle, by giving the individual a kind of private property in his job and income—for example, through civil service protections, seniority rights, etc. However, the prediction as to whether such guarantees will in fact be maintained depends, in any particular case, on an assessment of the strength of liberal traditions and institutions existing in the particular society in question. Moreover, if a competitive political system is to be maintained, a practical prerequisite is that private individuals and groups must be able to acquire and control money and resources without asking the permission of the regime in power. For this reason, among others, few democratic socialists are today inclined to argue that government should be the sole employer. The precise meaning of "socialism," in consequence, has become increasingly hazy.

p. 40: ". . . the notion that government by consent . . . means . . . a kind of giant and continuing town-meeting."

The history of democratic ideas is in part the story of the attempt to take this conception of government, which originated in highly unusual conditions, and to transport it from the small community to a context in which political affairs have become national and global in scope and political relations have become impersonal relations between great masses of men. One result has been the invention of vicarious substitutes for the feeling of direct democracy. Thus, in small groups there occasionally emerges a "sense of the meeting." When this notion is applied to a nation-state, a new and remarkable entity appears—"the will of the people." But to assert that a vast modern society has a unitary will is to venture into the occult. Similarly, the idea has been developed that the State is to be identified with the community as a whole, that it necessarily speaks for the community's supreme interests, and that it therefore has the real consent of its citizens to its actions even when it does not go through the form of asking for their opinions. Probably the most important consequence of the town-meeting conception of democracy for modern political theory and practice is the rise of such ideas and of the institutions that go with them. Rousseau is the great source of this kind of "totalitarian democracy," but his ideas are ambiguous, and there are other, more liberal elements in them as well. (J. L. Talmon's *The Origins of Totalitarian Democracy*, London: Secker & Warburg, 1952, is an interesting but one-sided and tendentious exploration of these issues.)

p. 41: ". . . critics . . . have offered the fact that there was no general public debate before the atom bomb was dropped . . ."
     The best-known exposition of the thesis discussed in this paragraph is the late C. Wright Mills' *The Power Elite*, New York: Oxford University Press, 1956. Chapter III of Daniel Bell's *The End of Ideology* presents an extended critique of the arguments in this book.

p. 41: "The majority . . . is not a cohesive social group . . ."
     There are exceptions. Sometimes a single great issue, like slavery before the Civil War, dominates the scene, piling up all other issues around it, and dividing a society into two great, mutually hostile formations (although there are always some who would like to avoid being counted in either group). Under such circumstances, one can speak of two stable groups, one "the majority," the other "the minority." When this happens, a democratic society is likely to obtain neither majority rule nor minority rule, but only trouble.

p. 43: "The proper phrase, as Robert Dahl has suggested, is rule by minorities."
     A Preface to Democratic Theory, p. 133.

p. 47: "Politics is a democracy's official business . . ."
     If the tools of democratic government are the bargain and the compromise, if the goal of a democratic government is to win the next election, what of the quality of democratic decision-making? What about "the common good" or "the public interest"? It should be pointed out, in the first place, that while a democratic government must aim at winning elections, its decisions may serve other purposes as well, just as the desire of a factory owner for profits or of a novelist for fame may serve the ends of more efficient production or better literature. The point is simply that unless a government wins elections, it will not be making the decisions; and so its decisions must be means to the end of winning elections.

Still, a larger question can be raised about the relation of the democratic bargain to the public interest. Is the democratic process simply a matter of giving Peter and Paul their say, and then striking a bargain between them? Peter may be the owner of a race track, Paul a man who likes to be sure in advance about the outcome of horse races. A bargain between the two, though it would be easy to strike, would not be attractive. Again, one interest group may wish to keep our defense program at its present level, opposing all efforts for the reduction of armaments; a second group may favor immediate, complete, unilateral disarmament. Does a good compromise consist simply in splitting the difference between them? The result might leave nobody happy but the morticians. At some point, clearly, a third element, something outside the interests and opinions of the parties to the conflict, must be introduced. It is what Felix Frankfurter has called "that vague, impalpable but all-controlling consideration, the public interest."

But what is this vague, impalpable, but all-controlling consideration? There are peculiar difficulties in trying to define "the public interest" in democratic terms. For democratic habits, not to mention the demands of intellectual clarity, require us to define "the public interest" in terms of interests that are actually or potentially held by definite individuals. The public interest cannot be the disembodied interest of a state or a society apart from the disagreeing and sometimes disagreeable individuals who compose such collective entities.

The beginning of an answer to the question lies in the recognition, I think, that the phrase "the public interest" has a number of different meanings. Among these, four in particular seem most important.

1. We may define "the public interest," first, in psychological terms. So considered, it stands for the unspoken presuppositions which, at a given time and place, govern the process of democratic competition. For while men may enter the political arena with nothing on their minds but the cause that agitates them, that is not all that is on their minds. They carry preconceptions with them, and the people on the other side are likely to share some of these preconceptions. For the process of competition and negotiation goes on within a surrounding culture.

A democratic society, for example, may choose to abolish all censorship and to protect even purveyors of pornography. Yet if the man who makes a profit from pornography lobbies for cheaper postal rates in the halls of Congress, he will still suffer from certain inherent disadvantages. Similarly, but at the other extreme, prevailing conventions exclude Negro groups from full access to the decision-making procedures of most Southern states. The groups that are "legitimate" and that confer legitimacy on others do not regard the Negro groups as legitimate or as part of the public whose interest is in question. In short, there are attitudes which, for better or worse, confine and direct democratic political competition by implicitly determining what kind of interest and what sort of person has a rightful claim to be admitted to the democratic political club. The most important revolutions in democratic politics—for example, the entrance of organized labor into the circle of groups that must be regularly consulted—take place only when these moral and cultural attitudes erode or change.

2. But this is to define "the public interest" simply in terms of the opinions and values, enlightened or unenlightened, that happen to be held by the legitimate or respectable sections of the community. There is a second meaning of the phrase, however, which makes "the public interest" something more than a matter of mere opinion. In this meaning of the term, "the public interest" covers the institutions and policies that objectively serve common interests. Whatever the special problems of a government may be, it has to see to it that the streets are reasonably clean, that the traffic moves, that the mails are delivered, that the public utilities work, and that the laws are enforced with sufficient orderliness to allow men to make some plausible predictions about the consequences of their intended actions. People may have different private interests and purposes, but when they occupy the same terrain and use the same physical and social facilities, their paths intersect and overlap. The most heavily traveled paths, the common facilities on which many different interests mutually depend, compose the public interest.

Currency, national defense, police, education, hospitals, the maintenance of the democratic political system itself, are standard examples of public interests in this sense of the term. The list is obviously elastic. Under the impact of population pressures, technology, urbanization, and unremitting international rivalries it is, indeed, steadily growing. One pitfall in approaching this conception of "the public interest" is to assume that its content is fixed. And a second is to assume that to serve the public interest is to serve everybody's interest equally. But this is not true. A road that has been improved so that ten times as many people can use it is a deprivation to the one man who enjoyed the quiet country road that existed before. When we have found "the public interest" we have still not found the answer to the political maiden's perennial prayer—the place where all unselfish citizens can stand together, without having to make any disagreeable decisions. The public interest is not a single and harmonious whole. It is plural and discordant. Different public interests collide—parks and new housing, national defense and welfare programs. The disagreements between men who all have the common good in mind are no less acrimonious than the disagreements between men who are only thinking of themselves.

Responsible judgments about the public interest, therefore, are not ineluctable conclusions from undeniable premises. A determination has to be made about the kinds of interest that ought to be given priority and, ultimately, about the kind of society at which one is aiming. Neither "the public interest" nor "national goals" nor a "national purpose" just exists, waiting to be discovered or rediscovered. Such phrases, if they have any content, express the resolutions, the commitments and preferences, conscious or unconscious, of particular men.

3. Moreover, the quest for the public interest has another complicating element. For there is a third meaning to the phrase. We often speak of the public interest when we mean to call attention to the existence of third parties, not directly involved in a problem, but indirectly affected by it. The interest of consumers is a public interest when labor and management strike a wage bargain, when a proposal is made for subsidies to farmers, or when tariffs are reviewed. The interests of medical research are a public interest when tax laws and business mores combine to pour wealth into entertainment and expense accounts. Of course, those who personally enjoy such benefits may hold a public interest in them as well. The worker is also a consumer, and the man who lives on an expense account may need the benefits of medical research sooner than others. But these public interests are nevertheless external interests. They may be widely shared interests, or public interests in the second sense of the phrase, or merely the interests of limited groups, but whatever the case may be, they are on the outside looking in.

The public interest, conceived as the interest of third parties, is therefore a shifting thing. It is the particular interest endangered at a particular moment. And as a result, it is frequently at a disadvantage. It may be scattered, unorganized, and voiceless. It can play a part in influencing social decisions only if the members of the public in question succeed in finding each other and in finding a voice. Private agencies like a civil liberties union, a legal aid society, or a settlement house can undertake this task. But one of the major responsibilities of democratic government is to speed the organization and empowerment of important publics. The formation of a federal department of urban affairs is a case in point. The interest that is on the outside looking in is unquestionably the interest that is endangered by the democratic decision-making process. It is endangered by any decision-making process that can be imagined. But democratic institutions can make it possible to discover these interests and harder to ignore them.

4. Yet none of these meanings of the phrase "the public interest" quite catch the reason why the belief that there is such a thing as the public interest is an essential condition of democratic politics and of any social arrangements that deserve the respect of civilized men. In its final meaning, it is a regulative ideal. The ideal of truth, as Charles Peirce remarked, expresses "the great hope" that different minds, starting out with the most antagonistic views, will still, with the progress of investigation, be carried "by a force outside of themselves to one and the same conclusion." Preferences count in politics as they do not count where the pursuit of truth is concerned, but the concept of the public interest expresses a similar great hope for the political sphere.

The ideal of the public interest calls on men, despite their egoism, to set their preferences side by side with the preferences of others and to examine them all with the same disinterestedness and impartiality. It asks them to seek as tolerable and comprehensive a compromise among these interests as is possible. And it reminds them that every decision they make is a limited one, that some interests may have been overlooked, that something better may be possible. "It is not from the benevolence of the butcher, the brewer, or the baker, that we expect our dinner," wrote Adam Smith, "but from their regard to their own interest." But the ideal of the public interest at least allows the butcher, the brewer, and the baker to see self-interest for what it is, and to recognize that there may be other interests besides their own. This is the final meaning of the concept of "the public interest," and it is what makes it at once vague and impalpable yet all-controlling. Without it, the belief that politics can rise above the level of a cat fight is impossible.

(For contrasting expositions of the idea of "the public interest," see Glendon Schubert, *The Public Interest,* Glencoe: The Free Press, 1960; also Gerhard Colm, "In Defense of the Public Interest," *Social Research* [Autumn, 1960], Vol. XXVII, No. 3, pp. 295–307. *Philosophy and the Public Interest,* prepared by W. A. R. Leys and C. M.

Perry for the Committee to Advance Original Work in Philosophy [American Philosophical Association] contains a useful bibliography and sample of opinions.)

p. 47: ". . . democratic politics requires ideas."

In the last public speech he delivered as Prime Minister, Stanley Baldwin said: "It seems to me that one of the reasons why our people are alive and flourishing, and have avoided many of the troubles that have fallen on less happy nations, is because we have never been guided by logic in anything we have done." (Quoted by L. Susan Stebbing, *Thinking to Some Purpose*, Harmondsworth: Penguin Books, 1939, p. 12.) After paying this compliment to his fellow countrymen, Mr. Baldwin was elevated to the peerage.

Opposition to doctrinaire ideologies has led to exaggerated statements concerning the dangers of systematic thought for democratic politics. Jacques Barzun, in the course of defending the rights of "intellect," has written: "The greatest danger to a democratic state is probably the contamination of its politics by Intellect. . . . To introduce strictness and rigor into the politics of adaptation, variety, and pluralism would be to give birth at once to a dozen groups of eternal enemies." (Jacques Barzun, *The House of Intellect,* New York: Harper & Brothers, 1959, p. 149.) But this is true only if the sole contribution that "Intellect" can make to politics is the production of encompassing, deductive ideologies. On the one hand, few of the great political ideologies are notable, in fact, for their strictness and rigor; they are notable rather for the narrowness of their premises and the looseness of the inferences drawn from these premises. On the other hand, names like Madison, Mill, or Holmes suggest that "Intellect" can make another and more useful kind of contribution to democratic politics. It is true that the accommodations required in politics are different from the conditions required for disciplined intellectual inquiry. But the quality of political accommodations depends at least in part on the quality of the ideas accommodated.

CHAPTER IV: RECOVERING GOVERNMENT BY CONSENT

p. 49: Quotation from Sartre.

Jean-Paul Sartre, *The Age of Reason,* translated by Eric Sutton, New York: Bantam Books, 1959, pp. 123–4.

p. 54: Quotation from Tocqueville.

Democracy in America, Vol. II, p. 110.

p. 57: "*. . . the more successful the association . . . the less the . . . members feel impelled . . . to take an active part . . .*"

See S. M. Lipset, M. Trow, J. Coleman, *Union Democracy,* Glencoe: The Free Press, 1956; also J. Seidman, J. London, B. Karsh, D. L. Tagliacozzo, *The Worker Views His Union,* Chicago: University of Chicago Press, 1958.

p. 57: "*. . . a large inert membership controlled by a small active minority . . .*"

See Robert Michels, *Political Parties,* Glencoe: The Free Press, 1949; Oliver Garceau, *The Politics of the American Medical Association,* Cambridge: Harvard University Press, 1941; also Bernard Barber, "Participation and Mass Apathy in Associations," in A. W. Gouldner, ed., *Studies in Leadership,* New York: Harper & Brothers, 1950. Among labor unions a notable exception to the oligarchic pattern is the International Typographical Union. Lipset, Trow, and Coleman, *Union Democracy,* is an invaluable and detailed study of this deviant case. Not only does it indicate that "the iron law of oligarchy" is oversimplified, but it also suggests some of the conditions conducive to the development of democratic arrangements within associations.

p. 59: "*. . . 'the scientific community' . . . is an undefined entity.*"

See Bernard Barber, *Science and the Social Order,* Glencoe: The Free Press, 1952; also Wallace Sayre, "Scientists and American Science Policy," *Science* [March 24, 1961], Vol. 133, No. 3456.

p. 60: Reference to Adolf Berle.

Adolf Berle, *Power Without Property,* New York: Harcourt, Brace and Company, 1959.

p. 61: Quotation from Collingwood.

R. G. Collingwood, *The New Leviathan,* Oxford: Clarendon Press, 1942, p. 193.

The classic statement is Mosca's: "Among the constant facts and tendencies that are to be found in all political organisms, one is so obvious that it is apparent to the most casual eye. In all societies . . . two classes of people appear—a class that rules and a class that is ruled. The first class, always the less numerous, performs all political functions, monopolizes power, enjoys the advantage that power brings, whereas the second, the more numerous class, is directed and controlled by the first in a manner that is now more or less legal, now more or less arbitrary and violent. . . . The power of any minority is irresistible as against each single individual in the majority, who stands alone before the totality of the organized minority. At the same time, the minority is organized for the very reason that it is a minority. . . ." (Gaetano Mosca, *The Ruling Class*, New York: McGraw-Hill Book Company, 1939, pp. 50, 53.) The eye is too casual. The fact that a few people, relatively speaking, make the key decisions affecting the lives of great numbers does not in itself imply that these few are a social class. Those who have great power, it is safe to assume, have a common desire to keep their power. But specific evidence about the character of a particular society is needed before this can be used to prove that those with such power have common interests. In fact, the conditions of their power may be such that they are in conflict with one another. Moreover, "each single individual in the majority" does not necessarily "stand alone." He may belong to an organized minority of his own.

Broadly speaking, in discussing the character of social power as it is exercised in a society, two different sets of consideration are relevant: (1) the composition of the groups that hold such power—their backgrounds, class, interests, and ideologies; (2) the conditions under which they hold their power—specifically, the groups that can influence the decisions made by those in power because they can reward or punish the holders of power, and can support, evade, or defy the decisions that are made.

p. 62: "Professional leadership and bureaucratic management . . . help to maintain the texture of a pluralistic society."

See Franz Neumann, "Approaches to the Study of Political Power," *Political Science Quarterly* [1950], Vol. 65.

p. 63: ". . . the less interested are apparently necessary . . ."

See B. R. Berelson, P. F. Lazarsfeld, W. N. McPhee, *Voting*, Chicago: University of Chicago Press, 1954; for second thoughts on the question of "apathy," see also W. H. M. Jones, "In Defense of Political Apathy," *Political Studies* [1954], Vol. 2.

p. 66: ". . . individual rights . . . within . . . organizations . . ."

An interesting study of one program for the protection of individual rights is *Democracy and Public Review: An Analysis of the UAW Public Review Board*, by Jack Stieber, Walter E. Oberer, and Michael Harrington (Center for the Study of Democratic Institutions, 1960).

p. 68: "Tocqueville . . . in arguing for local autonomy . . ."

This is a major theme of *Democracy in America*. See especially chapters V, XIV, XVI, in Vol. I, and chapters VI, VII, in Vol. II.

p. 69: ". . . the day-to-day government of the plant community."

See Peter Drucker, *The New Society*, New York: Harper & Brothers, 1949.

CHAPTER V: THE DILEMMAS OF AN OPEN SOCIETY

p. 74: Quotation from Zechariah Chafee.

Zechariah Chafee, *Government and Mass Communications*, Chicago: University of Chicago Press, copyright 1947 by The University of Chicago; in B. Berelson and M. Janowitz, *Reader in Public Opinion and Communication*, Glencoe: The Free Press, 1953, p. 238.

p. 75: "The pictures . . . created by the mass media react back upon what is pictured."

Arthur T. Hadley has said: "In considering the effect of the drive for circulation on news selection and therefore our knowledge of the world, the key is that bad news draws more people than good news, and exciting, shocking bad news does the best. . . . Then the self-reflexive principle starts to work. Through the press the body politic is informed about a continuous series of crises. . . . The human organism either reacts by becoming numb or else by lashing out blindly. . . . Then each of these reactions, being bad news, becomes in itself news. . . ." ("Modern Communication in an Age of Crisis," *Texas Quarterly* [Winter, 1959]; reprinted in *Current* [May, 1960], No. 1, pp. 52–3.

p. 76: Quotation from Zechariah Chafee.

In Berelson and Janowitz, *Reader in Public Opinion . . .* , p. 239.

p. 78: Quotation from Hannah Arendt.

The Human Condition, pp. 3–4. Copyright 1958 by The University of Chicago.

p. 80: Quotation from John Plamenatz.

In Richard McKeon, ed., *Democracy in a World of Tensions*, p. 317. Copyright 1951 by The University of Chicago.

p. 83: ". . . no alchemy which turns a society into a mass society simply because it possesses mass media of communication."

Yet this is the import of many standard sociological definitions of a "mass." Consider the following:

". . . the mass has a number of distinguishable features. First, its membership may come from all walks of life. . . . Secondly, the mass . . . is composed of anonymous individuals. Third, there exists little interaction or change of experience between the members of the mass. They are usually physically separated from one another. . . . Fourth, the mass is very loosely organized. . . .

"The fact that the mass consists of individuals belonging to a wide variety of local groups and cultures is important. . . . The object of mass interest can be thought of as attracting the attention of people away from their local cultures and spheres of life and turning it toward a wider universe, toward areas which are not defined or covered by rules, regulations, or expectations. In this sense the mass can be viewed as constituted by detached and alienated individuals who face objects or areas of life which are interesting, but which are also puzzling and not easy to understand and order. . . . Further, in not being able to communicate with each other, except in limited and imperfect ways, the members of the mass are forced to act separately, as individuals." (Herbert Blumer, "The Mass, The Public, and Public Opinion," in Berelson and Janowitz, *Reader in Public Opinion* . . . , pp. 43–4.) Daniel Bell discusses this and similar views in *The End of Ideology*, especially pp. 21–36.

p. 84: Quotation from Lord Acton.

Lord Acton's Letters to Mary Gladstone, New York: The Macmillan Company, 1904, pp. 193–6.

p. 89: ". . . the best example is the role . . . available to the scientific community."

See the statement, "Science and Human Welfare," of the Committee on Science in the Promotion of Human Welfare, of the American Association for the Advancement of Science, *Science* [July 8, 1960]; reprinted in *Current* [August, 1960], No. 4, pp. 57–64.

CHAPTER VI: THE REORGANIZATION OF WORK AND PLAY

p. 93: "In January, 1813, a group of English workers were brought to trial . . ."

"Proceedings at York Special Commission, January, 1813," in *Introduction to Contemporary Civilization in the West: A Source Book*, New York: Columbia University Press, 1946, pp. 176–83.

p. 96: "The British census of 1841 listed 431 occupations. A century later, the Occupational Dictionary listed 25,000 occupations."

See Theodore Caplow, *The Sociology of Work,* Minneapolis: University of Minnesota Press, 1954, pp. 21–2.

p. 96: ". . . technological specialization . . . defines specialized skills in terms of a process . . ."
See Peter Drucker, *The New Society.*

p. 97: ". . . the satisfactions of work seem . . . removed from the process of work itself."
Thus, some unions in automated plants in Great Britain are asking for extra pay—not pay for more demanding or responsible work, but "lonesome pay." (See the *Report and Recommendations of the Executive Council, International Association of Machinists,* September 13, 1960.) Charles R. Walker reports similar reactions in his *Toward the Automatic Factory,* New Haven: Yale University Press, 1957. For discussions of the larger theme of industrialism and satisfactions in work see Georges Friedmann, *The Anatomy of Work,* Glencoe: The Free Press, 1961; Daniel Bell, "Work and Its Discontents," and "Two Roads from Marx," reprinted in *The End of Ideology;* and C. R. Walker and R. H. Guest, *The Man on the Assembly Line,* Cambridge: Harvard University Press, 1952.

p. 98: Quotation from Veblen.
Thorstein Veblen, *The Instinct of Workmanship,* New York: The Macmillan Company, 1914, p. 307.

p. 99: Quotation from Andrew Ure.
Andrew Ure, *The Philosophy of Manufactures* (1835); in *Introduction to Contemporary Civilization . . . ,* p. 169. But note another of Ure's comments: "By the infirmity of human nature it happens that the more skillful the workman, the more self-willed and intractable he is apt to become, and, of course, the less fit a component of a mechanical system, in which, by occasional irregularities, he may do great damage to the whole."

p. 100: ". . . the . . . instrument of production is the organization . . ."
See Peter Drucker, *The New Society,* and also Robert Merton's "The Machine, The Worker and the Engineer," in his *Social Theory and Social Structure.*

p. 101: ". . . the art . . . of making a mesh of things . . ."
See "Managing Complexity," by Paul Appleby, in *Ethics* [January, 1954], Vol. LXIV, No. 2, Part I, pp. 79–99.

p. 101: "It was Emile Durkheim who stated . . ."
In *The Division of Labor.*

p. 103: Quotation from Balzac.
From his novel *The Civil Service.*

pp. 106–107: Quotation from J. L. and Barbara Hammond.
J. L. and Barbara Hammond, *The Town Labourer,* London, New York: Longmans, Green and Co., 1925, pp. 18–19.

p. 112: "The massive scale of contemporary organizations . . ."
The discussion of this theme leans heavily on Kenneth Boulding, *The Organizational Revolution,* New York: Harper & Brothers, 1953; see as well his article, "The Jungle of Hugeness," in *The Saturday Review,* March 1, 1958.

p. 114: ". . . 'centralization' . . . is an ambiguous term."
There is a fuller discussion of this issue in Herbert Simon, *Administrative Behavior,* New York: The Macmillan Company, 1947; see especially pp. 234 ff.

p. 115: "A man is a member of a community when he is on the job . . ."
"Nothing stands out more emphatically in all our research [on industrial work] than the individual's demand for social status and social function." (Peter Drucker, *The New Society,* p. 49.)

p. 115: "The struggle over work rules . . ."
The rules imposed by the working group itself on its members are frequently aimed at preventing the over-fulfillment of any agreement. Deplorable as this may be, it is important to remember that "the factory worker is subject to much heavier coercion than most other employees" and that the function of such rules is "to relieve the psychological pressure created by this coercion." To the extent that working routines seem to be imposed wholly from above, and without the advice and consent of those who must abide by them, they invite protective and retaliatory action. This is particularly the case where democratic attitudes towards authority are in the air. (See Theodore Caplow, *The Sociology of Work,* pp. 116–17.)

p. 116: ". . . costly though featherbedding is, the alternatives may be more costly."
An excellent discussion of this issue is the article by James Kuhn and Ivar Berg, "The Trouble with Labor Is 'Featherbedding,'" *Columbia University Forum* [Spring, 1960], Vol. III, No. 2. The complexities buried in the word "featherbedding" are illustrated by the

following passage: "A little examination reveals that often work rules benefit everyone, as in the following case. In the loading yard of a midwestern steel company, each crew was expected to load three flat cars with steel pipe in an eight-hour shift. A change in the pickup schedule of the railroad required flat cars to be ready for travel two hours before the end of the shift. To avoid costly and embarrassing delays in the shipments, the yard foreman approached the work crews with a deal: if the men worked extra fast and loaded the flat cars in time for the daily train pickup, he would let them take the extra two hours off with no penalty and, of course, with the same pay. The men agreed. . . . Thus they enjoyed the benefits of leisure after their extra effort, and the resourceful foreman maintained the shipping schedule to the benefit of the company.

"What was a beneficial work rule to the foreman and the traffic department was a rule that fostered featherbedding in the judgment of a new yard superintendent who arrived eight months later, fresh from engineering school. He was outraged. The men were equally outraged when he assigned them a fourth flatcar to load each shift. They charged him with introducing a speedup." (Quoted with permission of the publisher, Columbia University.)

p. 116: Quotation from Robert Merton.
Robert Merton, *Social Theory and Social Structure*, p. 325.

p. 117: Quotation from Frederick Taylor.
Quoted by Daniel Bell, *The End of Ideology*, p. 227.

p. 117: "As Herbert Simon has pointed out . . ."
Herbert Simon, *Administrative Behavior*, pp. 238–40.

p. 119: "Many workers . . . resist . . . changes that require more personal discretion and responsibility . . ."
But the other side of the coin, as Georges Friedmann points out, is that "the worker's satisfaction often increases with the complexity of the work performed . . ." (*The Anatomy of Work*, p. 14.)

p. 120: "In a period in which it is possible to speak of a thirty-hour week . . . it is also possible . . . to think differently about work itself . . ."
But there is a limit, of course, to what the rearrangement of the work process can do. This is why the issue of leisure bulks so large. "For anyone unwilling to delude himself . . . it must seem highly probable that for several generations yet there will remain a multitude of jobs in which the worker can find no outlet for his tastes, his deeper

wishes, or his personality. Even a radical reform of society . . . will not endow such work with the scope and interest necessary to make it the centre of his life and a means of self-fulfillment. Thus everything points to the growing importance of leisure time for the humanization of our technical civilization." (Georges Friedmann, *The Anatomy of Work*, p. 121.)

p. 122: ". . . an occasion, in Richard Hoggart's phrase, for 'sensation without commitment' . . ."

Richard Hoggart, *The Uses of Literacy*, London: Chatto and Windus, 1957.

p. 122: Quotation from Ernest Nagel.

Ernest Nagel, "The Place of Science in a Liberal Education," *Daedalus* [Winter, 1959], pp. 66–7.

CHAPTER VII: THE WELFARE STATE: POSTSCRIPT AND PRELUDE

pp. 125–126: Quotation from Tocqueville.
Democracy in America, Vol. II, pp. 318–9.

p. 126: ". . . the phrase 'the Welfare State' is an inflated way of describing . . . modest facts."

Broadly speaking, the functions performed by the modern Welfare State fall into four main categories. (1) The State has undertaken to reduce the general extent of economic insecurity by attempting to prevent violent fluctuations in the business cycle and in the value of money. In principle, this sort of effort is continuous with such traditional efforts as preventive medicine and the control of contagious diseases. (2) The Welfare State offers legal instrumentalities, such as minimum-wage laws and protections for collective bargaining, whose purpose is to ensure individuals adequate pay for the work they do. (3) The Welfare State offers a variety of special services, like the guaranteeing of bank deposits, intended to protect individuals against interruptions in the flow of income. (4) The Welfare State sometimes provides an alternative income when, for reasons foreseeable or unforeseeable, the normal income of the individual drops. Unemployment insurance and old-age benefits are obvious examples. We may also include in this category programs such as subsidized housing and rent control, which are aimed at protecting individuals against abnormal demands on their income rather than the reduction in their income.

Plainly, these categories of activity undertaken by the Welfare State are different, and cannot be judged by a single set of standards or adequately described by the same slogan. Taken together, they do not protect any single class of people; nor do they represent new principles of social action suddenly introduced during the last thirty years. The attempt to protect individuals against abnormal but unavoidable demands on their incomes by distributing the costs socially is represented in a practice as old as the provision of free public schools.

(For a general discussion of these points, see Eveline M. Burns, *Social Security and Public Policy*, New York: McGraw-Hill Book Co., 1956.)

p. 127: ". . . the Welfare State . . . is a postscript to emergency . . ."

Far from having been conceived in the councils of Socialists, most of what is now incorporated in the British Welfare State, for example, is the consequence of measures that had to be taken to marshal and protect a people at war, to distribute sacrifices equitably, and to readjust the British economy to the diminished resources of Great Britain after the war. (The *locus classicus* for the discussion of these issues is Richard Titmuss, *Problems of Social Policy*, London: Longmans, Green and Co., 1950.)

p. 128: "Grant only two assumptions, and most of the major programs of the Welfare State automatically unfold."

A large part of the argument that follows this sentence is based on the analysis offered by one of the Welfare State's most noted opponents. The culprit in question is Professor Friedrich Hayek; the guilty passage is in his *The Constitution of Liberty*, Chicago: University of Chicago Press, 1960, pp. 285–6. Professor Hayek offers the argument, of course, as a concession to necessity; but the necessities are so evident, and the concession so generous, that it is difficult to see what existing programs of the Welfare State could not then be justified.

p. 129: Quotation from Schumpeter.

Joseph Schumpeter, *Capitalism, Socialism and Democracy*, p. 142.

p. 130: ". . . the minimal material resources necessary to personal autonomy."

"In the general course of human nature, a power over a man's subsistence amounts to a power over his will." (Alexander Hamilton, *The Federalist Papers*, No. 79.)

pp. 130–131: Quotation from Mencken.

Alistair Cooke, ed., *The Vintage Mencken*, New York: Vintage Books, 1955, p. 75.

p. 131: Quotation from Holmes.
   The Holmes-Laski Letters, Cambridge: Harvard University Press, 1953, vol. II, p. 942.

p. 131: "The Welfare State . . . a product of democratic pressures."
This can be exaggerated. The idea that political intervention in the economy is due simply to the spread of democratic attitudes bespeaks a kind of historical amnesia. Abstract economic arguments on the advantages of the free market did not prevail, and are unlikely ever to prevail, when confronted by mass unemployment:

> I am sure that we are all a debtor for
> Mr. Hoover's delectable metaphor
> When he said that three years
> Would bring balm to our fears—
> Which the starving no doubt feel much better for.

p. 133: ". . . egalitarianism . . . manufactures new distinctions in the very process of destroying old ones."
   This is illustrated by one of the most notable features of modernized twentieth-century societies—the introduction of elaborate systems of impersonal examinations and tests for the selection and assignment of talents. The process has led to some justified fears, and to an amusing satire, Michael Young's *The Rise of the Meritocracy, 1870–2033,* London: Thames and Hudson, 1958. No doubt the ability to put one's best foot forward on examinations is only one peculiar capacity among others. But many of the fears which have been expressed are immoderate. At the very least, the new tests have weakened the influence of favoritism and snobbishness. And there is in fact little evidence that the purely technical and specialized abilities which tests can measure are the only qualifications that are needed to move to the top. We need only think of advancement in any university, business, or government bureaucracy to recognize that more intangible personal traits still have a very large influence on any individual's chances.
   The importance of technical competence in a modern society, however, can undoubtedly bring to positions of social power men who have no social convictions, or innocent and ill-informed ones. In an egalitarian and rationalized society, the liberal education of specialists is therefore an urgent necessity. (For a more pessimistic estimate of the significance of the emergence of the "new men," read Andrew Hacker's article, "Liberal Democracy and Social Control," *The American Po-*

litical Science Review [December, 1957], Vol. LI, No. 4, pp. 1009–
26.)

p. 134: Quotation from Mr. Galbraith.

J. K. Galbraith, *The Affluent Society,* Boston: Houghton Mifflin
Company, 1958, pp. 113–15.

p. 136: Quotation from Bertrand Russell.

Bertrand Russell, *The Prospects of Industrial Civilization,*
London: George Allen & Unwin, 2nd edition, 1959, p. 230. And note
another remark: "Assuming such an organized framework for the
material side of life, would it be possible to preserve mental freedom?
Or would those who controlled the economic organization use their
power to persecute any set of people whose opinions or behaviour they
happened to dislike? I think it must be taken as perfectly certain that
the officials in charge . . . would wish to use their power to crush out
all originality and all mental or moral progress. They would have an
outlook not unlike that of employers of labour at present. If their
power were unchecked, I do not doubt that they would kill art and
science and every kind of free speculation about life and the world."
(Pp. 273–4.)

*p. 137: "The question of personal liberty in a democratic Welfare
State . . ."*

Apart from the problem of controlling administrative officials,
there are, of course, other problems affecting personal liberties under
the Welfare State. It is plain that the Welfare State has restricted certain traditional liberties in the economic area. But before the judgment
can be made that this represents a net contraction in the total sphere
of liberties, at least two points have to be considered. First, every
legally guaranteed liberty enjoyed by the individual—for example, his
freedom of speech, or his property rights—spells out legal restrictions
on the behavior of others. Second, although the Welfare State has restricted various economic liberties, it has also expanded others, such
as the liberties of labor unions.

The question, in short, is not simply a question of more or less
liberty; it is a question of whose liberties and which liberties. The
Welfare State has changed the distribution of liberties, presumably in
the interest of greater economic stability and social justice. If that
presumption is wrong, the redistribution is unjustified. But the issue is
obscured so long as it is discussed in terms of liberty in the abstract,
without specifying the particular liberties that have been gained or
lost by particular individuals and groups. Moreover, the greater

economic well-being of large sections of the population means that a larger number of people possess the material powers that are the prerequisites to the enjoyment of their liberties—for example, the right to an advanced education or the consumer's right to spend his money as he pleases. Liberty is not the same thing as power, and serious intellectual confusions arise when the two are identified. But power—money, health, education, the aid of the appropriate organization—is often the condition for using a liberty and coming to value it.

It remains true, however, that the growth in the comparative economic power of any institution threatens the power and therefore the liberties of other institutions. The growing economic power of the State endangers liberties, just as the ungoverned power of private corporations once endangered liberties. But this truism has to be supplemented with three additional observations. Our present structure of basic personal and political liberties is seriously threatened from abroad, and would also have difficulty surviving another major economic disturbance such as the Depression of the Thirties: the growing powers of the State are a response to these dangers. Secondly, the centralized economic powers now exercised by the State, which are still limited, are countervailing powers against the centralization of economic power in private hands. Finally, there are safeguards against the danger of overweening government authority. Our legal system protects a sphere of private rights, and the burden of proof still remains with government when it wishes to extend any of its powers. Moreover, private centers of authority with powerful economic resources of their own still exist. Not least, political democracy provides those who are governed with powers over their governors.

p. 139: "A problem is 'residual' . . ."
> For other formulations of the distinction between "residual" and "institutional" problems, see Alfred J. Kahn, "The Function of Social Work in the Modern World," in Alfred J. Kahn, ed., *Issues in American Social Work*, New York: Columbia University Press, 1959; and also Harold L. Wilensky and Charles N. Lebeaux, *Industrial Society and Social Welfare*, New York: Russell Sage Foundation, 1958, especially Chapter VI.

p. 140: "Planning, as Gunnar Myrdal has pointed out . . ."
> Gunnar Myrdal, *Beyond the Welfare State*, New Haven: Yale University Press, 1960, p. 93. This book presents a highly illuminating analysis of the relations between "centralization," "decentralization," "regulation," and "planning."

CHAPTER VIII: THE RESPONSIBLE SOCIETY

p. 147: "*. . . responsibility for decisions concerning fundamental values . . . seems to fall through the mesh of all our organization . . .*"

Various aspects of this issue are discussed by Robert Merton, *Social Theory and Social Structure*, pp. 151–78, 317–38. See also Kenneth E. Boulding, "Decision-Making in the Modern World," in Lyman Bryson, ed., *An Outline of Man's Knowledge of the Modern World*. Other relevant works include Herbert Simon, *Administrative Behavior;* Chester I. Barnard, *The Functions of the Executive*, Cambridge: Harvard University Press, 1938; Philip Selznick, *TVA and the Grass Roots*, Berkeley: University of California Press, 1949; Peter M. Blau, *Bureaucracy in Modern Society*, New York: Random House, 1956.

p. 152: Quotation from C. P. Snow.

Address to the American Association for the Advancement of Science, New York, December 27, 1960; reported in *The New York Times*, December 28, 1960, p. 14.

p. 154: Quotation from Max Weber.

H. H. Gerth and C. Wright Mills, eds., *From Max Weber*, London: Kegan Paul, Trench, Trubner & Co., 1947, p. 146.

p. 160: Quotation from John Stuart Mill.

Representative Government, edited by R. B. McCallum, Oxford: Basil Blackwell, 1957, p. 138.

pp. 163–164: Quotation from Robert Heilbroner.

Robert Heilbroner, *The Future as History*, New York: Harper & Brothers, 1960, p. 153.

CHAPTER IX: EPILOGUE: WHY CHOOSE DEMOCRACY?

p. 166: "*. . . the inside truth about the universe . . . [and] democratic ideals.*"

Much effort has been spent by classic social philosophies in demonstrating that the particular social system they espouse is justified, quite apart from human preferences, by fundamental laws of nature or history. Although the issue cannot be argued here as it deserves, such an effort confuses the kind of reasoning that is appropriate in morals and politics with the kind of reasoning appropriate to geometry or to the nonevaluative study of the facts. The creation of such ideologies, however, is not the only function of social philosophy. If it serves its other functions well—for example, the clarification of fundamental ideas, the examination of fundamental values in their actual modes of operation, and the formulation of coherent strategies of action—it can provide an effective substitute for ideologies. Unhappily, the association of rigid ideologies with totalitarianism has led many political intellectuals to adopt a kind of teetotalitarianism—a general unwillingness to deal in general ideas.

p. 169: ". . . democracy is a technique for the socialization of conflict."

See E. E. Schattschneider, *The Semi-Sovereign People,* New York: Holt, Rinehart and Winston, 1960.

p. 172: Quotation from Bertrand Russell.
The Prospects of Industrial Civilization, p. 152.

p. 173: "Political democracy and a socially mobile society . ... invite the individual to a greater degree of consciousness . . ."

"This ceaseless agitation which democratic government has introduced into the political world influences all social intercourse. I am not sure that, on the whole, this is not the greatest advantage of democracy. . . . It is incontestable that the people frequently conduct public business very badly; but it is impossible that the lower orders should take a part in public business without extending the circle of their ideas and quitting the ordinary routine of their thoughts. The humblest individual who co-operates in the government of society acquires a certain degree of self-respect. . . . He is canvassed by a multitude of applicants, and in seeking to deceive him in a thousand ways, they really enlighten him. . . . He is perhaps neither happier nor better than those who came before him, but he is better informed and more active." (Tocqueville, *Democracy in America,* Vol. I, p. 251.)

INDEX

Acton, Lord, 84
Alienation, 71
  in Marxism, 97, 102
  of members of voluntary associations, 68
  See also Mass society
American dream, 37
"Americanization," 3
Anomie, 186
Anxiety of modern age, 1–3
Appleby, Paul, 101
Arendt, Hannah, 78
Aristotle, 24
Authority
  as permanent problem of government, 10–13
  See also Consent of the governed
Automation, 119–20
  "lonesome pay" in, 206
  See also Technology

Bagehot, Walter, 20
Balzac, Honoré de, 103
Banfield, Edward, 187
Bentham, Jeremy, 4, 28
Berle, Adolf, 60
Bourne, Randolph, 139
Bureaucracy
  alternative is system of closed classes, 103
  as effect of technology, 99–105
  hugeness in, 112–15
  informal organization in, 104–5, 113
  morality and, 106–10, 148–56
  obstruction in, 152–53
  responsible government and, 157–58
  in voluntary associations, 57–58, 61–62

Camus, Albert, 4
Capitalism, "power without property" in, 60, 129
Carr, E. H., 183–84
Centralization, problems of, 112–15, 144, 160
Chafee, Zechariah, 74, 76
Chaplin, Charlie, 4
Christianity, modernity and, 15
Citizenship, struggle for full, 19–20
Civil disobedience, 151–53
Civil liberty
  as effective instrument of democracy, 22
  See also Freedom
Coercion, *see* Force
Collectivism, *see* Mass society
Collingwood, R. G., 61
Communication
  in bureaucracy, 112–13, 155
  mass media of, 36
    do not turn society into mass society, 83–84
    modern impact of, 72–78
    present system incompatible with open society, 90–91
    television and radio as one-way communication, 71

Communism, 108
  as only one form of deeper dan-
    ger, 6
  See also Marxism
Competition
  in democracy, 176–77; *see also*
    Voluntary associations
  economic, 162–63
Comte, Auguste, 4
Conrad, Joseph, 185–86
Consent of the governed (consensus)
  always limited, 12–13
  coercion and, 193
  disillusionment about, 49–52
  as ideal of democracy, 33–35
  misconceptions concerning, 40–48
  nature of, in democracy, 24–29,
    168
    and ultimate philosophies, 26–
      29, 189–92
  voluntary associations and, *see*
    Voluntary associations
Cromwell, Oliver, 190
Custom, politics as substitute for, 11

Dahl, Robert, 43
Democracy
  bureaucracy seems essential to, 103
  debate about social priorities de-
    sirable in, 165
  decisive arrangements of
    civil liberty, 22
    pluralistic society, 22–24, 187–
      88; *see also* Groups
  defined, 30
    characteristics of democratic so-
      ciety, 167–71
  "democratic prospect," defined, ix
  ideals of, xi, 31–33
    consent of the governed, 33–35;
      see also Consent of the Gov-
      erned
    individual autonomy, 36–38;
      see also Individualism
    open society, 35–36; *see also*
      Open society
    responsible government, 38–39;
      see also Government, respon-
      sible
  intellectual rationale of, 174

  modernity and, *see* Modernization
    of society
  our image of, 8–9
  persisting issues in
    redistribution of wealth, 18–19,
      130–34, 186
    struggle for full citizenship, 19–
      20
  pressure groups essential to, 46–
    47; *see also* Groups; Volun-
    tary associations
  professional obedience in, 152–53
  "public interest" in, 196–200
  "savor" of, x
  shared rules of, 25–26, 188
  Tocqueville on despotism of, 7,
    125–26, 139
  two traditions of, 32–33
  why choose democracy? 170–79
  See also Freedom; Mass society;
    Politics; Welfare State
Divided loyalty, 24
Durkheim, Emile, 101, 186, 187–88

Economic abundance
  and democracy, 19, 186
  See also Redistribution of wealth
Economic insecurity, as essential for
    efficiency, 134
Economic system, competitive, 162–
    63
Education
  democracy as contribution to,
    169–70
  role of professions in, 89–90
Elections
  advantages of, 167–68
  "free," 45–46
  and "majority rule," 41–42
  mass media and, 75
Emerson, Ralph Waldo, 194
Epicureanism, 7
Equality
  conformity and, 171–72
  meaning of term, 132–33
  Welfare State and, 130–34
Ethics, *see* Morality
Examinations and tests, 133, 211

Featherbedding, 116, 207–8
Fitzgerald, F. Scott, 37

Force (coercion), implicit in all government, 12–13, 34, 193
Forster, E. M., 4
France, 1, 26
  French Revolution, 194
  symbols of government in, 21
Freedom
  Anglo-Saxon tradition of, 32–33
  of competition, 162–63
  not absolute value, 172–73
  technology has expanded range of, 97–99, 109–10
  and Welfare State, 136–38, 212–13
Freedom of speech in an open society, 36
Fromm, Erich, 6

Galbraith, John Kenneth, 120, 134
Government
  as always experimental, 16
  force implicit in, 12–13, 34, 193
  permanent problem of, 11–13; see also Consent of the Governed
  personal vs. impersonal, 105–6
  private, 39
  "representative," 43–46
  responsible
    bureaucracy and, 157–58; see also Bureaucracy
    conditions for, 158–61
    as ideal in democracy, 38–39
    public and, 160–65
    seems increasingly uncertain, 39, 145–48
  secrets in, 79–80
  test of, 85
  theatrical aspect of, 20–22
Germany, Weimar Republic in, 20
Great Britain, 1
  Welfare State in, 210
Greece, democracy in, 38
Groups
  in decision-making process, 42–43
  form a pluralistic society, 22–24, 187–88
  pressure groups essential to democracy, 46–47
  as private governments, 39
  See also Voluntary associations
Guilds, 96

Hadley, Arthur T., 204
Hall, Helen, 138
Hammond, J. L. and Barbara, 106–7
Hawthorne Study, 114
Heilbroner, Robert, 163
Hellenistic Age, 7
Hobbes, Thomas, 12, 169
Hoggart, Richard, 122
Holmes, Oliver Wendell, Jr., 73, 131, 168
Human nature, 15, 164
Huxley, Aldous, 4

Ideals
  of democracy, see Democracy
  modern attitude toward, 14–15
Individualism (individual autonomy)
  as ideal in democracy, 36–38
  impact of technology on
    concern today with security, 101–2
    technology as enemy of individualism, 93–95
    technology has bureaucratized work, 99–105
    technology has expanded range of choice, 97–99, 109–10
  and problem of control of technology, 110–12
    control of hugeness, 112–15
    a new ideal of work, 120–24
    reform of work process, 115–20
  voluntary associations as other side of, 54
  See also Welfare State
Industrial Revolution
  evils in, 106–7
  struggles against, 93–94
  See also Technology
"Influentials" and mass media, 84
"Institutional" problems
  defined, 139
  Welfare State and, 139–44
Ionesco, Eugene, Rhinoceros, 6

Japanese, wartime relocation of, 184

Kafka, Franz, 4
Keynes, John Maynard, 15
Kitto, H. D. F., 38

Labor, division of, 95–99
  centralized plans for, 117–18
  See also Individualism; Technology
Labor unions, 62–63, 163
  featherbedding in, 116, 207–8
  no longer clearly voluntary, 56, 202
  responsibility of local unions, 68–69
  rights of members of, 66
Leighton, Alexander, 184
Leisure as central problem in society, 120–24, 208–9
Lerner, Daniel, 17, 185
Liberalism
  malaise of, xii, 1–9, 164–65
  See also Democracy
Lindsay, Lord, 193
Lippmann, Walter, 6, 77, 84
  on philosophical consensus in democracy, 27, 188–92
Locke, John, 153

Machines
  vs. tools, 95
  See also Technology
Majority rule, misconceptions concerning, 41–43
Management, see Bureaucracy
Marxism, 6, 20, 193
  alienation in, 97, 102
  on democracy, 192–93
  as infallible doctrine, 189
  See also Communism
Mass culture, 122–23
Mass media, see Communication; Mass society
Mass society, 71
  books on, 183
  misleading definitions of "mass," 204–5
  not to be confused with pluralistic society, 83
  specter of, 3–9
    disappearance of public, 76–78, 83
    rise of mass media, 74–76, 83–84
    rise of technology, 78–81, 82–83

Medieval society, 37; see also Society, modern vs. traditional
Mencken, H. L., 130
Merton, Robert K., 116, 186
Michels, Robert, 57, 202
Middle East, modernization in, 17, 185
Mill, John Stuart, 77, 93, 160
Mills, C. Wright, 6
Milton, John, 84
Modern, defined, 14–15
Modernization of society, 13–20
  symbols in, 21–22
  See also Open society
Morality (ethics)
  of civil disobedience, 151–53
  of the expert, 148–56
  feeling that it is anachronism, 145–48
  of technology and bureaucracy, 106–10
  of Welfare State, 134–36
Mosca, Gaetano, 202–3
Myrdal, Gunnar, 140
"Mystery," origin of word, 96

Nagel, Ernest, 122
Natural Law, 27, 189–92
News in modern mass media, 74–76
Nightmare visions, 4
Nuclear tests, 151

Occupations, increase of, 96
Old age, 142
Oligarchy, iron law of, 57, 202
Open society
  classical idea of public in, 76–78, 83
    professions as substitute for classical public, 87–92
  as ideal of democracy, 35–36
  assertion that this ideal has collapsed, 81–86
  mass media in, see Communication, mass media of
  problem of technical knowledge in, 78–81, 82–83
  purposes of, 86
  See also Modernization of society

Organization
  as instrument of production, 100–1
  See also Bureaucracy
Orwell, George, 4
"Overpopulation," 139

Panter-Downes, Mollie, 6
Peirce, Charles, 200
Penology, 88–89
Philosophy
  ambiguities of word, 191–92
  ultimates as basis for consent of
    governed, 26–29, 189–92
Plamenatz, John, 80
Planning
  as supplement to economic com-
    petition, 163
  Welfare State and, 140–44
Plato, ix, 73, 131
Play, distinction between work and,
    120–24
Pluralistic society, *see* Society, plu-
    ralistic
Politics
  as indicator of disequilibrium, 11–
    13
  of malaise, 1–9, 55
  as official business of democracy,
    47–48
  See also Government
Popular will, 43–44
Potter, David, 186
Pressure groups essential to democ-
    racy, 46–47; *see also* Groups;
    Voluntary associations
Professions
  associations of
    local responsibility for, 69
    as shadow organizations, 58–59
    See also Voluntary associations
  distinction between professional
    knowledge and moral judg-
    ments, 148–56
  as substitutes for classic public,
    87–92
Progress, a modern attitude, 13–15
Public
  assertion that it has become a
    mass, 76–78, 83
  professions as substitutes for clas-
    sical, 87–92

and responsible government, 160–
    65
Public interest, defined, 196–200
Puritanism, 5, 15

Redistribution of wealth
  as persisting issue in democracy,
    18–19, 186
  and Welfare State, 130–34
Referenda, 40–41
Religion
  function of, 17
  rise of exotic cults, 7
"Residual" problems, defined, 139
Responsibility, *see* Government, re-
    sponsible; Morality
Rhinoceros (Ionesco), 6
Riesman, David, 5
Rousseau, Jean Jacques, 16, 40, 193
Russell, Bertrand, 136, 172, 212

Santayana, George, 17
Sartre, Jean-Paul, 50
Schumpeter, Joseph, 21, 129
Science
  has made our ignorance more evi-
    dent, 82
  need for education of layman in,
    91–92
  problem of democracy and, xi, 78–
    81, 82–83
  See also Technology
Scientific community
  should develop educational role,
    89–90
  as undefined entity, 58–59
  See also Professions
Secrets, governmental, 79–80
Security
  concern today with, 101–2
  economic advance and, 134
Simon, Herbert, 117
Skinner, B. F., 4
Smith, Adam, 200
Snow, C. P., 152
Social classes
  in democracy, 18–20, 32–33, 171
  modern attitude toward, 15–17
  rulers and ruled as, 61, 202–3

Social welfare
  misunderstood by layman, 89
  See also Welfare State
Socialism, 195
Society
  "dual societies," 39
  government as distinct from, 11,
    171
  modern vs. historical, 13–20
    groups in, 52–54
    technology in, 106–10
  open, see Open Society
  pluralistic, 22–24, 187–88
    not to be confused with "mass
      society," 83
    See also Groups; Voluntary as-
      sociations
  produces its own mad dream, 37
  See also Mass society
Stoicism, 7, 158
Symbols of democracy, 20–22

Taylor, Frederick, 100
  "Taylorism," 117, 118
Technology, 164
  individual and, see Individualism
  moral significance of, 106–10
  organization of work under, 95–99
    "lonesome pay," 206
    technology bureaucratizes work,
      99–105
  seems to be enemy of individual-
    ism, 93–95
  suspicion that it is a trap, 7
  See also Science
Tocqueville, Alexis de, 15, 58, 68,
  179, 215
  on the despotism of democracy, 7,
    125–26, 139
  on individualism, 54, 194
Town meeting, inapplicable today as
  model of government, 40–41,
  195–96

Urban planning, 141
  local autonomy in, 70
Ure, Andrew, 99, 206
Utopias, 4–5, 120

Variety, an advantage of democracy,
  171–74
Veblen, Thorstein, 98, 157
Voluntary associations
  emergence of shadow associations,
    58–61
  and government by consent, 52–
    55, 61–71
    democracy within voluntary as-
      sociations, 57–58, 61–62, 65–
      68
  no longer voluntary, 56–57
  See also Groups

Walden II, 4
Weber, Max, 154
Welfare State
  assumptions behind, 128–30, 134–
    36
  challenges personal autonomy,
    125–26
  democratic equality and, 130–34
  freedom and, 136–38, 212–13
  functions of, 209–10
  morality of, 134–36
  as postscript to emergency, 126–
    28, 210
    should have institutional—not
      emergency—orientation, 138–
      44
Whyte, William Holly, Jr., 5
Work
  and play (leisure), 120–24, 208–9
  reform of process of, 115–20
  See also Individualism; Technology

Young, Michael, 211
Youth problem, 142–43

ABOUT THE AUTHOR

Charles Frankel has been Professor of Philosophy at Columbia University since 1939. He also teaches at the New York School for Social Work. Born in New York City, he was educated at Cornell and Columbia. During the war he was a lieutenant in the Navy on active duty from 1942 to 1946. In 1947 Mr. Frankel received the Woodbridge Prize in Philosophy and in 1953–54 was a Guggenheim Fellow. Mr. Frankel has lectured throughout the United States and also in France, Belgium, Turkey, Ireland and elsewhere. He was host in 1959 for the CBS-TV program "The World of Ideas," and he has frequently been host on the CBS-Radio program "Invitation to Learning." Mr. Frankel's books are: *The Faith of Reason, The Bear and the Beaver, The Case for Modern Man,* and *The Democratic Prospect.* He was the principal author for "The Power of the Democratic Idea"—the Rockefeller Brothers Panel Report on American Democracy. Mr. Frankel has edited four books and has contributed to many magazines and periodicals. He is a member of various professional and civic organizations, such as the American Philosophical Association and the Civil Liberties Union. He lives in New City, New York, with his wife and two children.

Format by Howard Burg
Set in Linotype Caledonia
Composed by and printed by York Composition Co., Inc.
Bound by The Haddon Craftsmen, Inc.
HARPER & ROW, PUBLISHERS, INCORPORATED